PERENNIAL
GARDENING
IN
TEXAS

PERENNIAL GARDENING IN TEXAS

ALAN DEAN FRANZ

TAYLOR TRADE PUBLISHING
Lanham • New York • Dallas • Boulder • Toronto • Oxford

Published by Taylor Trade Publishing
An imprint of The Rowman & Littlefield Publishing Group, Inc.
4501 Forbes Boulevard, Suite 200
Lanham, Maryland 20706

Distributed by National Book Network

Book composition by Susan Mark
Coghill Composition Company
Richmond, Virginia

Library of Congress Cataloging-in-Publication Data

Franz, Alan Dean, 1961–
    Perennial gardening in Texas / Alan Dean Franz.—1st Taylor Trade Publishing ed.
      p. cm.
    Includes bibliographical references and index.
    ISBN 1-58979-115-0 (hardcover : alk. paper)
    1. Perennials—Texas.   I. Title.

SB434.F73 2005
635.9'32'09764—dc22   2004005277

♾™The paper used in this publication meets the minimum requirements of American National Standard for Information Sciences—Permanence of Paper for Printed Library Materials, ANSI/NISO Z39.48-1992.

Manufactured in the United States of America.

To my parents, Don and Joyce Franz

And in memory of my grandfathers,
John Loewen and Herman Franz
Gardeners, farmers, and book lovers

Contents

Foreword

There is a great secret those of us in Texas know, but others may not. Those not from our area think of beautiful gardens and Texas as contradictions. Although the natural beauty of our state and prairies, overflowing with wildflowers, is familiar to many, the magnificent landscapes of our botanical gardens, private homes, and estates often go unnoticed.

The gardening styles so popular elsewhere in the world seldom flourish in Texas without adaptations. But as with so many other things, Texans are ingenious as gardeners. Our own version of muted and soothing English-style cottage gardens, striking architectural Southwest landscapes, formal structured French gardens, and many others can be found throughout the state—all testaments to the resourcefulness of Texans.

A particular challenge to gardening in this great state is the lack of information tailored to us. Garden writing focused on the Northeast and Northwest does not apply to us, nor does Texas fit into the true Southern gardening information. As with so many other things, our state is unique. By necessity, Texas gardeners have learned to sieve kernels of information that apply to us from any source available. I am so delighted that the monumental effort of providing an informative work on perennials for Texas has been taken on by Alan Franz. I believe it will exist as a reference not only for us locally but also for gardeners who face similar plant selection and design problems across the nation.

Designing any garden, but especially a perennial border, is like conducting a great symphony. For harmony, one must orchestrate the design so certain flowers counterbalance each other during the season. This requires the conductor, or designer, to know his or her instruments, or plants, and when best to utilize them. In order for a perennial garden to look good all year, the designer must have an eye for design, an ability to mix colors, and the foresight to look into the future. This is no easy matter, especially with so little reference material available to beginning gardeners. This book is one step toward introducing the nation to the diversity of Texas gardens.

Perennial gardening has particular challenges, especially for Texans. We are blessed with a very long growing season, punctuated by occasional minor problems such as drought, flash floods, 100-degree-plus summer temperatures, and 50-degree overnight drops in temperature! We are a state of not only climatic but also geographic extremes. What other state can claim subtropical coasts, pine forests, majestic prairies, mountains, and desert areas? And, few others encompass as many USDA hardiness zones as Texas does: from 6a to 9b. What better place to explore all the possibilities of gardening?

If you can garden in Texas, you can garden almost anywhere. Texas is a unique area, and I'm glad that finally we have this book on perennials to call our own, a valuable resource for gardeners looking for the perfect perennial or design idea to bring harmony to their landscape.

MARY BRINEGAR
President
The Dallas Arboretum

Acknowledgments

Tim Host for support and editing

Janet Harris for guidance

My family and friends for support

Sally Wasowski for direction

Britton & Associates for time

Sandra Bolain for "continuous encouragement"

Photo 0.6 *(opposite page)*
Two of the author's favorites:
purple coneflower, *Echinacea
purpurea*, and liatris,
Liatris spicata, line his walk
in summer

A Note from the Author
A PLACE IN THE SUN

When I was about 10, I asked my parents for a piece of the garden that I could call my own. *Weeding the large vegetable patch and mowing the 3-acre yard on our Kansas farm was not enough. They gave me a 15 × 15 foot plot of land on the east side of the house. It was perfect. It was close to the water spigot, it got morning sun, and it was protected from summer and winter winds. It was my own place in the sun.*

This was the moment I became a budding gardener. Since my funds were limited, I began digging up and dividing existing daylilies, phlox, peonies, and iris, which were growing freely about the yard. Any new plants had to be permanent to keep costs down, so I chose perennials over the more immediate gratification of showy annuals. The process of arranging the little garden patch began my passion, or obsession, with gardening and an eventual career as a landscape architect and garden designer. Despite hot, dry summers and bitterly cold winters, the perennials returned every year, bigger and more beautiful than the year before. A budding photographer as well, I burned many rolls of film on that patch.

Now that I have lived in Texas for almost half of my life, this is home. What I learned as a child became the building blocks to what I learned in my career and as a gardener. My patch of yard has gotten much bigger, and my enthusiasm has grown as well. I guess gardeners are dreamers. The garden is in a constant state of change, and we constantly dream about the possibilities to come. So I hope you enjoy dreaming and creating your own place in the sun.

Introduction
AN ENGLISH GARDEN GROWS IN TEXAS

When the woman who lived next door to me was moving away, she told me that she was going to miss my yard. The front walk from the curb to the front door is bordered by a bed of perennial plants that bloom continuously from March to November. The plants sprawl and creep over the sidewalk edges, supplying nectar for busy bees and butterflies. My neighbor enjoyed watching the ever-changing display from her front porch; she said that it reminded her of pictures she had seen of English gardens. That was the best compliment she could have given me. Never let anyone tell you that you cannot grow an English garden in your own front yard. You just have to do it with a Texas twist.

Many people think the extreme heat, shallow soils, humidity in East Texas, and dryness in West Texas make replicating perennial gardening impossible here in Texas. On the contrary, a wide variety of colorful and exciting plants thrive with a little planning and care. The winters tend to be mild, and the springs and autumns can be quite moist, giving us the advantage of using plants not found in other parts of the country. And, of course, most natives grow with little care. Think of the wildflowers that bloom in the ditches. Using the natives and other adaptable plants, you can create your dream garden.

The same basic principals of design—layout, form, and color—apply anywhere in the world. My goal for this book is to guide you in choosing the right materials for your yard here in Texas where the South, Southwest, and Great Plains converge, and to display the plants that work best. As a visual person, and an impatient one, I prefer plant books that are big on pictures and short on words. I want just the facts on what conditions the plants will need and what they will look like.

"Gardens are like people, each one has its own character and history, and I suppose one might go on describing them indefinitely and still find something new to chronicle about each one."

THEODORE THOMAS,
Our Mountain Garden

Although I write from my experiences here in North Texas, this book need not be limited to this area. Heat is heat whether you're on the

Photo 0.8
The author's garden explodes with vibrant colors in summer.

South Texas Coast or in the Panhandle. You must just choose plants that will survive harsher winters for the more northern regions. Likewise, plants that live in the red clays of East Texas may have problems with the alkalinity and dry soils of West Texas. Using the guides you should find this book helpful not only for Dallas/Ft. Worth, but for Houston, Lubbock, and everywhere in between.

I have learned about gardening by researching, by talking to experts, and most importantly, by experimenting. Not everything listed will automatically be a star in your yard because every site is different. Light and shade, exposure to winds and sun, and soil makeup all play a role in what will grow in your yard. When I moved across town, some of my favorites from the first house never took off, even though I provided comparable conditions. Gardening is not wallpaper you apply once and forget about it. It is a process.

Experiment in your own yard. Find out what thrives, blooms, and excites you in your own corner of paradise. Once established, perennial gardens require small amounts of care for the lasting return they provide. But be careful: You may get hooked. Once you get started, it's hard to stop. You may find yourself sacrificing more plots of pristine emerald lawn for additional bands of rubies, sapphires, and golds. Never let anyone tell you that you can't have an English garden in Texas. This is Texas after all, and we can do anything we want to. We just have to do it our own way.

Photo 0.9
The author at Hidcoate Gardens, Glostchestershire, England

Chapter One
GETTING STARTED:
PLANNING A PERENNIAL GARDEN

*I*f you are planting a perennial garden for the first time, you may need a little help getting started. How should you start? What should you plant? When should you plant? Developing a plan will ultimately give you a garden that is beautiful as well as easy to maintain. It can be an exciting process as you anticipate the possibilities.

The first section of this book, chapters 1 through 4, establishes the site guidelines that will help you plan a perennial garden: soils and site, design and layout, background and structure, and maintenance and care. Being familiar with all of these conditions will give you a solid starting point for laying out new beds and choosing the right plants and will ultimately save you time and money.

The second section, chapters 6 through 12, deals with the specific elements that make up a perennial garden: color, texture and form, sun and shade, wet and dry sites, the five senses, wildlife, and the five seasons. Understanding these elements not only helps you design your garden, but also allows you to set the tone or mood for your personal piece of Texas. Once you have determined the conditions of the site and the elements of design that will control the look of your garden, you can choose the specific plants you need. This section also lists plants associated with each of the design elements that make up a garden.

> *"Gardening is a language with vocabulary, syntax, and above all punctuation. We often find that architecture provides the pause, the comma, that a garden needs amongst long paragraphs of plants. . . ."*
>
> JULIAN AND ISABEL BANNERMAN

The third section, chapters 13 through 15, gives descriptions of the perennials and the companion plants listed in the previous section. These detailed descriptions will aid you in choosing the right plants

Photo 1.2
Pincushion flower detail,
Scabiosa caucasica
'Butterfly Blue'

summer and from cold, northern winds in winter. And, if the lowest part of your yard allows water to stand after it rains, it will require raised beds or plant species that tolerate wet soils.

Take a long look at the area you want to plant before you begin. If you already know what kind of plants you want but have no particular spot in mind, determine the best conditions for your chosen plants and then find the location with those conditions in your garden.

CREATING A NEW BED

When creating a new bed, you will need to find out what your soil type and acidity/alkalinity levels are. This will help you determine what kind of amendments you should add to improve the soil. Always provide a bed that is high in organic matter and drains well. In poor soils, the new soil level should be higher than the existing level of the yard, unless you are using plants that prefer boggy conditions. Either mound the beds or build them up using a low wall (12 inches to 18 inches), as shown on the sketch, to accomplish this. The wall can be built out of timbers, stone, brick, or pavers, as long as it retains the soil. Choose what looks best in your garden.

First remove any existing grass, plants, or stones. Then, spade up the soil to at least 6 inches deep. If the soil is very poor, you may want to remove some of it. Add plenty of amendments and mix with existing soil. Mix in fertilizers as well. Push it down firmly to remove air pockets, but never compact it heavily.

based on their requirements and compatibility with other plants.

SELECTING THE SITE

The particular site where you want to plant your perennial garden has an enormous effect on what you plant. Every little space in the garden has its own microenvironment of conditions. Beds on the north side of the house or under trees need shade-tolerant plants. On the other hand, beds in full sun or on the south or west side of the house that are fully exposed need plants that will thrive in sunny, hot conditions. In large cities, the winter temperatures tend to be a bit warmer than those out in the countryside. Fences, hedges, and buildings also protect plants from dry, hot, southern winds in

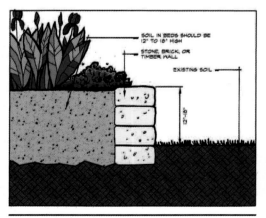

Photo 1.3
Section showing mounded landscape bed with a low wall

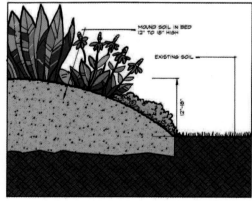

Photo 1.4
Section showing mounded landscape bed with no wall

PREPARING THE SOIL

If you take nothing else away from this book, know this: good soil is the most important key to successful gardening. The best soil for growing plants is loamy, deep, and neutral to slightly acidic. Because most soils in Texas do not have these qualities, you must know your soil and prepare it well. Good soil preparation will give your plants a better chance of survival by increasing growth and vigor, which ultimately helps them fight off diseases and pests. Good soils retain moisture when needed but drain off excess moisture easily, and they provide ample nutrients for growth.

If you don't know what your soil type is, for a nominal cost, you can have samples tested by a local nursery or agricultural extension service. Larger cities will have labs that do this testing for engineers and architects. The test will tell you the pH level and the type of soil.

SOIL TYPES

You'll need to know some basics about soil and soil types.

pH: The pH level tells you if the soil is acidic (below 7.0), neutral (7.0), or alkaline (above 7.0). Typically the best soils for growing plants are close to neutral or lower. Soils that are too alkaline are high in salts and low in iron, which is essential for healthy, green color in plants. Plants that are low in iron usually grow and bloom poorly and are susceptible to disease. Soil can be enhanced by the additions of peat moss, acidic soil amendments, and acidifiers. However, many plants native or adaptable to Texas grow naturally in alkaline soils and do not need amendments to alter the pH levels. East Texas naturally has acidic soils. If your soil is too acidic for your garden, you can add lime to help neutralize it.

Loam: Loam is the optimal type of soil. It is deep and rich with organic matter and may have a combination of clay and sand in it. Organic matter holds in moisture and is rich in nutrients. Loamy soils do not compact tightly, so they drain well. You will not find deep loamy soils regularly in Texas.

Clay: Clay soils have particles that are very small, which pack together so tightly they do not drain. Poor drainage can lead to poor plant health and disease problems. Clay soils tend to be low in nu-

trients, as well. Many plants will simply not grow if the soil has too much clay. Mix in plenty of organic matter and sand to increase the drainage of the soil.

Sand and Gravel: Sandy and gravely soils have large particles. They drain extremely well but do not hold moisture or nutrients. If you have sandy soil, add large amounts of organic matter and loam to increase moisture retention.

SOIL AMENDMENTS AND FERTILIZERS

A variety of effective amendments and fertilizers exist, including the following major ones.

Earthworm Castings: Earthworms are nature's soil conditioners. They digest the particles in the ground and aerate the soil. Their leftovers are high in nutrients and organic matter that is perfect for plants to absorb. Mix liberal amounts into your beds; they will not burn the plants like excessive chemical fertilizers can.

Greensand: Greensand is a natural rock powder that helps provide major trace elements and minerals for the plants, like vitamins do for people. It also aids in conducting moisture and exchanging nutrients, as well as loosening heavy, clay soils.

Lava Sand: Lava sand is similar to Greensand and is probably the best amendment for providing elements and minerals.

Lime: Lime is very alkaline, so add it only to soils that are extremely acidic and need to be neutralized.

Photo 1.5

Organic Fertilizers: Organic fertilizers are usually forms of decomposed cow, sheep, or poultry manure. Fish emulsion, made up of fish by-products, is also a common organic fertilizer. Since these animals eat plant material, their wastes are high in nitrogen and full of the minerals that are valuable to plants. They provide a well-rounded supply of all the nutrients your plants need, and they will be better for your plants in the long run than heavy chemicals will be.

Organic Matter/Humus: Organic matter and humus can include anything that was once alive and has now decomposed. The most common is compost, which you can make yourself from yard clippings, leaves, and raw vegetable food scraps. Soil conditioners with humus, manure, and composts are available at nurseries and garden centers. Mix large amounts of organic matter into your beds. They provide nutrients and air to the plants while both loosening clay soils and retaining moisture in sandy soils. Composted pecan leftovers are used as another common, available amendment. Peat moss is commonly used to provide acidity for azaleas, but it is expensive and has little nutrient value. Organic matter and humus produced from local materials are the best option for returning local minerals to your soil.

Sulfur: Sulfur products are added to soil to make it less alkaline. High alkalinity prevents many plants from absorbing minerals. In turn, the plants get chlorotic, or are weak and have yellow foliage. Many evergreens living in alkaline soils need additional sulfur to stay healthy.

Planting and Mulching

Once you have analyzed your soil and prepared a bed, you can plant. If you are planting in fall or winter, start with spring bulbs. They will emerge and bloom before most perennials start to leaf out in the spring. Plant your perennials from seeds or from growing pots. Plants that are already growing will develop and bloom faster. Many perennials will not bloom their first season if planted from seed. Some perennials, such as irises and peonies, may take several years from the time they are planted before they bloom heavily.

Plant so the crown where the foliage meets the roots is level with the soil. Planting too deep can

---

SOAPBOX ALERT

Use organic solutions whenever possible. Heavy chemicals for fungicides, fertilizers, and of course pesticides not only kill the problem pests but hurt the beneficial animals in the garden—the bees, butterflies, earthworms, lizards, birds, toads, and ladybugs. Remember, they all lived here long before we took over. Besides, who knows what effect these chemicals will have on us in the long run? Use preventive cures like good soil amendments to hold off the problems. They are not invasive to the environment, and they prevent problems with disease and pests in the future. Chemical fertilizers are high in salts, which are not good for the plants. These same chemicals also tend to give the plants too much food at once, causing them to grow too fast, in turn making them more susceptible to disease and insects. If you must use chemical fertilizers, use slow, time-released types.

suffocate the plant, and planting too shallow may cause the plant to dry out quickly. Press out any pockets of air around the plant and water thoroughly.

After planting, add a layer of mulch. A 2-inch-thick layer is usually best, but be careful not to suffocate the plants. Keep the level low at the base of most plants to prevent fungus problems.

Always add mulch to the top of your beds once they have been planted. Mulches hold in moisture, block weeds, and insulate the soil from extreme temperatures. As they decay, they add organic matter to the soil. Replace mulch in your bed one to two times a year. The type of mulch you choose depends on the region where you live. In most of Texas, hardwood mulch, such as shredded pine, cypress, or cedar mulch works well. Avoid using the large nuggets because they don't break down as well, and they allow too much evaporation. Cedar mulch also has the advantage of repelling insects. In East Texas, pine straw is readily available and provides an acidic mulch. In the deserts of far West Texas, gravel and decomposed granite may be the best option because hardwood mulches will simply dry out too easily, and then blow away.

Photo 1.6
Texas Hill Country near Austin

THE REGIONS OF TEXAS

Since Texas is a large state, the soils and climatic conditions vary widely from region to region. Texas is comprised of roughly seven different zones that range from the Piney Woods of East Texas, where the rainfall is high and the soils are acidic, to the Trans-Pecos highlands of far West Texas, where rainfall is low and the soils are alkaline. Understanding

Photo 1.7
Limestone outcrops typical of the Black Land Prairie

Photo 1.8
Piney Woods of East Texas

what region you live in is important to understanding which plants grow best based on general soil types, moisture levels, humidity levels, and hot and cold temperatures. The seven basic regions are as follows.

PINEY WOODS

The Piney Woods encompasses the eastern part of the state and includes the cities of Tyler, Texarkana, Houston, Longview, Palestine, and Beaumont. This area is part of the great pine forests of the southeastern United States. Pine and oak woods, with natural bogs and wetlands, typify this area. The rainfall and humidity levels here are the highest in the state, making it the most conducive area for growing a wide array of plants. The soils, as a rule, are red sandy-clay or silty sand and acidic.

PRAIRIES AND CROSS TIMBERS

The Black Land Prairies and the Cross Timbers include the cities of and areas surrounding Dallas/Ft. Worth, Waco, and Bryan/College Station as well as the areas encompassing the very southern regions of what was once the Great Plains. The majority of this area is the Black Land Prairies, which have dark, shallow, heavy clay layers on top of limestone bedrock. The soil tends to be quite alkaline and sticky. The Cross Timbers areas are fingers that run through the region typified by dry, sandy, slightly acidic soils once dominated by sporadic post oak woods. The rainfall in these Cross Timbers is moderate, with heavy periods of rain in spring and fall and dry spells in summer. Winter temperatures are fairly moderate with sudden dips into the 20s and even lower.

HILL COUNTRY

The Hill Country includes the rolling rugged landscape from San Antonio and Austin west to the Edwards Plateau, which extends farther west to the Pecos River and includes San Angelo. The Hill Country is the beloved heart of Texas with shallow, alkaline, clay soils on top of rolling limestone hills. Lady Bird Johnson has immortalized this area and its wildflowers. The rainfall here is moderate, and the summers are hot. The Edwards Plateau is drier, with colder winters, and its soil tends to be sandy and neutral to alkaline, with pockets of woodlands, such as those found in Lost Maples State Park.

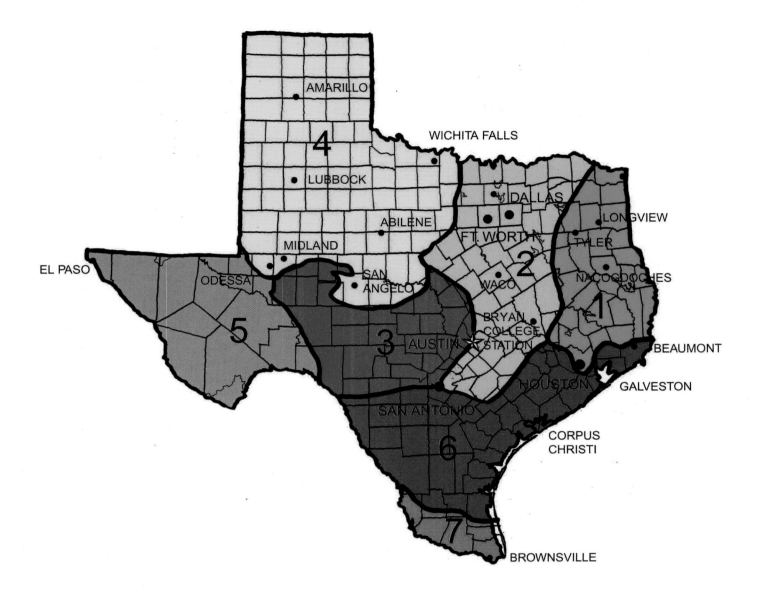

High Plains Country

The High Plains Country encompasses the northwest part of Texas, which includes the High Plains of the Panhandle, Amarillo, and Lubbock, as well as the adjacent Rolling Red or West Texas Plains, which includes Midland/Odessa, Wichita Falls, and Abilene. Along with the Prairies and Cross Timbers of north central Texas, this area forms the southern base for the Great Plains. Since this area of the state is the highest in elevation, it is also the coldest. Hard freezes and snow are common in the Panhandle. Rainfall is moderate in the eastern portions of the High Plains Country and low in the western portions, where drought spells are also common. Summers

here are hot and windy. The soils can range from clay to sandy and are generally neutral to alkaline.

Trans-Pecos

The Trans-Pecos encompasses the westernmost part of the state including El Paso. North and east of El Paso is somewhat mountainous. The mountains receive some moderate rainfall in summer and have well-drained, alkaline soils of clay, sand, and gravel. To the southeast is the Chihuahuan Desert, the driest part of the state. The desert is extremely dry with alkaline soils; it does not rain enough to flush the salts out of the soil.

Photo 1.9
Regions of Texas

1. Piney Woods
2. Prairies and Cross Timbers
3. Hill Country
4. High Plains Country
5. Trans-Pecos
6. Gulf Coast & South Texas Plains
7. Lower Rio Grande Valley

GULF COAST AND SOUTH TEXAS PLAINS

The Gulf Coast region extends from the Houston/Galveston area down along the coast and includes Corpus Christi. The South Texas Plains extend inward to the south end of San Antonio. The soils in the plains tend to be black, alkaline clay with alkaline sandy zones along the coast. The temperatures here in winter are buffered by the Gulf and are very moderate. Semitropical plants can be grown here. The rainfall is moderate to low in the western portions of this area.

LOWER RIO GRANDE VALLEY

The Lower Rio Grande Valley encompasses the southern tip of Texas including Brownsville. Winter temperatures here are very moderate, and subtropical plants can be grown easily. However, rainfall is low, and the natural landscape is quite arid. Soils are alkaline clay that is poorly drained.

HARDINESS AND CLIMATIC ZONES

The country has been divided into hardiness zones by the United States Department of Agri-

Photo 1.10
USDA Hardiness Zone Map

Temperatures are average minimums listed in Fahrenheit

Zone 6a: –5 to –10
Zone 6b: 0 to –5
Zone 7a: 0 to 5
Zone 7b: 5 to 10
Zone 8a: 10 to 15
Zone 8b: 15 to 20
Zone 9a: 20 to 25
Zone 9b: 25 to 30
Zone 10a: 30 to 35
Zone 10b: 35 to 40

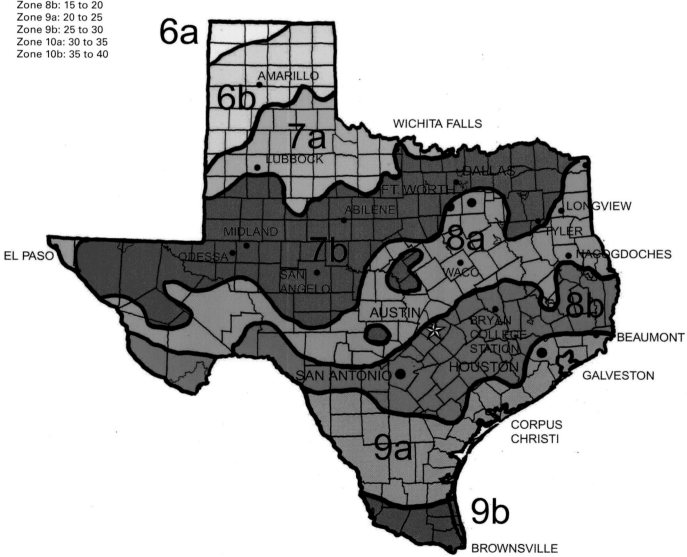

culture (USDA). There are two different types of zones: Cold Hardiness zones and Heat Hardiness zones.

Cold hardiness is determined by the average low temperatures in winter. The cold hardiness zones in Texas range from zone 6 (–10° to 0°) to zone 9 (20° to 30°). The hardiness zones are listed for all plants in the book.

Heat Hardiness zones refer to the average number of days an area experiences temperatures above 86 degrees. Texas is generally found in zone 8 (90 to 120 days) to zone 11 (180 to 210 days). This is a relatively new classification and not available for many plants. However, most plants listed in this book are tolerant of Texas heat.

SUMMARY

Once you have located a site for your new bed, familiarized yourself with your soil types, regional influences, and hardiness, and you have determined what types of amendments you must add to the soil, you can begin putting in your perennial garden. This step is important in achieving a beautiful and healthy perennial garden. If you do not think of planning as the fun part of gardening, think of it as the most worthwhile. Just as every beautiful house starts with a good foundation of stone or concrete, a beautiful garden starts with a good foundation of location and soil.

Chapter Two
STYLE: DESIGN AND LAYOUT

When deciding on a design for your perennial garden, start by examining the various styles of perennial gardens commonly used in landscape design. Just as light, soil moisture, exposures, and colors are significant, the style of your garden is an important element that must be considered before you begin.

Certain factors already exist on the site, like mature trees, size and shape of the yard, and the style of your house, that will help you determine your garden style. For example, if you have a naturally wooded, shady site with lots of trees, you won't want to impose a rigid geometric shape through the existing, random tree pattern.

Likewise, the character of the house and other buildings may dictate the style of garden you choose. A very formal, symmetrical house may be complemented by a formal symmetrical garden. In such a situation, if your yard is large enough, you may choose formality at the base of the house, then loosen up as you progress outward to more casual areas of the yard. On the other hand, a quaint cottage house suggests a cottage garden approach. And a sprawling, ranch-style house invites an informal garden layout, either with straight lines or curving shapes.

"Nothing is more completely the child of Art than a Garden."
SIR WALTER SCOTT

Finally, the shape of the yard may suggest a style of garden. For example, a long narrow yard sets up the geometry for a traditional border garden that follows a walk, fence, or hedge.

Photo 2.2
Plan of small formal knot garden

SECRET GARDEN

Photo 2.3
Dunbarton Oaks,
Washington, D.C.

Photo 2.4
Dunbarton Oaks,
Washington, D.C.

Photo 2.5
Formal Garden at Hampton
Court in England

The Formal Garden: Symmetry and Knotty-ness

The garden designers of the early Italian Renaissance used intricate, formal, symmetrical designs to reflect the rebirth of interest in classical architecture. Rather than colorful herbaceous plants, they used clipped evergreens like box- wood and yew, in conjunction with water features, colored gravel, and statuary. The intricate patterns of the gardens increased with the size and scope of the palaces, and by the fifteenth century, gardens such as those at Versailles in France featured huge panels of carefully controlled plantings. This style eventually found its way to England and the New World, but in a scaled-down, human size that also employed col-

Photo 2.6
Formal Knot Garden at the
Dallas Arboretum and
Botanical Gardens

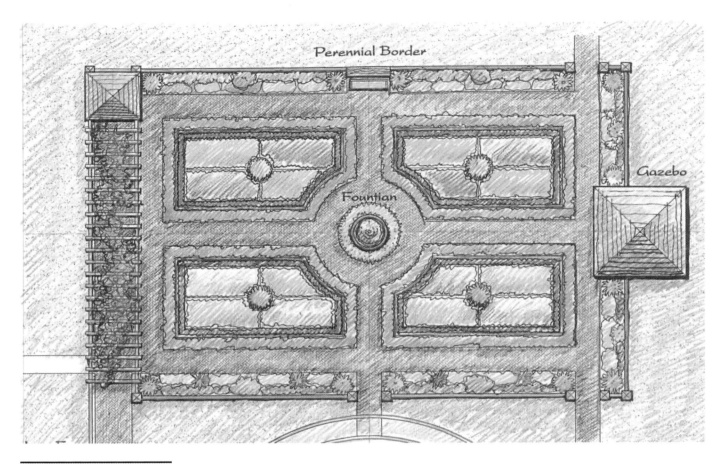

Photo 2.7
Formal garden plan

orful flowers. The Pioneers who settled North America applied the geometric patterns to their herb and vegetable gardens; this influence is still seen in modern formal gardens.

The basic elements of a formal garden include a symmetrical design, employing cross axials and centralized focal points. Evergreen hedges, stonewalls, and iron borders provide a skeleton

Photo 2.8
Informal Garden at the Dallas Arboretum and Botanical Gardens designed with curvilinear beds

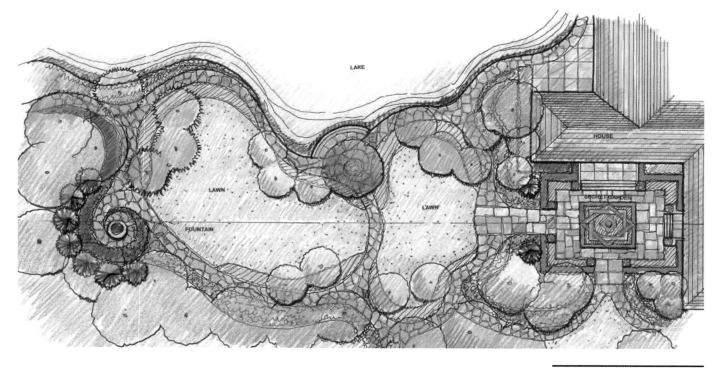

for the free flowing form of perennial and annual plants. Stoneware, sundials, benches, planters, and sculptures act as focal points for symmetrical views. The use of a formal structure can be employed as the overall design in a garden adjacent to a formal house, or in a small, separate garden room.

INFORMALITY: SHIFTING VIEWS

After the Renaissance peaked in England, pervasive styles of both architecture and landscape design began to change, and formality

was no longer the rage. Garden designers took their cue from Asian gardens and the Romantic artists of the seventeenth and eighteenth centuries, who painted broad landscapes depicting wild countryside scenes and the rural life of the gentry. The gardens featured a series of continually changing views, unfolding with mystery and surprise as one strolled the paths. The merging of the Japanese style with the Romantic Landscape movement resulted in the zenith of the English Landscape School. Designers ripped out the formal gardens, carved out lakes and ponds, and surrounded them with wild woodlands, sheep meadows, curving paths, and classical buildings made to be viewed from various vantage points. This style has prevailed in some form until the present time. New York's Central Park is a good example.

Because most gardeners do not have fifty extra acres to put in a reflecting pond large enough for boating or a meadow complete with happily grazing sheep, they must use a style with scaled-down elements. Loose, flowing garden shapes and informal paths have been adapted to the more casual ranch-style houses popular in suburban America in the last half of the twentieth century. Whether the lines are curving or straight, views can change and be framed. Landscape beds can complement the natural slopes and tree patterns of an existing

site. Objects in the landscape have also been scaled down; Roman temples and rowing ponds have become arbors and small gurgling fountains.

The Cottage Garden: Charm and Simplicity

The cottage garden and herbaceous borders grew out of the Arts and Crafts movements that hit England and the United States in the mid-1800s. The Arts and Crafts movement tried to counter the inhumanity of the Industrial Revolution by reconnecting art and architecture with the handmade artisans and craftsmen that were fading away. The architecture resulted in cottage houses in England and the bungalow style in the United States in the twentieth century. The gardens reflected the simplicity and old-fashioned nature of the architecture. Common plants like those that had been grown for generations and passed from neighbor to neighbor were used in simple, free flowing patterns. This garden style was in direct conflict with the Victorian gardens, which used many exotics and featured fussy, intricate beds and patterns. The new cottage gardens worked with nature while the Victorian counterparts controlled nature.

The modern cottage garden has retained simplicity and charm. It features a house or a build-

Photo 2.11
Cottage garden nearly hides this house

Photo 2.12
Perennial border at Hampton
Court in England

ing as a backdrop and is contained by walls, hedges, or fences. Usually a path leads visitors from the front gate to the front door of the house or some other destination. The path may be straight, curved, or broken, using irregular stones. Invariably the garden sprawls onto the path. Taller plants are placed along the back, with lower plants in front and along the paths. Vegetables, roses, annuals, vines, and other ornamental plants are mixed in with perennials to achieve a romantic effect. Flowers, colors, and butterflies flow into each other and across and over garden paths.

THE HERBACEOUS BORDER: COLOR AND DESIGN

What many gardeners think of as the zenith of perennial garden design came when Gertrude Jeckyll and others developed border gardens at the end of the nineteenth century. When Jeckyll, a floral painter and tapestry designer, began to lose her eyesight, she took up gardening and applied what she knew of color and design to long narrow beds, producing some of the most stunning gardens in history. She paid close at-

Photo 2.13
Perennial border plan

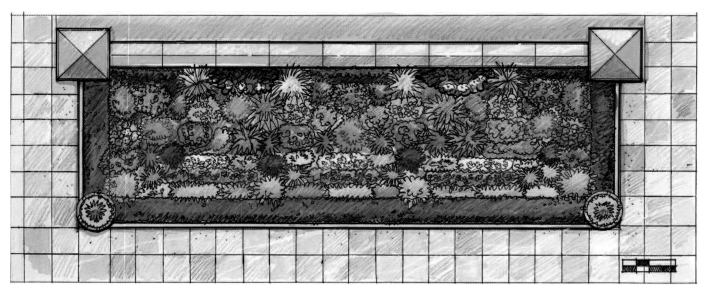

Photo 2.14
Sculpture Gardens at the Chicago Art Institute uses perennials in a modern garden design

tention to the details of the plants and worked them into seemingly random patterns and designs. Her repetition of color, texture, size, and scale all became important elements of the borders. The effect was much like an Impressionist painting where the color and light patterns define the bed. The gardens, even when not in bloom, were always given structure by elements like walls and hedges.

Even though the herbaceous border has become a staple of the British gardens, the same principles can be seen successfully transplanted anywhere. In Texas, foxglove and delphiniums can be replaced with drought-tolerant sages and yuccas. The effect is still that of a long tapestry full of colors, shapes, and textures.

A Modern Border: Boldness and Art

With the informality of the twentieth century and the advent of modern architecture and art, forms were distilled to their essence in shape, color, and texture. While Mies van der Rohe created the glass box skyscraper, Piet Modrian painted simple geometric shapes that still evoke mood and composition, and Henry Moore turned the human body into graceful sweeping forms in bronze. Gardens have also been transformed into pieces of art by the use of earth shaped forms, rock sculptures, and bold colors.

Brazilian landscape architect, Roberto Burle Marx transformed landscapes with large, bold patterns of color and texture. Even as a setting for a sculpture garden, the landscape holds its own as a work of art.

In the perennial garden, artiness can be applied in large bold sweeps of color and form, whether soft or geometric. Wolfgang Oehme and James van Sweden have made bold romantic gardens using the textures and colors of common grasses and perennials in both small-scale residences and large estates. They feature large sweeps of single types of plants. Likewise, the natural color combinations, sizes, and textures of plants can be combined to form intricate geometric patterns. The garden makes a wonderful setting for any sculpture even if you can't afford a Moore.

The Wild Garden: Woodland and Meadow

If you do not like structure, but do like to color in-between the lines, the natural or wild garden may be for you. Although they are carefully planned, planted, and maintained, these gardens look as if the plants grew naturally without any help from a green thumb. Meadows of low, native grasses are interplanted with annuals and perennials that waft in soft colors. The diversity of a natural or wild garden provides these kinds of plantings good habitats, while also creating

Chapter Two · *Style: Design and Layout*

Photo 2.15
Woodland garden at the
Dallas Arboretum and
Botanical Gardens

food for wildlife and insects. Perennials and annuals are left to seed, providing textures, new plantings, and food for animals. The Wildflower Center near Austin, Texas, is a prime example of this type of gardening. Many native wildflowers are, in fact, perennials. Plants that are native or highly adaptive to our climate work well in this type of garden and need less water, fertilizer, and maintenance.

The opposite of the meadow garden is the woodland. Nestled beneath tall canopies of trees are the shade-loving cousins of the sun-loving meadow flowers. These plants flourish in the dappled light along bark-covered paths. Most of these plants also prefer the increased moisture of the forest floor. Ferns, violets, and columbine drift quietly along with understory shrubs like oakleaf hydrangea. Sun or shade, the effect is

Photo 2.16
Wildflower meadow garden

wild and natural—no matter how premeditated the design. Followers of these styles have forgone the lawnmower and sprinkler system in favor of a more earth-friendly front yard.

If designing your garden seems more like a daunting task than an exciting endeavor, start small. A little piece of the yard can be any style you want: a knot garden, a herbaceous border, or a sunny meadow. As you look at other gardens and experiment with your own, you will find what works for you. In your own garden, what makes you happy is the right solution.

Chapter Three
BACKGROUND AND STRUCTURE

A garden can look quite bare in winter because most of the plants used in a perennial border are herbaceous, that is, they do not develop woody stems. Unless you are installing a natural garden, like a woodland area or a meadow, you should provide elements that give the garden structure, no matter what season. Some of these elements, like walls and fences, may already be in your garden. During the growing season, they become backdrops, edgers, or subplayers to the stars of the beds, the perennials. Some perennials are evergreen and look good year-round, but most are not. An attractive bed needs good structure, as these elements become the "bones" of the garden. Although hedges and walls imply straight lines, your garden need not be formal or regimented. Structural elements you should consider for your garden include background and edging.

BACKGROUNDS

Providing a background is a key element when designing a perennial border. It need not be tall, but it must provide structure year-round. It can be a permanent material or a growing plant.

WALLS

The material used for the walls should match or complement the house and the style of the garden. It can be formal or informal. Brick walls and stone walls make good backdrops for formal gardens. Stacked stone walls have no mortar and have a more casual look. Stucco and tiled walls lend more of a Southwestern flair and can be formal or informal.

"Gardening is a language with vocabulary, syntax, and above all punctuation. We often find that architecture provides the pause, the comma, that a garden needs amongst long paragraphs of plants. . . ."

JULIAN AND ISABEL BANNERMAN

FENCES

You may already have a fence on the perimeter of your yard made of wrought iron, cedar, redwood, or even bamboo. A fence used as a

Photo 3.2
A stone wall provides an edge to a garden

Photo 3.3
Boxwood hedges define a formal garden

background does not have to be completely solid. Picket fences provide a nice backdrop to plantings in the front of a house with a cottage garden, while providing an edge to the public sidewalk. Screen and trellis-type fences allow some views and air movement while giving structure and providing a framework for vines.

HEDGES

Hedges are a common part of almost every style of garden. The most favored are evergreen. However, many deciduous shrubs have enough structure from their branches to carry themselves

Photo 3.4
A brick wall forms a permanent backdrop to a perennial border

Photo 3.5
A wood screen fence provides a backdrop while allowing views and breezes

Photo 3.6
Clipped hedge of dwarf Burford holly, *Ilex cornuta 'Burfordii Nana'*

Photo 3.7
Mondo grass, *Ophiopogon japonicas*, provides a soft, evergreen edge

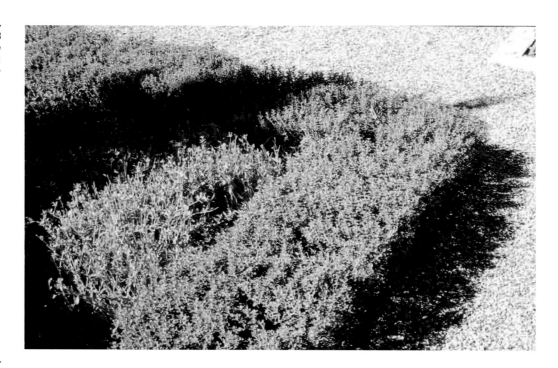

Photo 3.8
Germander, *Teucrium chaemedrys*, can be trimmed into a low, evergreen edger

Photo 3.9
Creeping thyme, *Thymus vulgaris*, and lavender, *Lavandula species*, make loose, evergreen edgers that spill over paving

as a structural element through winter. They can be sheared, formal hedges or informal groupings of two or three types of shrubs that make a nice border by themselves. Plant lower blooming shrubs in front of tall foliage or evergreen shrubs to give an added layering effect to the border.

SHRUBS FOR HEDGES

Abelia grandiflora
Abelia+*

Berberis thunbergii
Redleaf Barberry+

Buxus species
Boxwood+*

Caesalpinia species
Desert Bird of Paradise

Callicarpa americana
American Beautyberry

Camellia species
Camellia*

Euonymus alata
Burning Bush+

Fatsia japonica
Japanese Fatsia*

Forsythia species
Forsythia

Gardenia jasminoides
Gardenia*

Hibiscus syracuse
Rose of Sharon, Althea

Hydrangea species
Hydrangea

Ilex species
Holly+*

Juniperus species
Junipers+*

Leucophyllum species
Texas Sage, Texas Ranger*

Loropetalum chinensis rubrum
Fringe Flower*

**Magnolia grandiflora
'Little Gem'**
Little Gem Magnolia*

Myrica pusilla
Dwarf Wax Myrtle*

Nandina domestica
Nandina+*

Nerium oleander
Dwarf Oleander*

Pittosporum tobira
Mock Orange, Pittosporum+*

Raphiolepis indica
Indian Hawthorn*

Rosa species
Shrub and Landscape Roses

Sophora secundiflora
Texas Mountain Laurel*

Spiraea species
Spirea

Viburnum species
Viburnum*

Weigela florida
Weigela

+ Can be sheared
* Evergreen or semievergreen

VINES AND CLIMBERS

**Bignonia caprolata
(Anisostichus capreolata)**
Cross Vine*

Campsis radicans
Trumpet Vine

Clematis species
Clematis*

Ficus pumila
Fig Ivy*

Gelsemium sempervirens
Carolina Jessamine*

Lonicera sempervirens
Coral Honeysuckle*

Rosa species
Climbing Roses

Trachelospermum jasminoides
Confederate Jasmine,
Star Jasmine*

Wisteria sinensis
Wisteria

* Evergreen

CLIPPED EDGERS

Berberis thunbergii
Redleaf Barberry

Buxus species
Boxwood*

Ilex vomitoria 'Nana'
Dwarf Yaupon Holly*

Nandina domestica
Dwarf Varieties of Nandina*

Rhododendron species
Azalea*

Teucrium chaemedrys
Germander*

SPILLING EDGERS

Gardenia radicans
Dwarf Gardenia*

Hemerocallis species
Dwarf Daylily

Heuchera species
Coral Bells*

Ilex species
Holly*

Juniperus species
Creeping Junipers*

Liriope species
Liriope, Monkey Grass*

Ophiopogon species
MondoGrass, Ophiopogon*

Phlox subulata
Creeping Phlox

**Rosemarinus officinalis
'Prostratus'**
Creeping Rosemary*

Thymus vulgaris
Creeping Thyme*

Zephyranthus candida
White Rain Lily*

* Evergreen

VINES AND CLIMBERS

Whether growing up walls and fences or twinning around trellises, vines add structure and create a backdrop to the border.

EDGERS

Like background elements, edgings provide structure to the beds. Living plants or hardscape materials like stone can be used as edgings. They can be formal like a low, clipped hedge, or they can be loose and spilling. Paths, walks, and stepping-stones also provide a low, flat edge. Low walls of brick, stone, or timber not only provide a hard edge, but also allow you to raise the soil level. Ornamental iron edges add a visual interest to the bed. Low clipped edges of boxwood and holly give a refined, formal look.

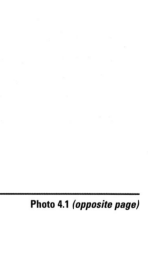

Photo 4.1 *(opposite page)*

Chapter Four
MAINTENANCE AND CARE

Maintenance for an established perennial bed can be minimal if you provide the right conditions and plant the right plants. However, you may find yourself constantly adding and changing things, so it never really ends. In late winter and early spring, you will need to spend more time cleaning out the beds for the upcoming year. If you don't want a lot of maintenance, choose plants that have few disease and pest problems, and make sure the soil and light conditions are favorable for what you plant. No garden is ever without maintenance, but making the right choices at the beginning can save time later on.

MAINTENANCE THROUGH THE YEAR

Use the following as a general annual to-do list.

January

* Winter is the least busy time for you in your garden. Most of the plants have gone dormant, and the temperatures are too cold to enjoy extended periods outside. After the rush of the holidays, mail-order nurseries start sending out their catalogues. Avid gardeners begin to dream about what projects they want to accomplish in the coming year. Allow your dreams to turn into a plan for upcoming projects, which will help you schedule your time and money to get those things accomplished.

* Add new beds and irrigation during the winter when the weather allows. By using winter months this way, you will be ready to do the fun stuff like buying and planting the plants as soon as temperatures rise and spring fever hits. Midspring and fall are the best times to plant perennials, grasses, and shrubs because the weather is mild and rainfall is higher. Fall planting is actually preferred for most plants because they don't suffer as much shock as they are going dormant. The roots will get established during the winter, and then they are ready to grow in spring.

∾ Enjoy what plants are providing color, like camellias and leopard plants. Plant them close to the house or by windows so you will enjoy the flowers from inside. You may want to cover them with tarps or blankets if the weather suddenly dips into freezing temperatures. Fruiting plants like hollies and beautyberries will be on display as well.

February

∾ By middle February, the earliest daffodils and other spring bulbs start to bloom. Remove faded flowers after they have finished blooming. Don't cut the foliage away until it is dry because the leaves store up food in the bulb for next year's flower.

∾ In mid-February, start pruning. Before the leaves and stems begin shooting out of the ground, remove any dead foliage from last year's perennials and dry leaves that have blown into the beds. Prune summer-blooming, woody perennials and perennial-like shrubs such as butterfly bush, crape myrtle, hummingbird bush, and caryopteris down 6 inches to 12 inches from the ground. Don't prune back spring-blooming plants. Grasses, liriope, and semievergreen ferns that have gotten ragged over the winter months can be cut down as well. Any pruning on roses should be done at this time, too. Trim any rose branches to right above an active, swelling leaf bud.

∾ If you don't already have a compost heap, start one with the dried foliage and cuttings. Do not add roses or other plants prone to diseases. Mix in ample amounts of grass cuttings and raw vegetable kitchen scraps, eggshells, and cow/sheep/horse manure. Never add cooked or processed food, meat, or cat/dog droppings. Keep it moist and turn it frequently. Once it decomposes into a dark, loamy material, you can add it back to your garden.

Photo 4.4
Daffodils, *Narcissus species*, line the authors' front walk in early spring after the perennials and grasses have been trimmed back

❧ Add soil and mulches where the beds have gotten low. Fertilize the garden with organic fertilizers and soil amendments. Add cornmeal around roses and other plants prone to fungus.

March

❧ Prune spring flowering shrubs and vines after they bloom. Shrubs that produce berries like holly and nandina must be pruned carefully or they will not retain their berries.

❧ Remove faded flowers from spring bulbs after they are done blooming. Don't cut the foliage away until it is dry because the leaves store up food in the bulb for next year's flower.

❧ Move or divide summer- and fall-blooming perennials that have become crowded.

❧ Plant new early blooming perennials, roses, shrubs, and vines.

❧ Choose wisteria that is already flowering, so that you will know that they bloom heavily from a young age.

❧ Fertilize perennials, shrubs, and roses.

April

❧ Fertilize and prune azaleas after they bloom. Add acidifiers to soils for azaleas, gardenias, maples, hydrangeas, and other acid-loving plants.

❧ The annual last freeze usually happens mid- to late March depending on where in Texas you live. When the chance of the last freeze has passed, begin planting summer annuals.

❧ Release beneficial insects such as ladybugs, lacewings, and praying mantis.

❧ Take a drive through the country. The beginning of April is peak season for the azaleas and dogwoods in East Texas. The end of April is also the peak of wildflower season, so pack up the family and take a drive through the country.

May

❧ Continue pruning spring shrubs and perennials after they have finished blooming.

❧ Remove faded foliage of spring bulbs once they have dried.

❧ Monitor plants closely and spray for infections. Powdery mildew on crape myrtles and blackspot on roses can be a problem in May.

ॐ Monitor and treat the rest of the garden for outbreaks of pests.

ॐ Remove faded flower stalks from daylilies and irises.

ॐ Take time to enjoy the garden. April and May are typically the most beautiful times in the garden. The weather is warmer yet not hot, the plants are lush and full of color, and the butterflies and bees are out in full force.

June

ॐ Mulch the beds with 2 inches of shredded hardwood mulch or pine straw for the summer to control weeds and to conserve moisture.

ॐ Pinch back fall bloomers like asters, chrysanthemums, and goldenrod to promote fuller, bushier plants.

ॐ Keep faded flowers of the summer perennials pinched off to promote continuous blooming.

ॐ Monitor plants for disease and pest problems.

ॐ Water potted plants daily.

July

ॐ Increase water as temperatures rise. However, do not overwater. Long, deep waterings no more than twice a week in the heat of summer help the plants develop deeper, healthier roots.

ॐ Fertilize the shrubs and perennials to help them get through the tough days ahead.

ॐ Remove faded flowers from perennials and shrubs.

ॐ Water potted plants daily.

August

ॐ Observe and learn which plants are truly drought and heat tolerant. They will suddenly take over the garden and thrive. Many of the grasses too will flourish and begin sending up plumes.

ॐ Water beds deeply during dry spells.

ॐ Remove faded flowers from perennials, shrubs, and annuals.

ॐ Water potted plants daily.

ॐ Stay cool. Cut the flowers and bring them indoors if you can't look at them from a pool outside.

ॐ Take a trip to the beach or mountains if you can.

September

ॐ Monitor the temperatures and rainfall amounts. Water deeply if rainfall is low. Even though it may not be as hot, the weather can still be quite dry. However in September, the temperatures will start to drop, and the rains typically return. The garden will start springing back to life. Watch as the late-summer- and fall-blooming perennials and grasses take over the flowerbeds for the next couple of months.

ॐ Monitor for fungal problems again as humidity rises.

ॐ Shop the nurseries for sales. They typically will try to get rid of perennials and shrubs to make room for Christmas trees.

ॐ Add hummingbird feeders to supplement your garden. August through October is usually the peak season for hummingbirds in Texas, and plants like hummingbird bush and firecracker plant are in full bloom at this time.

October

ॐ Plant spring bulbs like daffodils and grape hyacinths.

ॐ Move and divide spring flowering perennials and shrubs. Fall is the best time to plant most perennials, grasses, and shrubs, so this is an optimal time to start new beds. However, you may not be able to find the plants you want in the nurseries at this time, so plant spring bulbs and cover them with winter annuals for a great show. Then, as the winter annuals and the spring bulbs fade the following spring, you can plant more permanent perennials when they become available.

ॐ Add fallen leaves to the compost heap.

- Leave the faded flowers of yarrow, cone-flowers, and black-eyed Susans. They provide a nice dried texture into winter and provide food for birds.
- Dig up summer bulbs that may be damaged by the upcoming cold weather. Generally, in the Dallas area, gladiolas and cannas will survive in the ground through winter. In the panhandle, they will need to be dug up.

November

- Protect and mulch sensitive plants to protect against freezing in the northern parts of the state.
- Trim back perennials as they go dormant. Remember where they are planted if you are going to plant bulbs or annuals around them.

December

- Enjoy any leftover fall color, winter-berries, and winter annuals. December is usually a hectic month for most people. Fortunately, the garden is less demanding.
- Protect cold-sensitive plants from harsh temperatures with cloth or tarps.
- Put food out for the birds.
- Notice that the camellias will start to bloom.
- Transplant perennials, shrubs, vines, and trees when they are dormant.
- Finish planting spring bulbs.

SOAPBOX ALERT

Use organic solutions whenever possible. Heavy chemicals for fungicides, fertilizers, and pesticides not only kill the problem, but also hurt things that are beneficial in the garden such as bees, butterflies, earthworms, lizards, birds, toads, and ladybugs. Remember, they all lived here long before we took over. Besides, who knows what effect they will have on us? For plants like roses and crape myrtles that are susceptible to fungus, use preventive cures to hold off the problems. These preventive measures are typically less invasive to the environment than treating a problem once it has started.

The best advice on diseases and pests is to avoid plants that are prone to these problems. Sources are readily available on how to treat specific problems through your local nursery or through the Texas Agricultural Extension Service. Keep in mind not to plant perennials that get root rot easily where the natural soil does not drain. This will help you avoid fungal problems. Don't plant moisture-loving plants like Louisiana iris in gravelly soils in full, hot sun. And never plant acid-loving plants like azaleas directly in heavy, alkaline clay soil.

The maintenance and care of your perennial garden can be low key if you have prepared the garden properly. The goal is to enjoy the ever-changing display of colors, sounds, and smells, not to battle them. Once established, most of the plants listed will be quite self-sufficient with occasional attention from you.

Chapter Five
PLANNING A COLOR SCHEME

*O*nce the site and bed layout has been determined for your perennial garden, begin focusing on designing with the plants themselves. Of all the possible design elements, the colors of the flowers and foliage are the most important. Color combinations set the mood and ambience that the garden will take on. For example, hot colors like reds, yellows, and oranges tend to jump out and excite. On the other hand, cool colors like blues and purples are more calming, and tend to look distant and serene. Approach your bed as if it were a painting, and choose paints, or plants, that work with the mood you want to set and the color combinations you enjoy. Always repeat plants and colors to provide unity throughout the garden. Too many colors or not enough repetition of colors will cause a bed or a garden begin to look chaotic and messy.

If you are not sure what colors to start with, pick your personal favorites or pick those that will complement their surroundings. If you are planting next to your white painted house, darker, richer, and more vibrant colors will stand out better than whites and grays. If that white house has blue trim, you may choose blues to play off the trim or oranges and reds to complement it. If you are planting in front of a dark brick wall, choose light colors such as white, yellow, gray, and pink for contrast.

If you are still not sure where to start, go to the old trusted color wheel. The color wheel begins with the primary colors of red, yellow, and blue. All other colors are combinations of these three. The three secondary colors, purple, orange, and green, are each a combination of two of the primary colors. The rest of the hues are a combination of secondary and primary colors. Of course, adding whites, grays, lights, and darks embellish the palette.

> *"The plant is, to a landscape artist, not only a plant—rare, unusual, ordinary, or doomed to disappearance—but it is also a color, a shape, a volume, or an arabesque in itself."*
>
> ROBERTO BURLE MARX,
> LANDSCAPE DESIGNER

Photo 5.2
Lambsear, *Stachys lanata*,
and blue fescue,
Festuca ovina glauca

The Basics of Color Combinations

Using color combinations to your advantage requires just a little knowledge regarding primary colors, complementary colors, harmonious and monochromatic schemes, and pastels versus dark colors.

Photo 5.3
Gerbera daisy,
Gerbera species

Primary Colors

The three primary colors of red, yellow, and blue actually make a great combination. You can take that principle of three opposite colors and apply it anywhere on the color wheel to come up with a great triple treat. For example, you may use orange, purple and green; or yellow-green, blue-violet, and red-orange.

Complementary Colors

To make a very dynamic combination, choose two colors opposite each other on the color wheel. Together, they provide high contrast and pop out from each other. The opposite of red is green, blue is orange, purple is yellow, and so on. Sometimes using the complementary color simply as an accent may look better. For example, your border may consist mainly of blue shades, but you might add some oranges every now and then to add spice.

Harmonious Colors

Colors found close to each other on the color wheel tend to blend and make a unified appearance. For example, you may choose reds,

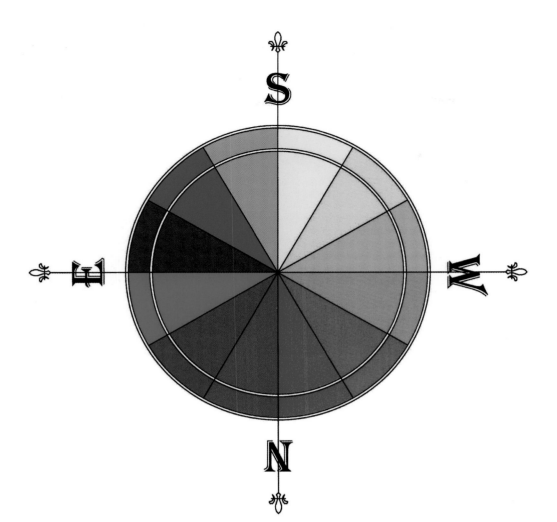

Photo 5.4
Color wheel

Photo 5.5
Primary color scheme garden
using yellows, reds, and blues

Photo 5.6
Monochromatic color scheme
garden using whites

oranges, and yellows; or you might choose blues, violets, and pinks.

MONOCHROMATIC SCHEMES

The use of one basic color can be striking. A wide range of plants can be used, provided they all share the same color or color family, and in most cases, green will always be a backdrop. The most popular monochromatic scheme is white. It gives a subtle, clean, sophisticated look. Whites also tend to brighten a dark space or pick up lights at night from windows and fixtures near the house. Whites are effective when planted along paths that will be used frequently at night.

If you find one color too subtle, try one hue in various tones of light to dark. A border of all red flowers can be a little strong. Adding darker reds and maroons for depth and lighter pinks and whites as highlights will make the bed more interesting, while relying on the strength and uniformity of one main color. Blues work especially well when mixed with blue-grays and silvers.

PASTELS VS. DARK COLORS

Pastels provide a soft, calming look, while richer, vibrant colors provide a livelier appear-

ance. You might choose plants that evolve from pastels (often found naturally in spring) and gradually change your border to richer, darker jeweled colors by the end of summer and autumn.

FAVORITE COLOR COMBINATIONS

BLUES, WHITES, AND GRAYS

This combination lends a soft and cool effect to a garden. These colors work well equally with white buildings as well as with darker ones. Gray and bluestone pavers blend nicely, too. For a little highlight, sprinkle in dashes of soft yellow, orange, or pink.

BLUES, YELLOWS, AND WHITES

This combination is also soft and bright. Use it with other white elements and bluestone pavers and gravel.

BLUES, PINKS, AND WHITE

The effect of this scheme is similar to the previous combination being soft and bright. Use it if you prefer the pinks to the yellows.

Photo 5.7
Blue/gray/white color scheme
garden

BLUES, PURPLES, LAVENDERS, AND PINKS

This classic combination of harmonious colors is cool and serene. The blues, violets, and purples provide a cool tapestry while the pinks provide pizzazz without competing too much for attention.

REDS, YELLOWS, AND ORANGES

This is another classic combination of harmonious colors with a hot and bold effect. Be careful not to let the entire border scream. Oranges may be the loudest. Use some darker reds and softer yellows to tone down the look. You can vary hues over the seasons with more pastel col-

Photo 5.8
Cool white/purple/pink color scheme garden

ors in spring and darker shades in autumn. But in summer, let them shout.

WHITES, PINKS, AND REDS

This combination works similarly to a blue-white-gray combination. The pinks and whites will stand out, leaving darker reds and maroons to fade back. This scheme works well with red bricks, reddish stones, gray woods, and gray stones.

YELLOWS, GREENS, AND BLUES

Like other harmonious color schemes, this combination provides unifying color. Although green is not a common flower color, various

Photo 5.9
Scarlet sage, *Salvia coccinea*

Photo 5.10
Texas Star hibiscus,
Hibiscus coccineus

shades of greens can be found in foliage plants like hostas, ferns, and grasses. The scheme can range from the cools of blues and blue-greens to the hotter tones of yellow, yellow-green, and chartreuse, which read well under the dappled light of trees.

OPPOSITES ATTRACT

If you want to get attention in the border or in a certain portion of a bed, remember that complementary colors work well together and offset each other. Complementary colors are those located opposite each other on the color wheel. Blues make oranges jump. Reds are offset by greens. Yellows are excited by violets, and so on.

PRIMARY COLORS

The combination of reds, blues, and yellows is a simple but dynamic combination. Be careful though; depending on the intensity of the colors chosen, it can be overwhelming.

YOUR FAVORITE COLORS

You may just pick your favorite colors. My favorites are blues, violets, and purples with a dash of sunny yellow. In my backyard, which gets a lot of shade, I use more pastels and soft colors. In my front yard, which faces the hot, sunny southwest, I use the gray, blue, purple color scheme with hot accents of yellow and an occasional orange in the summer months. The orange looks great against the blue-gray-purple combination. Use the color combination that pleases you, guided by some basic rules. Some of the most famous borders in the world use almost the entire gamut of colors relying on repetition of certain plants, colors, or textures to look great.

RED HOT

Plants that Have Red Flowers and Foliage

Red is the lowest and the most vibrant color of the visible spectrum. One of the warm colors, it represents heat, blood, and the heart, and it is associated with passion and love. Red tends to be stimulating and exciting. Its complementary color is green.

Photo 5.11
Japanese blood grass,
Imperata cylindrica
'Red Baron'

Red Hot

PERENNIALS

Achillea species
Yarrow, Milfoil

Anemone coronaria
Poppy Anemone, Windflower

Aniscanthus quadrifidus var. wrightii
Hummingbird Bush, Flame Acanthus

Aquilegia x hybrida 'Bierdermiere'
Dwarf Columbines

Asclepias tuberosa
Butterfly Weed

Aster species
Aster

Astilbe x arendsii
Astilbe, False Spirea

Belamcanda chinensis
Blackberry Lily, Candy Lily

Canna x generalis
Canna Lily

Centranthus ruber
Red Valerian

Chrysanthemum x morifolium
Garden Mum

Coreopsis rosea
Pink Coreopsis

Crocosmia x crocosmiflora
Crocosmia, Montbretia

Dianthus species
Dianthus, Carnation

Foeniculum vulgare
Fennel*

Gaillardia x grandiflora
Gaillardia, Indian Blanket

Geranium species
Hardy Geranium, Cranesbill

Gerbera species
Gerbera Daisy

Gladiolus species
Gladiolus

Hemerocallis species
Daylily

Heuchera sanquinea
Coral Bells

Hibiscus species
Hibiscus

Hippeastrum x johnsonii
Hardy Amaryllis

Hymenocallis species
Spider Lily

Iris species
Iris

Kniphofia uvaria
Red Hot Poker, Torch Lily, Tritoma

Lilium species
Lilies

Lobelia cardinalis
Cardinal Flower Lobelia*

Lycorus radiata
Autumn Crocus, Spider Lily

Malvaviscus drummondii
Turk's Cap**

Monarda didmyma
Bee Balm

Paeonia species
Peony

Penstemon species
Penstemon

Ratibida columnifera
Mexican Hat

Rudbeckia hirta
Gloriosa Daisy, Rudbeckia

Russelia equisetiformis
Firecracker Plant

Salvia coccinea
Scarlet Sage

Salvia greggii
Autumn Sage, Cherry Sage

Salvia penstemonoides
Penstemon Sage, Big Red Sage

Sedum spectabile
Showy Sedum

Sidalcea species
Prairie Mallow

Stokesia laevis
Stokes Aster

Tulipa clusiana
Species Tulip, Wild Tulip

Verbena species
Verbena

Veronica species
Veronica, Speedwell

GRASSES*

Andropogon species
Bluestem Grasses

Imperata cylindrica 'Red Baron'
Japanese Blood Grass

SHRUBS, VINES, AND ROSES

Acer palmatum
Japanese Maple*

Berberis thunbergii
Redleaf Barberry*

Bignonia caprolata
Cross Vine

Caesalpinia species
Desert Bird of Paradise

Camellia species
Camellia

Campsis radicans
Trumpet Vine

Clematis species
Clematis

Euonymus alata
Burning Bush*

Hesperaloe parviflora
Red Yucca

Hibiscus syriacus
Rose of Sharon, Althea

Ilex species
Holly**

Lagerstroemia indica
Dwarf Crape Myrtle

Nandina domestica
Nandina**

Nerium oleander
Dwarf Oleander

Rhododendron species
Azalea

Rosa species
Rose**

Spiraea x bumalda 'Anthony Waterer'
Anthony Waterer Spirea

Weigela florida
Weigela*

* Red foliage
** Red fruit

Photo 5.12
Daylily, *Hemerocallis species*

Photo 5.13
Butterfly weed,
Asclepias tuberosa

Photo 5.14
Trumpet vine,
Campsis radicans

OUTRAGEOUS ORANGE

Plants that Have Orange Flowers

Orange is a warm color that stimulates the emotions, unlike red, which stimulates the blood and body. It combines the cheerfulness of yellow with the boldness of red, and it represents bravery as well. Its complementary color is blue.

Outrageous Orange

PERENNIALS

Asclepias tuberosa
Butterfly Weed

Belamcanda chinensis
Blackberry Lily, Candy Lily

Bulbine frutescens
Bulbine

Canna x generalis
Canna Lily

Chrysanthemum x morifolium
Garden Mum

Crocosmia x crocosmiflora
Crocosmia, Montbretia

Gaillardia x grandiflora
Gaillardia, Indian Blanket

Gerbera species
Gerbera Daisy

Gladiolus species
Gladiolus

Iris germanica
German Bearded Iris

Kniphofia uvaria
Red Hot Poker, Torch Lily, Tritoma

Lantana camara
Lantana

Lilium species
Lilies

Narcissus species
Daffodils, Jonquils, and Narcissus

Phlox paniculata
Summer Phlox

Ratibida columnifera
Mexican Hat

Rudbeckia hirta
Gloriosa Daisy, Rudbeckia, Yellow Coneflower

Tagetes lucida
Mexican Mint Marigold, Mexican Taragon

Tecoma stans
Yellow Bells, Esperanza

SHRUBS, VINES, AND ROSES

Bignonia caprolata
Cross Vine

Caesalpinia
Desert Bird of Paradise

Campsis radicans
Trumpet Vine

Lonicera sempervirens
Coral Honeysuckle

Rhododendron species
Azalea

Rosa species
Rose

SUNNY YELLOWS

Plants that Have Yellow Flowers and Foliage

Yellow, another warm color, represents the warming nature of the sun. Because it stimulates the intellect, it also represents wisdom. Cheerful and happy, it reflects the sun when dominating the summer border. Purple is its complementary color.

Photo 5.15
Black-eyed Susan, *Rudbeckia fulgida 'Goldstrum'*

Photo 5.16
Daffodil, *Narcissus species 'February Gold'*

Photo 5.17
Golden Japanese forest grass,
Hakonechloa macro 'Aureola'

Sunny Yellows

PERENNIALS

Achillea species
Yarrow, Milfoil

Alchemilla mollis
Lady's Mantle

Allium moly
Golden Garlic

Alpinia species
Ginger*

Aquilegia chrysantha 'Hinckleyana'
Texas Gold Columbine

Artemisia ludoviciana abula 'Silver King'
Silver King Artemisia

Asclepias tuberosa
Butterfly Weed

Beloperone guttata
Gold and Brown Shrimp Plant

Belamcanda chinensis
Blackberry Lily, Candy Lily

Berlandiera species
Greeneyes, Chocolate Daisy

Buddleia x wyeriana 'Honeycomb'
Honeycomb Butterfly Bush

Bulbine frutescens
Bulbine

Calyophus hartwegii
Sun Drops

Canna x generalis
Canna Lily

Caryopteris x clandonensis
Caryopteris, Bluemist Spirea*

Chrysanthemum x morifolium
Garden Mum

Coreopsis species
Tickseed, Coreopsis

Crocosmia x crocosmiflora
Crocosmia, Montbretia

Crocus vernus
Crocus

Gaillardia x grandiflora
Gaillardia, Indian Blanket

Gerbera species
Gerbera Daisy

Gladiolus species
Gladiolus

Helianthus maximiliani
Maximillian Sunflower

Heliopsis helianthoides
False Sunflower

Hemerocallis species
Daylily

Hosta species
Hosta Lily, Plantain Lily*

Hymenoxys scaposa
4 Nerve Daisy

Iris species
Iris

Iris pseudacorus
Yellow Flag Iris

Kniphofia uvaria
Red Hot Poker, Torch Lily, Tritoma

Lantana camara
Lantana

Ligularia tussilaginea 'Aureo-maculata'
Leopard Plant*

Lilium species
Lilies

Lycorus aurea
Yellow Spider Lily

Morea bicolor
Butterfly Iris

Narcissus species
Daffodils, Jonquils, and Narcissus

Oenothera missouriensis
Missouri Primrose, Ozark Sundrop

Phlomis russeliana
Jerusalem Sage

Ratibida columnifera
Mexican Hat

Rudbeckia species
Black-Eyed Susan, Rudbeckia, Yellow Coneflower

Salvia greggii
Autumn Sage, Cherry Sage

Solidago sphacelata
Goldenrod

Tagetes species
Copper Canyon Daisy, Mexican Mint Marigold

Tecoma stans
Yellow Bells, Esperanza

Thalictrum aquilegifolium
Meadow Rue

Thymus citriodorus
Lemon Thyme*

Tradescantia virginiana
Spiderwort*

Zantedeschia species
Calla Lily

Zephyranthus sulphurea
Yellow Rain Lily

Zexmenia hispida
Zexmenia

GRASSES*

Acorus gramineus
Variegated Sweet Flag

Carex marrowii 'Aureo-Variegata'
Variegated Japanese Sedge

Hakonechloa macro 'Aureola'
Golden Japanese Forest Grass

Miscanthus sinensis
Miscanthus, Maiden Grass, Japanese Silver Grass

SHRUBS, VINES, AND ROSES

Acuba japonica
Acuba*

Bignonia caprolata
Cross Vine

Caesalpinia species
Desert Bird of Paradise

Campsis radicans
Trumpet Vine

Forsythia species
Forsythia

Gelsemium sempervirens
Carolina Jessamine

Hesperaloe parviflora 'Yellow'
Yellow Yucca

Hypericum henryi
St. John's Wort

Juniperus species
Junipers*

Mahonia bealei
Leatherleaf Mahonia

Opuntia species
Prickly Pear

Rhododendron species
Azalea

Rosa species
Rose

Yucca species
Yucca*

*Yellow variegated or yellow-green foliage

Photo 5.18
Variegated hosta, *Hosta species 'Albo marginata'*

GREEN WITH ENVY

Plants Grown for Their Foliage

Green is a cool color, representing stability, endurance, and peace. Since it is the most common color found outdoors, that may be why gardens have a calming effect on people. Green becomes the canvas upon which all the other colors are overlaid. Even when plants are not in bloom, a rich palette of greens sustain the border. Its complementary color is red.

Photo 5.19
Southern wood fern,
Thelypteris kunthii

Photo 5.20
Carissa holly leaves,
Ilex cornuta 'Carissa'

Green with Envy

PERENNIALS

Ajuga reptans
Ajuga, Bugleweed

Alchemilla mollis
Lady's Mantle

Alpinia species
Ginger

Aspidistra elatior
Aspidistra, Cast Iron Plant

Colocasia esculenta
Elephant Ears

Foeniculum vulgare
Fennel

Ligularia tussilaginea 'Aureo-maculata'
Leopard Plant

Liriope species
Liriope, Lilyturf

Ophiopogon japonicas
Ophiopogon, Mondo Grass

Rivina humilis
Pigeonberry

Rosemarinus officinalis
Rosemary

Santolina virens
Green Lavender Cotton,
Green Santolina

Sedum spectabile
Showy Sedum

Teucrium chaemedrys
Germander

Thymus vulgaris
Creeping Thyme

GRASSES

Andropogon species
Bluestem Grasses

Bouteloua curtipendula var. caespitosa
Sideoats Grama

Calamagrostis arundinacea 'Karl Foerster'
Karl Foerster Feather Reed Grass

Chasmanthium latifolium
Inland Sea Oats

Equisetum hyemale
Horsetail Reed

Eragrostis curvula
Weeping Love Grass

Miscanthus sinensis
Miscanthus, Maiden Grass,
Japanese Silver Grass

Muhlenbergia species
Muhly Grasses

Nasella tenuissima
Mexican Feather Grass

Panicum virgatum
Switch Grass

Pennisetum alopecuroides
Fountain Grass

Sorghastrum nutans
Indian Grass

Typha latifolia
Cattail Reed

FERNS

All Ferns

SHRUBS, VINES, AND ROSES

Abelia grandiflora
Abelia

Acer palmatum
Japanese Maple

Acuba japonica
Acuba

Agave species
Agave, Century Plant

Buxus species
Boxwood

Cycas revoluta
Sago Palm

Dasylerion species
Desert Spoon, Sotol

Euonymus alata
Burning Bush

Fatsia japonica
Japanese Fatsia

Ficus pumila
Fig Ivy

Hesperaloe species
Red Yucca

Ilex species
Holly

Juniperus species
Junipers

Magnolia grandiflora 'Little Gem'
Little Gem Magnolia

Mahonia bealei
Leatherleaf Mahonia

Myrica pusilla
Dwarf Wax Myrtle

Nandina domestica
Nandina

Opuntia species
Prickly Pear

Pittosporum tobira
Mock Orange, Pittosporum

Trachelospermum jasminoides
Star Jasmine

Yucca species
Adam's Needle, Yucca

Plants that Have Blue Flowers and Foliage

Blue is a cool color that has a calming and serene effect. It represents love, devotion, and harmony. It also represents the sky and water, thus giving a cooling effect to a hot summer garden. Its complementary color is orange.

Photo 5.21
Balloon flower, *Platycodon gradiflorus*

Photo 5.22
Globe thistle, *Echinops ritro 'Vetch's Blue'*

Photo 5.23
Blue fescue, *Festuca ovina glauca*

Singin' the Blues

PERENNIALS

Agapanthus species
Lily of the Nile, Agapanthus

Agastache species
Hyssop, Hummingbird Mint

Ajuga reptans
Ajuga, Bugleweed

Allium caeruleum
Blue Alliums

Anemone coronaria
Poppy Anemone, Windflower

Aquilegia x hybrida 'Bierdermiere'
Dwarf Columbines

Aster species
Aster

Baptisia australis
Blue False Indigo

Buddleia x davidii
Butterfly Bush, Summer Lilac

Caryopteris x clandonensis
Caryopteris, Bluemist Spirea

Ceratostigma plumbaginoides
Creeping Plumbago

Crocus vernus
Crocus

Echinops ritro 'Vetch's Blue'
Globe Thistle*

Eupatorium species
Hardy Ageratum

Geranium species
Hardy Geranium, Cranesbill

Gladiolus species
Gladiolus

Hosta species
Hosta Lily, Plantain Lily*

Ipeion uniflorum
Blue-Eyed Grass, Spring Star Flower

Iris species
Iris

Liriope species
Liriope, Lilyturf

Muscari species
Grape Hyacinth

Nepeta faassenii
Catmint

Perovskia atriplicifolia
Russian Sage

Phlox species
Phlox

Platycodon gradiflorus
Balloon Flower

Rosemarinus officinalis
Rosemary

Ruellia brittoniana
Ruellia, Mexican Petunia

Salvia 'Indigo Spires'
Indigo Spires Salvia

Salvia azurea var. grandiflora
Azure Sage, Pitcher Sage

Salvia bicolor
Bicolor Sage, Cocoa Sapphire Salvia

Salvia blepharophylla
Purple Leaf Sage

Salvia buchananii
Buchanan's Sage

Salvia chamaedryoides
Gray Shrub Sage

Salvia engelmannii
Engelmann's Sage

Salvia farinacea
Mealy Cup Sage

Salvia guarantica
Anise Scented Sage

Salvia lyrata
Lyre Leaf Sage

Salvia officinalis
Garden Sage

Salvia uliginosa
Bog Sage

Salvia x superba
Meadow Sage

Scabiosa caucasica 'Butterfly Blue'
Pincushion Flower

Scilla peruviana
Peruvian Scilla

Scilla siberica
Siberian Squill

Stokesia laevis
Stokes Aster

Teucrium chaemedrys
Germander

Teucrium fruticans
Bush Germander

Verbena species
Verbena

Veronica peduncularis 'Georgia Blue'
Creeping Speedwell

Veronica species
Veronica, Speedwell

GRASSES*

Andropogon species
Bluestem Grasses

Carex glauca
Blue Sedge

Elymus glaucus
Blue Wild Rye

Eragrostis curvula
Weeping Love Grass

Festuca ovina glauca
Blue Fescue

Muhlenbergia lindhiemerii
Lindhiemers Muhly

Panicum virgatum
Sorghastrum nutans

Indian Grass
Switch Grass

SHRUBS, VINES, AND ROSES

Agave species
Agave, Century Plant*

Clematis species
Clematis

Dasylerion species
Desert Spoon, Sotol*

Hibiscus syriacus
Rose of Sharon, Althea

Hydrangea macrophylla
Hydrangea

Ilex meserveae
Blue Hollies*

Juniperus species
Junipers*

Lagerstroemia indica
Dwarf Crape Myrtle

Rosa species
Rose

Sophora secundiflora
Texas Mountain Laurel

Vitex agnus-castus
Vitex, Chastetree

Wisteria sinensis
Wisteria

*Blue foliage

Photo 5.24
Spanish lavender,
Lavandula stoechas

PURPLE PASSION

Plants with Purple, Violet, or Lavender Flowers and Foliage

These cool colors represent the highest levels of the visible light spectrum as well as the higher ideals of spirituality, honor, and self-esteem. Purple is bold and draws attention. Lavender, on the other hand, is soft and calming. Yellow is the complementary color.

Photo 5.25
Iris, *Iris germanica
'Royal Touch'*

Photo 5.26
Purple heart, *Setcreasea
pallida 'Purple Heart'*

Purple Passion

PERENNIALS

Acanthus mollis
Bear's Breeches, Grecian
Leaf Plant

Ajuga reptans
Ajuga, Bugleweed*

Allium species
Allium

Anemone species
Anemone, Windflower

**Aquilegia x hybrida
'Bierdermiere'**
Dwarf Columbines

Aster species
Aster

Astilbe x arendsii
Astilbe, False Spirea

Belamcanda chinensis
Blackberry Lily, Candy Lily

Buddleia x davidii
Butterfly Bush, Summer Lilac

Callirhoe involucrata
Wine Cups, Poppy Mallow

Chrysanthemum x morifolium
Garden Mum

Crocus vernus
Crocus

Echinacea purpurea
Purple Coneflower

**Erysismum linifolium
'Bowles Mauve'**
Wallflower

**Eupatorium rugosum
'Chocolate'**
Chocolate Mist Flower*

Foeniculum vulgare
Fennel*

Geranium species
Hardy Geranium, Cranesbill

Gladiolus species
Gladiolus

Helleborus orientalis
Lenten Rose

Hemerocallis species
Daylily

**Heuchera americana
'Palace Purple'**
Palace Purple Coral Bells*

Hosta species
Hosta Lily, Plantain Lily

Hyacintoides hispanica
Woodland Hyacinths,
Spanish Bluebells

Iris species
Iris

Lantana sellowiana
Trailing Lantana

Lavandula species
Lavender

Liatris spicata
Liatris, Kansas Gayfeather

Lilium species
Lilies

Liriope species
Liriope, Lilyturf

Lythrum salicaria
Purple Loosestrife

Monarda didmyma
Bee Balm

Muscari species
Grape Hyacinth

Nepeta faassenii
Catmint

Nierembergia 'Purple Robe'
Nierembergia, Cupflower

Ophiopogon species
Black and Ebony Knight
Mondo Grass*

Oxalis triangularis
Purple Shamrock*

Paeonia species
Peony

Penstemon species
Penstemon

Phlox species
Phlox

Physostegia virginiana
Fall Obedient Plant,
False Dragonhead

Poliomintha longiflora
Mexican Oregano

Ruellia brittoniana
Ruellia, Mexican Petunia

Salvia officinalis
Garden Sage*

Salvia bicolor
Bicolor Sage, Cocoa
Sapphire Salvia*

Salvia blepharophylla
Purple Leaf Sage*

Salvia greggii
Autumn Sage, Cherry Sage

**Salvia greggii x lycioides
'Wild Grape'**
Wild Grape Sage

Salvia leucantha
Mexican Bush Sage

Salvia lyrata
Lyre Leaf Sage*

Salvia nemerosa 'Plumosa'
Plumosa Meadow Sage

**Salvia verticillata
'Purple Rain'**
Purple Rain Salvia

Salvia x superba
Meadow Sage

Scilla siberica
Siberian Squill

Setcreasea pallida
Purple Heart*

Stachys lanata
Lamb's Ear

Stokesia laevis
Stokes Aster

Teucrium chaemedrys
Germander

Thymus vulgaris
Creeping Thyme

Tradescantia virginiana
Spiderwort

Tulbaghia violacea
Society Garlic

**Tulipa bakeri
'Lilac Wonder'**
Species Tulip, Wild Tulip

Verbena species
Verbena

Viola species
Wood Violet

Zantedeschia species
Calla Lily

FERNS

Athyrium niponicum 'Pictum'
Japanese Painted Fern*

GRASSES*

Andropogon species
Bluestem

Deschampsia caespitosa
Tufted Hair Grass

SHRUBS, VINES, AND ROSES

Callicarpa americana
American Beautyberry**

Chilopsis linearis
Desert Willow

Clematis species
Clematis

Cotinus coggygria
Smoke Tree*

Hibiscus Syriacase
Rose of Sharon, Althea

Hydrangea macrophylla
Hydrangea

Lagerstroemia indica
Dwarf Crape Myrtle

Leucophyllum species
Texas Sage, Texas Ranger

Loropetalum chinensis rubrum
Fringe Flower*

Nandina domestica
Nandina*

Opuntia species
Prickly Pear*

Rhododendron species
Azalea

Rosa species
Rose

Sophora secundiflora
Texas Mountain Laurel

Weigela florida
Weigela

Wisteria sinensis
Wisteria

*Purple foliage
**Purple fruit

Photo 5.27
Oriental lily, *Lilium species*
'Stargazer'

Plants that Have Pink Flowers

Pink is the combination of red and white, mixing the vitality and excitability of red with the calming, soothing nature of white. Fresh and cheerful, it blends well with most colors. It can be a bold shocking pink or a restful light rose. Pink is the backbone of any pastel colored border.

Photo 5.28
Purple coneflower, *Echinacea purpurea* 'Magnus'

Photo 5.29
Lady Baltimore hibiscus, *Hibiscus moscheutos* 'Lady Baltimore'

PERENNIALS

Achillea species
Yarrow, Milfoil

Agastache species
Hyssop, Hummingbird Mint

Anemone species
Anemone, Windflower

Aquilegia x hybrida 'Bierdermiere'
Dwarf Columbines

Asclepias incarnata
Pink Butterfly Weed

Aster species
Aster

Astilbe x arendsii
Astilbe, False Spirea

Belamcanda chinensis
Blackberry Lily, Candy Lily

Buddleia x davidii
Butterfly Bush, Summer Lilac

Callirhoe involucrata
Winecups, Poppy Mallow

Canna x generalis
Canna Lily

Centranthus ruber
Red Valerian

Chrysanthemum x 'Clara Curtis'
Clara Curtis Chrysanthemum

Chrysanthemum x morifolium
Garden Mum

Coreopsis rosea
Pink Coreopsis

Crinum species
Crinum Lily

Dianthus 'First Love'
Hardy Carnation

Dianthus gratianopolitanus
Cheddar Pinks

Echinacea pallida
Prairie Coneflower, Pale Coneflower

Echinacea purpurea
Purple Coneflower

Eupatorium maculatum 'Gateway'
Joe Pye Weed

Geranium species
Hardy Geranium, Cranesbill

Gerbera species
Gerbera Daisy

Gladiolus species
Gladiolus

Guara lindhiemerii 'Siskiyou Pink'
Pink Guara, Whirling Butterflies

Helleborus orientalis
Lenten Rose

Hemerocallis species
Daylily

Heuchera sanquinea
Coral Bells

Hibiscus moscheutos
Hibiscus, Rose Mallow

Hippeastrum x johnsonii
Hardy Amaryllis

Hosta species
Hosta Lily, Plantain Lily

Hyacintoides hispanica
Woodland Hyacinths, Spanish Bluebells

Incarvillea delavayi
Chinese Foxglove

Iris species
Iris

Lantana camara
Lantana

Lavandula species
Lavender

Lilium species
Lilies

Lobelia cardinalis
Cardinal Flower Lobelia

Lycorus radiata
Autumn Crocus, Spider Lily, Surprise Lily

Lycorus squamigera
Belladonna Lily

Lythrum salicaria
Purple Loosestrife

Monarda didmyma
Bee Balm

Narcissus species
Daffodils, Jonquils, and Narcissus

Oenothera speciosa
Evening Primrose

Oxalis species
Wood Sorrel, Purple Shamrock

Paeonia species
Peony

Pavonia lasiopetala
Rock Rose

Penstemon species
Penstemon, Beardtongue

Phlox species
Phlox

Physostegia virginiana
Fall Obedient Plant, False Dragonhead

Platycodon gradiflorus
Balloon Flower

Ruellia brittoniana
Ruellia, Mexican Petunia

Salvia coccinea
Scarlet Sage

Salvia greggii
Autumn Sage, Cherry Sage

Salvia leucantha
Mexican Bush Sage

Salvia penstemonoides
Penstemon Sage, Big Red Sage

Salvia x superba
Meadow Sage

Scabiosa caucasica 'Pink Mist'
Pincushion Flower

Scilla siberica
Siberian Squill

Scutellaria suffrutescens
Pink Scullcap

Sedum spectabile
Showy Sedum

Sidalcea species
Prairie Mallow

Stachys officinalis
Woodland Betony

Stokesia laevis
Stokes Aster

Teucrium chaemedrys
Germander

Thalictrum aquilegifolium
Meadow Rue

Thymus vulgaris
Creeping Thyme

Tulipa species
Species or Wild Tulip

Verbena species
Verbena

Veronica species
Veronica, Speedwell

Viola odorata
Wood Violet, Sweet Violet

Zantedeschia species
Calla Lily

Zephyranthus robusta
Pink Rain Lily

GRASSES

Muhlenbergia capillaris
Gulf Muhly, Hairyawn Muhly

SHRUBS, VINES, AND ROSES

Abelia grandiflora
Abelia

Berberis thunbergii
Redleaf Barberry

Camellia species
Camellia

Chilopsis linearis
Desert Willow

Clematis species
Clematis

Cotinus coggygria
Smoke Tree

Hibiscus Syracuse
Rose of Sharon, Althea

Hydrangea macrophylla
Hydrangea

Lagerstroemia indica
Dwarf Crape Myrtle

Leucophyllum species
Texas Ranger, Texas Sage

Lonicera sempervirens
Coral Honeysuckle

Loropetalum chinensis rubrum
Fringe Flower

Magnolia lilliflora
Lily Magnolia

Nerium oleander
Dwarf Oleander

Raphiolepis indica
Indian Hawthorn

Rhododendron species
Azalea

Rosa species
Rose

Spiraea species
Spirea

Symphoricarpos orbiculatus
Coralberry**

Viburnum x burkwoodii
Burkwood Viburnum

Vitex agnus-castus
Vitex, Chastetree

Weigela florida
Weigela

Wisteria sinensis
Wisteria

** Pink fruit

Photo 5.30
Ox-eye daisy, *Chrysanthemum
leucanthemum*

THE CLEAN WHITES

Plants that Have White Flowers and Creamy or White Variegated Foliage

White is a combination of all the colors of the light spectrum. It represents purity and calmness and has a fresh, clean look. White unites various colors. At night, it is the only garden color visible by the moonlight.

Photo 5.31
Angel's trumpet,
Datura meteloides

Photo 5.32
Brazilian rock rose,
Pavonia hastata

The Clean Whites

PERENNIALS

Acanthus mollis
Bear's Breeches, Grecian Leaf Plant

Achillea species
Yarrow, Milfoil

Agapanthus species
Lily of the Nile, Agapanthus

Anemone species
Poppy Anemone, Windflower

Aster species
Aster

Astilbe x arendsii
Astilbe, False Spirea

Belamcanda chinensis
Blackberry Lily, Candy Lily

Buddleia x davidii
Butterfly Bush, Summer Lilac

Canna x generalis
Canna Lily

Centranthus ruber
Red Valerian

Chrysanthemum species
Ox-eye Daisy, Garden Mum, Shasta Daisy

Crinum species
Crinum Lily

Crocus vernus
Crocus

Crinum species
Crinum Lily

Datura meteloides
Angel's Trumpet

Dianthus 'First Love'
Hardy Carnation

Echinacea purpurea
Purple Coneflower

Engelmannia pinnatifida
Engelmann Daisy

Eupatorium rugosum 'Chocolate'
Chocolate Mist Flower

Geranium species
Hardy Geranium, Cranesbill

Gerbera species
Gerbera Daisy

Gladiolus species
Gladiolus

Guara lindhiemerii
Guara, Whirling Butterflies

Hedychium coronarium
Butterfly Ginger, Ginger Lily

Helleborus orientalis
Lenten Rose

Heuchera species
Coral Bells

Hibiscus moscheutos
Hibiscus, Rose Mallow

Hippeastrum x johnsonii
Hardy Amaryllis

Hosta species
Hosta Lily, Plantain Lily*

Hyacintoides hispanica
Woodland Hyacinths, Spanish Bluebells

Iberis sempervirens
Candytuft

Iris pallida 'Argentea Variegata'
Zebra Iris*

Iris species
Iris

Lantana montevidensis
Trailing Lantana

Lavandula angustifolia
English Lavender

Leucojum aestivum
Summer Snowflake

Liatris spicata
Liatris, Kansas Gayfeather, Blazing Star

Liriope species
Liriope, Lilyturf*

Lobelia cardinalis
Cardinal Flower Lobelia

Lycorus x albiflora
White Spider Lily

Lysimachia clethroides
Gooseneck Loosestrife

Malvaviscus drummondii
Turk's Cap

Melampodium leucanthum
Blackfoot Daisy

Monarda didmyma
Bee Balm

Morea iridiodes
African Iris, Fortnight Lily

Muscari botryoides 'Album'
White Grape Hyacinth

Narcissus species
Daffodils, Jonquils, and Narcissus

Nierembergia 'Mont Blanc'
Nierembergia, Cupflower

Ophiopogon jaburan
Aztec Grass*

Paeonia species
Peony

Pavonia hastata
Brazilian Rock Rose

Penstemon cobea
Prairie Penstemon, Prairie Foxglove

Phlox species
Phlox

Physostegia virginiana
Fall Obedient Plant, False Dragonhead

Platycodon gradiflorus
Balloon Flower

Polianthes tuberorsa
Mexican Tuberose

Rivina humilis
Pigeonberry

Ruellia brittoniana
Ruellia, Mexican Petunia

Salvia farinacea
Mealy Cup Sage

Salvia greggii
Autumn Sage, Cherry Sage

Salvia x superba
Meadow Sage

Saxifrage stolonifera
Strawberry Geranium

Scilla sibirica
Siberian Squill

Sidalcea species
Prairie Mallow

Thalictrum aquilegifolium
Meadow Rue

Thymus vulgaris
Creeping Thyme

Verbena species
Verbena

Veronica species
Veronica, Speedwell

Viola odorata
Wood Violet, Sweet Violet

Zantedeschia species
Calla Lily

Zephyranthus candida
White Rain Lily

GRASSES*

Acorus species
Variegated Sweet Flag

Carex marrowii 'Aureo-Variegata'
Variegated Japanese Sedge

Miscanthus sinensis
Miscanthus, Maiden Grass, Japanese Silver Grass*

SHRUBS, VINES, AND ROSES

Abelia grandiflora
Abelia

Callicarpa americana
American Beautyberry**

Camellia species
Camellia

Chilopsis linearis
Desert willow

Clematis odorata
Evergreen Clematis

Clematis paniculata
Sweet Autumn Clematis

Clematis species
Clematis

Gardenia jasminoides
Gardenia

Hesperaloe funifera
Giant Hesperaloe

Hibiscus syriacus
Rose of Sharon, Althea

Hydrangea arborescens
Anna Belle Hydrangea

Hydrangea macrophylla
Hydrangea

Hydrangea quercifolia
Oakleaf Hydrangea

Ilex species
Holly*

Lagerstroemia indica
Dwarf Crape Myrtle

Magnolia grandiflora 'Little Gem'
Little Gem Magnolia

Magnolia stellata
Star Magnolia

Pittosporum tobira
Mock Orange, Pittosporum*

Raphiolepis indica
Indian Hawthorn

Rhododendron species
Azalea

Rosa species
Rose

Spiraea nipponica 'Snowmound'
Snowmound Spirea

Spiraea prunifolia
Bridal Wreath Spirea

Trachelospermum jasminoides
Star Jasmine

Viburnum species
Viburnum

Vitex agnus-castus
Vitex, Chastetree

Weigela florida
Weigela

Wisteria sinensis
Wisteria

Yucca species
Adam's Needle, Yucca*

* White or creamy variegated foliage
** White fruit

Plants that Have Gray or Silver Foliage

Silver and gray are neutral, cool, backdrop colors that help weave other hues together. However, they also sparkle in the sunlight and add an extra dimension of luminescence to the border. Most silver leaved plants grow naturally in arid, sunny places like Texas and the Southwest United States.

Photo 5.33
Lamb's ear, *Stachys lanata*

Photo 5.34
Artemesia, *Artemisia x 'Powis Castle'*

Photo 5.35
Grey santolina,
Santolina incana

Cool Grays

PERENNIALS

Achillea species
Yarrow, Milfoil

Artemisia species
Artemisia

Dianthus gratianopolitanus
Cheddar Pinks

**Erysismum linifolium
'Bowles Mauve'**
Wallflower

Lavandula species
Lavender

Perovskia atriplicifolia
Russian Sage

Phlomis russeliana
Jerusalem Sage

Salvia chamaedryoides
Gray Shrub Sage

Salvia leucantha
Mexican Bush Sage

Salvia officinalis
Garden Sage

Santolina incana
Lavender Cotton,
Gray Santolina

Stachys lanata
Lamb's Ear

Thymus pseudolanuginosus
Wooly Thyme

SHRUBS, VINES, AND ROSES

Agave species
Agave, Century Plant

Dasylerion species
Desert Spoon, Sotol

Leucophyllum species
Texas Sage, Texas Ranger

Yucca species
Adam's Needle, Yucca

Photo 6.1 *(opposite page)*
Spiky form of red hot poker,
*Kniphofia uvaria
'Bressingham Comet'*

Chapter Six
FORM AND TEXTURE

Another key element in the design of a perennial border is the use of form and texture. Form is the overall shape or character of the plant. Placing strong forms like spikes against softer forms like curves gives focal points for the eye and makes a striking statement. Texture describes the overall boldness or softness of a plant, usually defined by the size of the foliage and flowers. Using a combination of different textures gives the garden interest. However, a good border depends on repetition of form and texture, just as it depends on the repetition of color. Too many forms and textures with no repetition can appear chaotic because the eye has nowhere to rest. Even if you use the plants that are different sizes or colors, repetition can be achieved through setting up patterns of similar forms and textures.

FINE TEXTURE

Plants that appear to have a fine texture have small leaves and flowers, and they give softness and flow to a garden. From any distance at all, your eye tends not to see the individual leaves or plants in a bed, but rather the picture as a whole—like in an Impressionist painting. Fine textured plants are also the glue that blends the other plants together. Bolder plants spring from a canvas of fine textures. Like cool colors, fine textures give a receding illusion. To give a small garden the illusion of being larger, plant finely textured plants and flowers at the far end.

Fine Texture

PERENNIALS

Ajuga reptans
Ajuga, Bugleweed

Artemisia species
Artemisia

Calyophus hartwegii
Sun Drops

Ceratostigma plumbaginoides
Creeping Plumbago

Coreopsis rosea
Pink Coreopsis

Coreopsis verticillata
Thread Leaf Coreopsis

Dianthus species
Cheddar Pinks, Hardy
Carnation

Engelmannia pinnatifida
Engelmann Daisy

Eupatorium species
Hardy Ageratum, Gregg's
Mist Flower

Foeniculum vulgare
Fennel

Geranium species
Hardy Geranium, Cranesbill

Guara lindhiemerii
Guara, Whirling Butterflies

Hymenoxys scaposa
4 Nerve Daisy

Iberis sempervirens
Candytuft

Ipeion uniflorum
Blue-Eyed Grass, Spring
Star Flower

Melampodium leucanthum
Blackfoot Daisy

Nepeta faassenii
Catmint

Nierembergia caerulea
Nierembergia, Cupflower

Ophiopogon japonicas
Ophiopogon, Mondo Grass

Perovskia atriplicifolia
Russian Sage

Phlox subulata
Creeping Phlox

Rivina humilis
Pigeonberry

Rosemarinus officinalis
Rosemary

Russelia equisetiformis
Firecracker Plant

Salvia azurea var. grandiflora
Azure Sage, Pitcher Sage

Salvia chamaedryoides
Gray Shrub Sage

Salvia greggii
Autumn Sage, Cherry Sage

Salvia engelmanii
Engleman's Sage

Salvia bicolor
Bicolor Sage, Cocoa
Sapphire Salvia

Santolina species
Lavender Cotton, Santolina

Scutellaria suffrutescens
Scullcap

Tagetes lucida
Mexican Mint Marigold

Teucrium chaemedrys
Germander

Thalictrum aquilegifolium
Meadow Rue

Thymus vulgaris
Creeping Thyme

Verbena bonariensis
Upright Verbena

Verbena tenuisecta
Moss Verbena

**Veronica peduncularis
'Georgia Blue'**
Creeping Speedwell

Zephyranthus species
Rain Lily

GRASSES

Acorus species
Sweet Flag

**Bouteloua curtipendula
var. caespitosa**
Sideoats Grama

Chasmanthium latifolium
Inland Sea Oats

Equisetum scirpoides
Dwarf Horsetail Reed

Eragrostis curvula
Weeping Love Grass

Festuca ovina glauca
Blue Fescue

Hakonechloa macro 'Aureola'
Golden Japanese Forest Grass

Imperata cylindrica 'Red Baron'
Japanese Blood Grass

Muhlenbergia capillaris
Gulf Muhly, Hairyawn Muhly

Muhlenbergia dumosa
Bamboo Muhly

Nasella tenuissima
Mexican Feather Grass

Typha minima
Dwarf Cattail Reed

FERNS

Adiantum capillus-veneris
Southern Maidenhair Fern

Athyrium niponicum 'Pictum'
Japanese Painted Fern

Dryopteris erythrosora
Autumn Fern

Thelypteris kunthii
Southern Wood Fern

SHRUBS, VINES, AND ROSES

Berberis thunbergii
Redleaf Barberry

Buxus species
Boxwood

Caesalpinia species
Desert Bird of Paradise

Chilopsis linearis
Desert Willow

Ficus pumila
Fig Ivy

Gelsemium sempervirens
Carolina Jessamine

Juniperus species
Junipers

Leucophyllum species
Texas Sage, Texas Ranger

Myrica pusilla
Dwarf Wax Myrtle

Nandina domestica
Nandina

Sophora secundiflora
Texas Mountain Laurel

Vitex agnus-castus
Vitex, Chastetree

Bold Texture

Bold texture has the opposite effect of fine texture. Plants with large leaves and flowers offer bold texture and stand out instead of recede. For a long, narrow garden, use large-leaved plants at the far end to give the illusion they are closer and the garden is not so long. Big, bold, colorful foliage and exotic flowers are indicative of the lush tropics, as well.

Photo 6.2
Bold texture of canna,
Canna x generalis

Bold Texture

Perennials

Alchemilla mollis
Lady's Mantle

Alpinia species
Ginger

Aspidistra elatior
Aspidistra, Cast Iron Plant

Acanthus mollis
Bear's Breeches, Grecian Leaf Plant

Canna x generalis
Canna Lily

Colocasia esculenta
Elephant Ears

Crinum species
Crinum Lily

Datura meteloides
Angel's Trumpet

Eupatorium maculatum 'Gateway'
Joe Pye Weed

Hibiscus moscheutos
Hibiscus, Rose Mallow

Hippeastrum x johnsonii
Hardy Amaryllis

Hosta species
Hosta Lily, Plantain Lily

Ligularia tussilaginea 'Aureo-maculata'
Leopard Plant

Malvaviscus drummondii
Turk's Cap

Phlomis russeliana
Jerusalem Sage

Rudbeckia maxima
Giant Rudbeckia, Giant Coneflower

Rudbeckia nitida 'Herbestonne'
Herbestonne Coneflower

Sedum spectabile
Showy Sedum

Tecoma stans
Yellow Bells, Esperanza

Shrubs, Vines, and Roses

Acuba japonica
Acuba

Agave species
Agave, Century Plant

Camellia japonica
Camellia

Clematis odorata
Evergreen Clematis

Cotinus coggygria
Smoke Tree

Cycas revoluta
Sago Palm

Dasylerion species
Desert Spoon, Sotol

Fatsia japonica
Japanese Fatsia

Hydrangea species
Hydrangea

Ilex latifolia
Luster Leaf Holly

Magnolia species
Magnolia

Mahonia bealei
Leatherleaf Mahonia

Opuntia species
Prickly Pear

Pittosporum tobira
Mock Orange, Pittosporum

Raphiolepis indica
Indian Hawthorn

Viburnum species
Viburnum

Yucca species
Adam's Needle, Yucca

Photo 6.3
Spiky form of liatris,
Liatris spicata

SPIKY FORMS

Nothing creates a focal point quite like a spiky form does. Whether with pointed, sword-like foliage or with vertical plume-like flowers, spiky shapes naturally draw the eye. Sprinkle spikes all over your garden for accents. They all don't have to be as bold and colorful as red hot pokers or yuccas. Using softer plants like grasses or irises repeat the form without competing for attention.

Spiky Forms

PERENNIALS

Agastache species
Hyssop, Hummingbird Mint, Agastache

Belamcanda chinensis
Blackberry Lily, Candy Lily

Bulbine frutescens
Bulbine

Crocosmia x crocosmiflora
Crocosmia, Montbretia

Gladiolus species
Gladiolus

Iris species
Iris

Kniphofia uvaria
Red Hot Poker, Torch Lily, Tritoma

Lavandula angustifolia
English Lavender

Liatris spicata
Liatris, Kansas Gayfeather, Blazing Star

Lysimachia clethroides
Gooseneck Loosestrife

Morea species
African Iris, Fortnight Lily

Muscari species
Grape Hyacinth

Penstemon species
Penstemon, Beardtongue

Physostegia virginiana
Fall Obedient Plant, False Dragonhead

Polianthes tuberorsa
Mexican Tuberose

Salvia 'Indigo Spires'
Indigo Spires Salvia

Salvia azurea var. grandiflora
Azure Sage, Pitcher Sage

Salvia coccinea
Scarlet Sage

Salvia guarantica
Anise Scented Sage

Salvia leucantha
Mexican Bush Sage

Salvia nemerosa 'Plumosa'
Plumosa Meadow Sage

Salvia penstemonoides
Penstemon Sage, Big Red Sage

Salvia x superba
Meadow Sage

Salvia verticillata 'Purple Rain'
Purple Rain Salvia

Solidago sphacelata
Goldenrod

Veronica species
Veronica, Speedwell

Zantedeschia species
Calla Lily

GRASSES

Most Grasses

SHRUBS, VINES, AND ROSES

Agave species
Agave, Century Plant

Dasylerion species
Desert Spoon, Sotol

Hesperaloe species
Red Yucca, Hesperaloe

Norlina species
Bear Grass

Yucca species
Adam's Needle, Yucca

FEATHERY, FLOWING, AND WEEPING FORMS

Like those with fine texture, plants that are feathery, flowing, or weeping give the garden softness and flow. These wispy forms catch the wind and wave in the breeze giving the added touch of movement. Feathery plants within a formal bed soften it and make it more casual. Flowing and weeping plants also mimic flowing water.

UPRIGHT AND VERTICAL FORMS

Upright and vertical plants lead the eye upward toward the sky. Tight, evergreen shrubs like skyrocket juniper and Nellie R. Stevens holly are examples of upright and vertical plantings that give a more formal look to the bed. Looser plants like Herbestonne rudbeckia and upright verbena achieve the same feel without the stiffness or formality. Most provide a good backbone for the perennial garden.

Feathery, Flowing, and Weeping Forms

PERENNIALS

Aquilegia species
Columbine

Artemisia species
Artemisia

Astilbe x arendsii
Astilbe, False Spirea

Buddleia x davidii
Butterfly Bush, Summer Lilac

Ceratostigma plumbaginoides
Creeping Plumbago

Engelmannia pinnatifida
Engelmann Daisy

Guara lindhiemerii
Guara, Whirling Butterflies

Liatris spicata
Liatris, Kansas Gayfeather, Blazing Star

Phlox pilosa
Prairie Phlox

Russelia equisetiformis
Firecracker Plant

Salvia azurea var. grandiflora
Azure Sage, Pitcher Sage

Salvia engelmanii
Engleman's Sage

Salvia x superba
Meadow Sage

GRASSES

Most grasses

FERNS

Most ferns

SHRUBS, VINES, AND ROSES

Acer palmatum
Japanese Maple

Caesalpinia species
Desert Bird of Paradise

Callicarpa americana
American Beautyberry

Chilopsis linearis
Desert willow

Cotinus coggygria
Smoke Tree

Juniperus species
Junipers

Lagerstroemia indica
Miniature Weeping Crape Myrtle

Nandina domestica
Nandina

Norlina species
Bear Grass

Symphoricarpos orbiculatus
Coralberry

Vitex agnus-castus
Vitex, Chastetree

Upright and Vertical Forms

PERENNIALS

Canna x generalis
Canna Lily

Centranthus ruber
Red Valerian

Echinops ritro 'Vetch's Blue'
Globe Thistle

Gladiolus species
Gladiolus

Guara lindhiemerii
Guara, Whirling Butterflies

Helianthus maximiliani
Maximillian Sunflower

Hibiscus coccineus
Texas Star Hibiscus

Hippeastrum x johnsonii
Hardy Amaryllis

Iris species
Iris

Lilium species
Lilies

Lobelia cardinalis
Cardinal Flower Lobelia

Lycorus radiata
Autumn Crocus, Spider Lily,
Surprise Lily

Lythrum species
Purple Loosestrife

Morea iridiodes species
African Iris, Fortnight Lily

Penstemon species
Penstemon, Beardtongue

Phlox paniculata
Summer Phlox

Physostegia virginiana
Fall Obedient Plant,
False Dragonhead

Polianthes tuberorsa
Mexican Tuberose

Rudbeckia maxima
Giant Rudbeckia,
Giant Coneflower

Rudbeckia nitida 'Herbestonne'
Herbestonne Coneflower

Salvia 'Indigo Spires'
Indigo Spires Salvia

Salvia azurea var. grandiflora
Azure Sage, Pitcher Sage

Salvia guarantica
Anise Scented Sage

Salvia leucantha
Mexican Bush Sage

Salvia uliginosa
Bog Sage

Verbena bonariensis
Upright Verbena

GRASSES

**Andropogon gerardii
var. Gerardii**
Bluestem

**Calamagrostis arundinacea
'Karl Foerster'**
Karl Foerster Feather
Reed Grass

Equisetum hyemale
Horsetail Reed

Miscanthus species
Miscanthus, Maiden Grass

Muhlenbergia lindhiemerii
Lindhiemers Muhly

Panicum virgatum
Switch Grass

Pennisetum species
Fountain Grass

Sorghastrum nutans
Indian Grass

Typha latifolia
Cattail Reed

SHRUBS, VINES, AND ROSES

Hesperaloe funifera
Giant Hesperaloe

Hibiscus syriacus
Rose of Sharon, Althea

Ilex species
Tree variety Hollies

Juniperus species
Upright Junipers

Lagerstroemia indica
Dwarf Crape Myrtle

Vitex agnus-castus
Vitex, Chastetree

CREEPING AND SPILLING FORMS

Creeping and spilling forms achieve the opposite effect of vertical forms. They grow horizontally, creeping along the ground and spilling over paths, stones, and walls. Instead of pushing your eye upward, they take your attention down and out. These plants are great in rock gardens and by gravel paths.

ROUNDED AND MOUNDED FORMS

Rounded and mounding forms are probably the most common shape of perennials or shrubs. The leaves, flowers, and stems all grow from a central point on the ground. No matter what the flower type, the overall rounded form unites many different plants.

Creeping and Spilling Forms

PERENNIALS

Ajuga reptans
Ajuga, Bugleweed

Callirhoe involucrata
Winecups, Poppy Mallow

Calyophus hartwegii
Sun Drops

Ceratostigma plumbaginoides
Creeping Plumbago

Dianthus gratianopolitanus
Cheddar Pinks

Geranium species
Hardy Geranium, Cranesbill

Hymenoxys scaposa
4 Nerve Daisy

Iberis sempervirens
Candytuft

Incarvillea delavayi
Chinese Foxglove

Lantana species
Lantana

Mentha species
Mint

Nierembergia caerulea
Nierembergia, Cupflower

Oenothera species
Missouri Primrose, Ozark
Sundrop, Evening Primrose

Phlox divaricata
Louisiana Phlox

Phlox pilosa
Prairie Phlox

Phlox subulata
Creeping Phlox

Rivina humilis
Pigeonberry

Rosemarinus officinalis
Rosemary

Russelia equisetiformis
Firecracker Plant

Salvia engelmanii
Engleman's Sage

Salvia bicolor
Bicolor Sage, Cocoa
Sapphire Salvia

Santolina species
Lavender Cotton, Santolina

Saxifrage stolonifera
Strawberry Geranium

Scutellaria suffrutescens
Pink Scullcap

Stachys lanata
Lamb's Ear

Stachys officinalis
Woodland Betony

Teucrium chaemedrys
Germander

Thymus vulgaris
Creeping Thyme

Verbena specie
Verbena

**Veronica peduncularis
'Georgia Blue'**
Creeping Speedwell

Viola odorata species
Wood Violet, Sweet Violet

GRASSES

Eragrostis curvula
Weeping Love Grass

Festuca ovina glauca
Blue Fescue

Hakonechloa macro 'Aureola'
Golden Japanese Forest Grass

SHRUBS, VINES, AND ROSES

Gardenia radicans
Dwarf Gardenia

Hypericum henryi
St. John's Wort

Juniperus species
Creeping Junipers

Lagerstroemia indica
Miniature Crape Myrtle

Rosa species
Ground Cover Roses

Rounded and Mounded Forms

PERNNIALS

**Aniscanthus quadrifidus
var. wrightii**
Hummingbird Bush,
Flame Acanthus

Artemisia x 'Powis Castle'
Powis Castle Artemisia

Aster x frikartii
Aster Hybrids

Baptisia australis
Blue False Indigo

Caryopteris x clandonensis
Caryopteris, Bluemist Spirea

**Erysismum linifolium
'Bowles Mauve'**
Wallflower

Paeonia species
Peony

Pavonia species
Rock Rose

Salvia greggii
Autumn Sage, Cherry Sage

Scutellaria suffrutescens
Pink Scullcap

Sedum spectabile
Showy Sedum

Tagetes lemmonii
Copper Canyon Daisy

Teucrium species
Germander

SHRUBS, VINES, AND ROSES

Abelia grandiflora
Abelia

Berberis thunbergii
Redleaf Barberry

Buxus species
Boxwood

Camellia species
Camellia

Euonymus alata
Burning Bush

Gardenia jasminoides
Gardenia

Hydrangea species
Hydrangea

Hypericum henryi
St. John's Wort

Ilex species
Holly

Leucophyllum species
Texas Ranger, Texas Sage

**Loropetalum chinensis
rubrum**
Fringe Flower

Myrica pusilla
Dwarf Wax Myrtle

Nandina domestica
Nandina

Nerium oleander
Dwarf Oleander

Pittosporum tobira
Mock Orange, Pittosporum

Raphiolepis indica
Indian Hawthorn

Rhododendron species
Azalea

Rosa species
Rose

Spiraea species
Spirea

Viburnum species
Viburnum

Weigela florida
Weigela

Photo 6.5
Daisy forms of black-eyed
Susan, *Rudbeckia species*,
asters, *Aster species*, and
purple coneflowers, *Echinacea
species*, in midsummer

Daisy Forms

No other flower form is as happy and carefree as a daisy. Just think of a sunny cottage garden or a meadow of waving flowers. Their quiet charm brightens any garden.

Cluster and Globe Forms

Like strong spiky accents, globes and clusters command a focal point. Usually atop long slender stems, they simply must be noticed. They can be large like giant alliums, which look good individually, or they can be small like drumstick alliums, which look better in groups. Clusters of small flowers like butterfly weed or yarrow give fine texture while providing a large bold quality. They also provide a landing pad for hungry butterflies and insects.

Photo 6.6
Globular form of blue alliums,
Allium caeruleum

CHAPTER SIX · *Form and Texture*

Daisy Forms

PERENNIALS

Anemone hupehensis
Japanese Anemone

Aster species
Aster

Berlandiera species
Greeneyes, Chocolate Daisy

Chrysanthemum species
Ox-eye Daisy, Garden Mum,
Shasta Daisy

Coreopsis species
Coreopsis

Echinacea purpurea
Purple Coneflower

Engelmannia pinnatifida
Engelmann Daisy

Gaillardia x grandiflora
Gaillardia, Indian Blanket

Gerbera species
Gerbera Daisy

Helianthus maximiliani
Maximillian Sunflower

Heliopsis helianthoides
False Sunflower

Hymenoxys scaposa
4 Nerve Daisy

Melampodium leucanthum
Blackfoot Daisy

Rudbeckia species
Black-Eyed Susans,
Coneflowers

Tagetes species
Copper Canyon Daisy,
Mexican Mint Marigold

Zexmenia hispida
Zexmenia

Cluster and Globe Forms

PERENNIALS

Achillea species
Yarrow, Milfoil

Allium species
Allium

Asclepias tuberosa
Butterfly Weed

Agapanthus species
Lily of the Nile, Agapanthus

Caryopteris x clandonensis
Caryopteris, Bluemist Spirea

Centranthus ruber
Red Valerian

Echinops ritro 'Vetch's Blue'
Globe Thistle

Eupatorium species
Hardy Ageratum, Joe Pye Weed

Foeniculum vulgare
Fennel

Lantana species
Lantana

Lycorus radiata
Autumn Crocus, Spider Lily,
Surprise Lily

Monarda didmyma
Bee Balm

Phlox paniculata
Summer Phlox

Scabiosa caucasica
Pincushion Flower

Sedum spectabile
Showy Sedum

Stokesia laevis
Stokes Aster

Tulbaghia violacea
Society Garlic

Verbena species
Verbena

SHRUBS, VINES, AND ROSES

Caesalpinia species
Desert Bird of Paradise

Hydrangea species
Hydrangea

Mahonia bealei
Leatherleaf Mahonia

Raphiolepis indica
Indian Hawthorn

Spiraea x bumalda 'Anthony Waterer'
Anthony Waterer Spirea

Viburnum species
Viburnum

Chapter Seven
SUN AND SHADE

While most of the plants listed in this book will tolerate and even appreciate a little afternoon shade in summer, a few thrive with full, bright sun. Although most of the plants are drought tolerant, a few prefer moist soils, so review the drought tolerant list when planning a Xeriscape. Almost all of them will tolerate a little shade and water in the hot months.

On the opposite end of the spectrum, many plants *prefer* the coolness of a shady garden. Few plants can take full, heavy shade, but those listed will do well in light, all-day shade, or morning sun with afternoon shade. Again, shady gardens tend to be moist, but a few plants, like columbine and lyre leaf sage, prefer drier conditions. Notice that a few plants, like ruellia and holly, can be found on both lists.

Photo 7.2
Hostas, *Hosta species,* and ferns need shade

Sun Worshipers: Plants for Sunny Gardens

PERENNIALS

Achillea species
Yarrow, Milfoil

Aniscanthus quadrifidus var. wrightii
Hummingbird Bush, Flame Acanthus

Artemisia species
Artemisia

Asclepias species
Butterfly Weed

Aster species
Aster Hybrids

Agastache species
Hyssop, Hummingbird Mint

Agapanthus species
Lily of the Nile, Agapanthus

Berlandiera species
Chocolate Daisy, Greeneyes

Buddleia x davidii
Butterfly Bush, Summer Lilac

Bulbine frutescens
Bulbine

Callirhoe involucrata
Winecups, Poppy Mallow

Calyophus hartwegii
Sun Drops

Canna x generalis
Canna Lily

Caryopteris x clandonensis
Caryopteris, Bluemist Spirea

Chrysanthemum leucanthemum
Ox-Eye Daisy

Chrysanthemum maximum
Shasta Daisy

Coreopsis species
Tickseed, Coreopsis

Echinacea purpurea
Purple Coneflower

Engelmannia pinnatifida
Engelmann Daisy

Gaillardia x grandiflora
Gaillardia, Indian Blanket

Guara lindhiemerii
Guara, Whirling Butterflies

Helianthus maximiliani
Maximillian Sunflower

Heliopsis helianthoides
False Sunflower

Hibiscus coccineus
Texas Star Hibiscus

Iris germanica
German Bearded Iris

Kniphofia uvaria
Red Hot Poker, Torch Lily, Tritoma

Lantana species
Lantana

Lavandula species
Lavender

Liatris spicata
Liatris, Kansas Gayfeather

Lythrum salicaria
Purple Loosestrife

Melampodium leucanthum
Blackfoot Daisy

Monarda fistulosa
Bergamot

Morea iridiodes
African Iris, Fortnight Lily

Nepeta faassenii
Catmint

Nierembergia caerulea
Nierembergia, Cupflower

Oenothera species
Missouri Primrose, Ozark Sundrop, Evening Primrose

Pavonia lasiopetala
Rock Rose

Penstemon species
Penstemon, Beardtongue

Perovskia atriplicifolia
Russian Sage

Phlomis russeliana
Jerusalem Sage

Poliomintha longiflora
Mexican Oregano

Ratibida columnifera
Mexican Hat

Rosemarinus officinalis
Rosemary

Rudbeckia species
Black-Eyed Susan, Rudbeckia

Ruellia brittoniana
Ruellia, Mexican Petunia

Russelia equisetiformis
Firecracker Plant

Salvia species
Salvia, Sage

Santolina species
Lavender Cotton, Gray Santolina

Scabiosa caucasica
Pincushion Flower

Scutellaria suffrutescens
Pink Scullcap

Stachys lanata
Lamb's Ear

Tagetes species
Copper Canyon Daisy, Mexican Mint Marigold

Tecoma stans
Yellow Bells, Esperanza

Teucrium chaemedrys
Germander

Thymus vulgaris
Creeping Thyme

Tulbaghia violacea
Society Garlic

Verbena species
Verbena

Zexmenia hispida
Zexmenia

GRASSES

Andropogon species
Bluestem Grasses

Bouteloua curtipendula var. caespitosa
Sideoats Grama

Elymus glaucus
Blue Wild Rye

Eragrostis curvula
Weeping Love Grass

Festuca ovina glauca
Blue Fescue

Miscanthus sinensis
Miscanthus, Maiden Grass, Japanese Silver grass

Muhlenbergia species
Muhly Grasses

Nasella tenuissima
Mexican Feather Grass

Panicum virgatum
Switch Grass

Pennisetum species
Fountain Grasses

Sorghastrum nutans
Indian Grass

SHRUBS, VINES, AND ROSES

Abelia grandiflora
Abelia

Agave species
Agave, Century Plant

Berberis thunbergii
Redleaf Barberry

Caesalpinia species
Desert Bird of Paradise

Campsis radicans
Trumpet Vine

Chilopsis linearis
Desert Willow

Cotinus coggygria
Smoke Tree

Dasylerion species
Desert Spoon, Sotol

Euonymus alata
Burning Bush

Hesperaloe species
Red Yucca

Hibiscus syriacus
Rose of Sharon, Althea

Ilex species
Holly

Juniperus species
Junipers

Lagerstroemia indica
Dwarf Crape Myrtle

Leucophyllum species
Texas Sage, Texas Ranger

Lonicera sempervirens
Coral Honeysuckle

Magnolia grandiflora 'Little Gem'
Little Gem Magnolia

Myrica pusilla
Dwarf Wax Myrtle

Nandina domestica
Nandina

Nerium oleander
Dwarf Oleander

Norlina species
Bear Grass

Opuntia species
Prickly Pear

Raphiolepis indica
Indian Hawthorn

Sophora secundiflora
Texas Mountain Laurel

Vitex agnus-castus
Vitex, Chastetree

Wisteria sinensis
Wisteria

Yucca species
Adam's Needle, Yucca

Photo 7.3 *(left)*
Mexican petunia, *Ruellia brittoniana,* tolerates sun and shade

Photo 7.4 *(below)*
Gaillardia, *Gaillardia x grandiflora*, and bergamot, *Monarda fistulosa,* need full sun

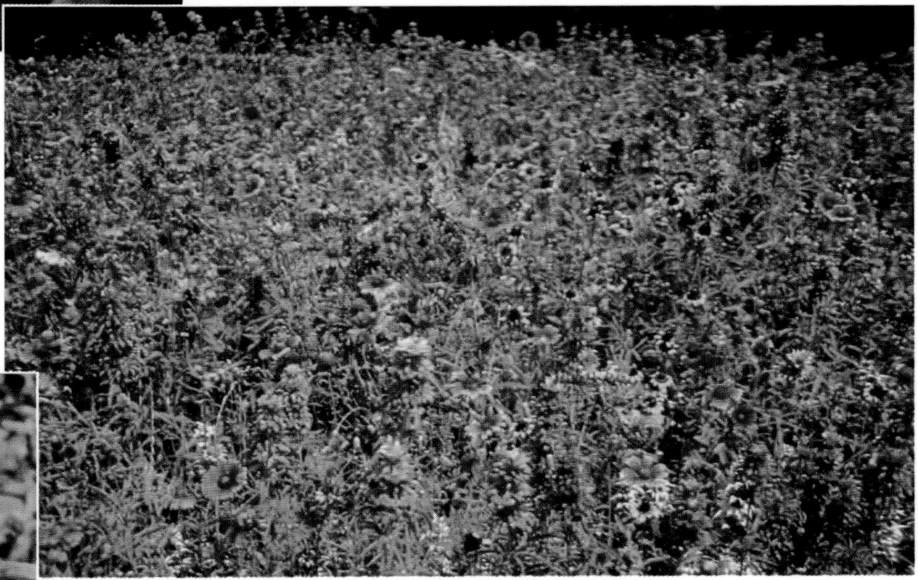

Photo 7.5 *(below)*
Firecracker plant, *Russelia equisetiformis,* loves full sun

Photo 7.6 *(left)*
Mexican hat, *Ratibida columnifera,* loves full sun

Photo 7.7
Dwarf columbines,
Aquilegia x hybrida,
prefer shade

Photo 7.8
Lenten rose,
Helleborus orientalis,
prefer shade

Photo 7.9
Holly fern,
Cyrtomium falcatum,
prefer shade

Shady Dealers: Plants for Shady Gardens

PERENNIALS

Ajuga reptans
Ajuga, Bugleweed

Alchemilla mollis
Lady's Mantle

Alpinia species
Ginger

Anemone hupehensis
Japanese Anemone

Aquilegia species
Columbine

Aspidistra elatior
Aspidistra, Cast Iron Plant

Astilbe x arendsii
Astilbe, False Spirea

Acanthus mollis
Bear's Breeches, Grecian
Leaf Plant

Beloperone guttata
Gold and Brown Shrimp Plant

Colocasia esculenta
Elephant Ears

Eupatorium species
Hardy Ageratum, Joe Pye Weed

Geranium species
Hardy Geranium, Cranesbill

Helleborus orientalis
Lenten Rose

Hemerocallis species
Daylily

Heuchera species
Coral Bells

Hosta species
Hosta Lily, Plantain Lily

Leucojum aestivum
Summer Snowflake

Liriope species
Liriope, Lilyturf

Lycorus radiata
Autumn Crocus, Spider Lily,
Surprise Lily

Malvaviscus drummondii
Turk's Cap

Narcissus species
Daffodils, Jonquils, and
Narcissus

Ophiopogon species
Ophiopogon, Mondo Grass,
Aztec Grass

Oxalis species
Wood Sorrel, Shamrock

Phlox divaricata
Louisiana Phlox

Phlox pilosa
Prairie Phlox

Rivina humilis
Pigeonberry

Ruellia brittoniana
Ruellia, Mexican Petunia

Salvia lyrata
Lyre Leaf Sage

Saxifrage stolonifera
Strawberry Geranium

Viola species
Wood Violet, Sweet Violet

Zantedeschia species
Calla Lily

GRASSES

Acorus species
Variegated Sweet Flag

Carex species
Sedge

Chasmanthium latifolium
Inland Sea Oats

Equisetum hyemale
Horsetail Reed

Hakonechloa macro 'Aureola'
Golden Japanese Forest Grass

FERNS

**Arachinoides simplicior
'Variegata'**
Variegated Shield Fern

Adiantum capillus-veneris
Southern Maidenhair Fern

Athyrium niponicum 'Pictum'
Japanese Painted Fern

Cyrtomium falcatum
Holly Fern

Dryopteris erythrosora
Autumn Fern

Thelypteris kunthii
Southern Wood Fern

SHRUBS, VINES, AND ROSES

Abelia grandiflora
Abelia

Acer palmatum
Japanese Maple

Acuba japonica
Acuba

Bignonia caprolata
Cross Vine

Buxus species
Boxwood

Callicarpa americana
American Beautyberry

Camellia species
Camellia

Clematis species
Clematis

Cycas revoluta
Sago Palm

Fatsia japonica
Japanese Fatsia

Ficus pumila
Fig Ivy

Gardenia jasminoides
Gardenia

Hydrangea species
Hydrangea

Hypericum henryi
St. John's Wort

Loropetalum chinensis rubrum
Fringe Flower

Mahonia bealei
Leatherleaf Mahonia

Myrica pusilla
Dwarf Wax Myrtle

Nandina domestica
Nandina

Pittosporum tobira
Mock Orange, Pittosporum

Rhododendron species
Azalea

Symphoricarpos orbiculatus
Coralberry

Viburnum species
Viburnum

Chapter Eight
WET AND DRY

hile most of the plants listed in
this book prefer well-drained soils
with regular irrigation in
summer, some plants grow naturally in more
extreme conditions: wet or dry soils. They generally
will tolerate only one of these conditions.
Although, the iris family includes some species that
thrive in wet conditions and other species that
thrive in dry conditions. The German bearded
iris, for example, needs good drainage and likes
dry periods. On the other hand, the yellow flag,
Siberian, and Louisiana irises grow naturally in
bogs and do not like to dry out.

The plants listed for wet soils are ideal if your garden is low and does
not drain well or if it is next to a pond or a fountain where spillover is
common. Most of the plants listed grow in well-drained soil provided
they get regular irrigation year-round. In fact, although most perennials do not grow well in yards that are watered heavily by an automatic
system in heavy Texas soils, the plants listed here for wet soil will
thrive in such conditions.

The plants listed for dry soils grow naturally in desert or semiarid conditions. Once established, they need little additional water except in
the hottest months. Desert plants like yuccas and agaves may never
have to be watered once established, especially if you live in the eastern half of the state. None of them will survive if their feet stay wet,
which will cause root rot. All of the plants listed are ideal for Xeriscape
gardens.

Photo 8.2 *(left)*
Yellow flag iris, *Iris pseudacorus*, prefers wet conditions

Photo 8.3 *(right)*
White rain lilies,
Zephyranthus candida,
bloom after rains in summer

Photo 8.4 *(below)*
Fall obedient plant,
Physostegia virginiana,
thrives in moist soils

Photo 8.5 *(above)*
Louisiana iris, *Iris fulva*
'Delta Star', is a bog dweller

Soggy Bottoms: Plants for Moist and Boggy Soils

PERENNIALS

Alchemilla mollis
Lady's Mantle

Alpinia species
Ginger

Asclepias incarnata
Pink Butterfly Weed

Astilbe x arendsii
Astilbe, False Spirea

Canna x generalis
Canna Lily

Colocasia esculenta
Elephant Ears

Coreopsis rosea
Pink Coreopsis

Crinum species
Crinum Lily

Helianthus maximiliani
Maximillian Sunflower

Hibiscus coccineus
Texas Star Hibiscus

Hosta species
Hosta Lily, Plantain Lily

Iris fulva, Iris giganticaerulea, Iris foliosa
Louisiana Iris

Iris pseudacorus
Yellow Flag Iris

Iris sibirica
Siberian Iris

Ligularia tussilaginea 'Aureo-maculata'
Leopard Plant

Lobelia cardinalis
Cardinal Flower Lobelia

Lythrum salicaria
Purple Loosestrife

Ophiopogon species
Ophiopogon, Mondo Grass, Aztec Grass

Physostegia virginiana
Fall Obedient Plant, False Dragonhead

Rudbeckia maxima
Giant Rudbeckia, Giant Coneflower

Ruellia brittoniana
Ruellia, Mexican Petunia

Salvia uliginosa
Bog Sage

Solidago sphacelata
Goldenrod

Tulbaghia violacea
Society Garlic

Zantedeschia species
Calla Lily

Zephyranthus species
White Rain Lily

GRASSES

Acorus species
Sweet Flag

Carex species
Sedge

Equisetum species
Horsetail Reed

Sorghastrum nutans
Indian Grass

Typha latifolia
Cattail Reed

FERNS

Arachinoides simplicior 'Variegata'
Variegated Shield Fern

Adiantum capillus-veneris
Southern Maidenhair Fern

Athyrium niponicum 'Pictum'
Japanese Painted Fern

Cyrtomium falcatum
Holly Fern

Dryopteris erythrosora
Autumn Fern

Thelypteris kunthii
Southern Wood Fern

Photo 8.6 (left)
Purple loosestrife, *Lythrum salicaria 'Mordens Pink'*, thrives in moist soils

Photo 8.7 (below)
Four nerve daisy, *Hymenoxys scaposa*, prefers dry soils

Photo 8.8
Pink skullcap,
Scutellaria suffrutescens,
prefers dry soils

Photo 8.9
Flowers of red yucca,
Hesperaloe parviflora,
prefers dry soils

PERENNIALS

Achillea species
Yarrow, Milfoil

Aniscanthus quadrifidus var. wrightii
Hummingbird Bush, Flame Acanthus

Aquilegia chrysantha 'Hinckleyana'
Texas Gold Columbine

Artemisia species
Artemisia

Asclepias tuberosa
Butterfly Weed

Aster species
Fall Aster

Agastache species
Hyssop, Hummingbird Mint

Acanthus mollis
Bear's Breeches, Grecian Leaf Plant

Baptisia australis
Blue False Indigo

Berlandiera species
Greeneyes, Chocolate Daisy

Bulbine frutescens
Bulbine

Callirhoe involucrata
Winecups, Poppy Mallow

Calyophus hartwegii
Sun Drops

Coreopsis species
Tickseed, Coreopsis

Echinacea purpurea
Purple Coneflower

Echinops ritro 'Vetch's Blue'
Globe Thistle

Engelmannia pinnatifida
Engelmann Daisy

Erysimum linifolium 'Bowles Mauve'
Wallflower

Eupatorium species
Hardy Ageratum, Gregg's Mist Flower

Gaillardia x grandiflora
Gaillardia, Indian Blanket

Guara lindhiemerii
Guara, Whirling Butterflies

Helianthus maximiliani
Maximillian Sunflower

Heliopsis helianthoides
False Sunflower

Hymenoxys scaposa
4 Nerve Daisy

Ipeion uniflorum
Blue-Eyed Grass, Spring Star Flower

Iris species
Bearded Iris

Kniphofia uvaria
Red Hot Poker, Torch Lily, Tritoma

Lantana species
Lantana

Lavandula species
Lavender

Liatris spicata
Liatris, Kansas Gayfeather, Blazing Star

Malvaviscus drummondii
Turk's Cap

Melampodium leucanthum
Blackfoot Daisy

Monarda fistulosa
Bergamot

Nierembergia caerulea
Nierembergia, Cupflower

Oenothera species
Missouri Primrose, Ozark Sundrop, Evening Primrose

Pavonia species
Rock Rose

Penstemon species
Penstemon, Beardtongue

Perovskia atriplicifolia
Russian Sage

Phlomis russeliana
Jerusalem Sage

Poliomintha longiflora
Mexican Oregano

Ratibida columnifera
Mexican Hat

Rivina humilis
Pigeonberry

Rosemarinus officinalis
Rosemary

Rudbeckia species
Black-Eyed Susan, Rudbeckia

Ruellia brittoniana
Ruellia, Mexican Petunia

Salvia species
Most Sages

Santolina species
Lavender Cotton, Gray Santolina

Scabiosa caucasica
Pincushion Flower

Scutellaria suffrutescens
Pink Scullcap

Sedum spectabile
Showy Sedum

Stachys lanata
Lamb's Ear

Tagetes species
Copper Canyon Daisy, Mexican Mint Marigold

Teucrium species
Germander

Thymus vulgaris
Creeping Thyme

Verbena species
Verbena

Zexmenia hispida
Zexmenia

GRASSES

Andropogon species
Bluestem Grasses

Bouteloua curtipendula var. caespitosa
Sideoats Grama

Elymus glaucus
Blue Wild Rye

Eragrostis curvula
Weeping Love Grass

Festuca ovina glauca
Blue Fescue

Muhlenbergia species
Muhly, Deer Grass

Nasella tenuissima
Mexican Feather Grass

Panicum virgatum
Switch Grass

Pennisetum species
Fountain Grass

Sorghastrum nutans
Indian Grass

SHRUBS, VINES, AND ROSES

Agave species
Agave, Century Plant

Berberis thunbergii
Redleaf Barberry

Bignonia caprolata
Cross Vine

Caesalpinia species
Desert Bird of Paradise

Callicarpa americana
American Beautyberry

Chilopsis linearis
Desert willow

Cycas revoluta
Sago Palm

Dasylerion species
Desert Spoon, Sotol

Hesperaloe species
Red Yucca

Juniperus species
Junipers

Lagerstroemia indica
Dwarf Crape Myrtle

Leucophyllum species
Texas Sage, Texas Ranger

Lonicera sempervirens
Coral Honeysuckle

Mahonia bealei
Leatherleaf Mahonia

Myrica pusilla
Dwarf Wax Myrtle

Nandina domestica
Nandina

Opuntia species
Prickly Pear

Raphiolepis indica
Indian Hawthorn

Sophora secundiflora
Texas Mountain Laurel

Vitex agnus-castus
Vitex, Chastetree

Yucca species
Adam's Needle, Yucca

Chapter Nine
THE SENSES

While seeing colors, shapes, and light patterns is the primary way to experience a garden, the other four senses play an important part in the overall enjoyment as well. A well-planned garden can excite all of your senses: the sweet scents of an antique rose or the intense fragrance of rosemary; the satin softness of lamb's ear or the sharp poke of the prickly pear; the sweet taste of mint and the spiciness of thyme; the rustling of grasses and the song of the birds and bees.

"The greatest gift of a garden is the restoration of the five senses."

HANNA RION,
Let's Make a Flower Garden

Photo 9.2
Garden sage, *Salvia officinalis*, is an herb used for flavoring food

Plants for the Nose: Plants with Fragrant Flowers or Foliage

PERENNIALS

Allium species
Alliums, Garlic*

Alpinia species
Ginger

Anemone hupehensis
Japanese Anemone

Artemisia species
Artemisia*

Agastache species
Hyssop, Hummingbird Mint*

Berlandiera species
Greeneyes, Chocolate Daisy

Buddleia x davidii
Butterfly Bush, Summer Lilac

Chrysanthemum species
Garden Mums, Ox-Eye and
Shasta Daisy

Datura meteloides
Angel's Trumpet

Dianthus species
Cheddar Pinks,
Hardy Carnation

**Erysismum linifolium
'Bowles Mauve'**
Wallflower

Hedychium coronarium
Butterfly Ginger,
Ginger Lily

Helleborus orientalis
Lenten Rose

Hemerocallis species
Daylily

Iberis sempervirens
Candytuft

Iris species
Iris

Lantana species
Lantana

Lavandula species
Lavender*

Leucojum aestivum
Summer Snowflake

Lilium species
Lilies

Mentha species
Mint*

Monarda species
Bee Balm*

Muscari species
Grape Hyacinth

Narcissus species
Daffodils, Jonquils,
and Narcissus

Nepeta faassenii
Catmint*

Oenothera species
Missouri Primrose, Ozark
Sundrop, Evening Primrose

Oxalis species
Wood Sorrel, Shamrock

Pavonia lasiopetala
Rock Rose

Perovskia atriplicifolia
Russian Sage*

Phlox species
Phlox

Polianthes tuberorsa
Mexican Tuberose

Poliomintha longiflora
Mexican Oregano*

Rosemarinus officinalis
Rosemary*

Salvia species
Salvia, Sage*

Santolina species
Lavender Cotton, Santolina*

Saxifrage stolonifera
Strawberry Geranium

Scabiosa caucasica
Pincushion Flower

Scilla species
Scilla

Tagetes species
Copper Canyon Daisy,
Mexican Mint Marigold*

Teucrium species
Germander*

Thymus species
Creeping Thyme*

Tulbaghia violacea
Society Garlic*

Tulipa species
Species or Wild Tulip

Verbena species
Verbena

Viola species
Wood Violet, Sweet Violet

Zantedeschia species
Calla Lily

Zexmenia hispida
Zexmenia*

SHRUBS, VINES, AND ROSES

Bignonia caprolata
Cross Vine

Camellia species
Camellia

Clematis species
Clematis

Forsythia species
Forsythia

Gardenia jasminoides
Gardenia

Gelsemium sempervirens
Carolina Jessamine

Hibiscus syriacus
Rose of Sharon, Althea

Juniperus species
Junipers*

Leucophyllum species
Texas Sage, Texas Ranger*

Magnolia species
Magnolia

Myrica pusilla
Dwarf Wax Myrtle*

Pittosporum tobira
Mock Orange, Pittosporum

Rhododendron species
Azalea

Rosa species
Rose

Sophora secundiflora
Texas Mountain Laurel

Spiraea species
Spirea

Trachelospermum jasminoides
Star Jasmine

Viburnum species
Viburnum

Vitex agnus-castus
Vitex, Chastetree*

Weigela florida
Weigela

Wisteria sinensis
Wisteria

* Fragrant foliage

Photo 9.3
Lamb's Ear, *Stachys lanata*,
is soft to the touch

Plants for the Fingers: Plants with Interesting Textures to Touch

PERENNIALS

Achillea species
Yarrow, Milfoil

Artemisia species
Powis Castle Artemisia

Echinacea purpurea
Purple Coneflower+

Echinops ritro 'Vetch's Blue'
Globe Thistle+

Eupatorium species
Hardy Ageratum, Gregg's
Mist Flower

Foeniculum vulgare
Fennel

Hosta species
Hosta Lily, Plantain Lily

Lavandula species
Lavender

Liatris spicata
Liatris, Kansas Gayfeather,
Blazing Star

**Ligularia tussilaginea
'Aureo-maculata'**
Leopard Plant

Liriope species
Liriope, Lilyturf

Mentha species
Mint

Monarda didmyma
Bee Balm

Nepeta faassenii
Catmint

Perovskia atriplicifolia
Russian Sage

Phlomis russeliana
Jerusalem Sage

Rosemarinus officinalis
Rosemary+

Salvia chamaedryoides
Gray Shrub Sage

Salvia officinalis
Garden Sage

Salvia leucantha
Mexican Bush Sage

Santolina species
Lavender Cotton, Gray
Santolina+

Stachys species
Lamb's Ear, Woodland Betony

Thymus pseudolanuginosus
Wooly Thyme

Verbena tenuisecta
Moss Verbena

GRASSES

Calamagrostis arundinacea
Feather Reed Grass

Chasmanthium latifolium
Inland Sea Oats

Equisetum hyemale
Horsetail Reed

Eragrostis curvula
Weeping Love Grass

Festuca ovina glauca
Blue Fescue

Miscanthus sinensis
Miscanthus, Maiden Grass,
Japanese Silver Grass

Muhlenbergia species
Muhly

Nasella tenuissima
Mexican Feather Grass

Panicum virgatum
Switch Grass

Pennisetum species
Fountain Grass

Sorghastrum nutans
Indian Grass

Typha latifolia
Cattail Reed

SHRUBS, VINES, AND ROSES

Agave species
Agave, Century Plant+

Berberis thunbergii
Redleaf Barberry+

Cotinus coggygria
Smoke Tree

Dasylerion species
Desert Spoon, Sotol+

Hesperaloe species
Red Yucca+

Ilex species
Holly+

Juniperus species
Junipers+

Leucophyllum species
Texas Sage, Texas Ranger

Norlina species
Bear Grass+

Opuntia species
Prickly Pear+

Yucca species
Adam's Needle, Yucca+

+Thorns or prickliness

Photo 9.4
Grasses add sound and movement, as well as color at the end of summer

Warning

Never cook with plants that have been sprayed with pesticides or chemical fungicides.

Plants for the Tongue: Plants Used in Cooking

Perennials

Alpinia species
Ginger

Chrysanthemum x morifolium
Garden Mum

Foeniculum vulgare
Fennel

Mentha species
Mint

Salvia officinalis
Garden Sage

Teucrium chaemedrys
Germander

Thymus species
Thyme

Shrubs, Vines, and Roses

Rosa species
Rose

Yucca species
Adam's Needle, Yucca

Photo 10.1 ***(opposite page)***
Swallowtail butterfly on burkwood viburnum, *Viburnum x burkwoodii*

Chapter Ten
THE BIRDS AND THE BEES

*B*irds, bees, butterflies, and other wildlife are important components of nature. The garden will come to life with the colors of butterflies and cardinals, the music of songbirds and bumble bees, and the busy activity of hummingbirds and dragonflies. Earthworms, ladybugs, toads, and lizards also will take up residence in your garden depending on the plants provided for food and shelter. You should use organic fertilizers and pesticides because chemical compounds, especially pesticides, can damage and kill the garden creatures. While you may get rid of the mosquitoes and ants, you'll end up sacrificing the birds and bees, as well.

PLANTS FOR BUTTERFLIES AND OTHER INSECTS

Butterflies prefer flowers that are large, fragrant, and colorful, especially reds, purples, oranges, and yellows. Any native flower is a good nectar source. Flowers with clusters or large surfaces (the ultimate bug landing pads), like daises, are preferred since the butterflies can rest a bit while feeding. Many flowers bloom in late summer and fall when butterflies are at their peak. Keep in mind, any flower rich in nectar will be attractive not only to butterflies, but to bees and other insects, as well. Usually, bees don't care when you work around them. However, they will get aggressive when someone gets close to their hive or nest.

Asclepias tuberosa, butterfly weed, also known as the milkweed, has a poisonous sap. The caterpillar from the monarch butterfly is the only one that can eat these leaves. The adult butterfly then retains the poison and is not eaten by birds and lizards. *Foeniculum vulgare*, fennel, is a popular food source for swallowtail butterfly caterpillars.

NOTE:

While most plants are listed for their flowers, two are also listed for their foliage, butterfly weed and fennel. Butterflies lay their eggs on these plants, so the caterpillars have food once the eggs are hatched. Don't remove the caterpillars; the plants will survive.

Photo 10.2 *(left)*
Bumble bee on vitex, *Vitex Agnus-castus*

Photo 10.4 *(below)*
Swallowtail butterfly caterpillar on fennel, *Foeniculum vulgare*

Photo 10.3 *(left)*
Swallowtail butterfly on lantana, *Lantana camera 'New Gold'*

Photo 10.5 *(below)*
Butterfly on lantana, *Lantana camera*

Photo 10.6 *(below)*
Honey bee on Gregg's mist flower, *Eupatorium greggii*

Plant for Butterflies and Other Insects

PERENNIALS

Achillea species
Yarrow, Milfoil*

Allium species
Allium

Anemone species
Anemone

Aniscanthus quadrifidus var. wrightii
Hummingbird Bush, Flame Acanthus

Aquilegia species
Columbine

Asclepias species
Butterfly Weed*

Aster species
Aster*

Agastache species
Agastache, Hyssop, Hummingbird Mint*

Baptisia australis
Blue False Indigo

Beloperone guttata
Gold and Brown Shrimp Plant*

Belamcanda chinensis
Blackberry Lily, Candy Lily

Berlandiera species
Greeneyes, Chocolate Daisy*

Buddleia x davidii
Butterfly Bush, Summer Lilac*

Callirhoe involucrata
Winecups, Poppy Mallow*

Calyophus hartwegii
Sun Drops

Caryopteris x clandonensis
Caryopteris, Bluemist Spirea*

Centranthus ruber
Red Valerian

Chrysanthemum species
Ox-Eye Daisy, Shasta Daisy, Chrysanthemum *

Coreopsis species
Tickseed, Coreopsis*

Crocosmia x crocosmiflora
Crocosmia, Montbretia

Dianthus species
Cheddar Pinks, Hardy Carnation

Echinacea purpurea
Purple Coneflower*

Engelmannia pinnatifida
Engelmann Daisy

Eupatorium species
Hardy Ageratum, Joe Pye Weed*

Foeniculum vulgare
Fennel*

Gaillardia x grandiflora
Gaillardia, Indian Blanket*

Gerbera species
Gerbera Daisy

Gladiolus species
Gladiolus

Guara lindhiemerii
Guara, Whirling Butterflies*

Helianthus maximiliani
Maximillian Sunflower

Heliopsis helianthoides
False Sunflower

Hemerocallis species
Daylily

Hibiscus species
Hibiscus, Rose Mallow

Hymenocallis species
Spider Lily

Hymenoxys scaposa
4 Nerve Daisy

Iberis sempervirens
Candytuft

Kniphofia uvaria
Red Hot Poker, Torch Lily, Tritoma

Lantana species
Lantana*

Lavandula species
Lavender*

Liatris spicata
Liatris, Kansas Gayfeather, Blazing Star*

Lobelia cardinalis
Cardinal Flower Lobelia

Lycorus radiata
Autumn Crocus, Spider Lily, Surprise Lily

Lythrum salicaria
Purple Loosestrife

Malvaviscus drummondii
Turk's Cap

Melampodium leucanthum
Blackfoot Daisy

Mentha species
Mint

Monarda species
Bee Balm*

Nepeta faassenii
Catmint

Oenothera species
Missouri Primrose, Ozark Sundrop, Evening Primrose*

Paeonia species
Peony

Pavonia species
Rock Rose*

Penstemon species
Penstemon, Beardtongue

Perovskia atriplicifolia
Russian Sage

Phlox species
Phlox

Physostegia virginiana
Fall Obedient Plant, False Dragonhead

Platycodon gradiflorus
Balloon Flower

Polianthes tuberorsa
Mexican Tuberose

Poliomintha longiflora
Mexican Oregano

Ratibida columnifera
Mexican Hat*

Rudbeckia species
Rudbeckia, Black-Eyed Susan*

Ruellia brittoniana
Ruellia, Mexican Petunia*

Salvia species
Sage, Salvia*

Scabiosa caucasica
Pincushion Flower*

Scutellaria suffrutescens
Pink Scullcap

Sedum spectabile
Showy Sedum

Sidalcea species
Prairie Mallow

Solidago sphacelata
Goldenrod*

Stokesia laevis
Stokes Aster*

Tagetes species
Copper Canyon Daisy, Mexican Mint Marigold

Tecoma stans
Yellow Bells, Esperanza

Thalictrum aquilegifolium
Meadow Rue

Tulbaghia violacea
Society Garlic

Tulipa species
Species or Wild Tulip

Verbena species
Verbena*

Veronica species
Veronica, Speedwell

Viola species
Wood Violet, Sweet Violet

Zexmenia hispida
Zexmenia

SHRUBS, VINES, AND ROSES

Abelia grandiflora
Abelia

Caesalpinia species
Desert Bird of Paradise

Chilopsis linearis
Desert Willow

Clematis species
Clematis

Forsythia species
Forsythia

Gelsemium sempervirens
Carolina Jessamine

Hesperaloe species
Red Yucca*

Hibiscus syriacus
Rose of Sharon, Althea

Hypericum henryi
St. John's Wort

Lonicera sempervirens
Coral Honeysuckle*

Opuntia species
Prickly Pear

Rosa species
Rose*

Sophora secundiflora
Texas Mountain Laurel

Spiraea species
Spirea

Trachelospermum jasminoides
Star Jasmine

Viburnum species
Viburnum

Vitex agnus-castus
Vitex, Chastetree

Weigela florida
Weigela

Wisteria sinensis
Wisteria

Yucca species
Adam's Needle, Yucca*

*Particularly attractive to butterflies

Plants for Hummingbirds

PERENNIALS

Aniscanthus quadrifidus var. wrightii
Hummingbird Bush, Flame Acanthus

Agastache species
Hyssop, Hummingbird Mint

Asclepias tuberosa
Butterfly Weed

Buddleia x davidii
Butterfly Bush, Summer Lilac

Bulbine frutescens
Bulbine

Crocosmia x crocosmiflora
Crocosmia, Montbretia

Hemerocalis species
Daylily

Heuchera sanquinea
Coral Bells

Hibiscus coccineus
Texas Star Hibiscus

Hibiscus moscheutos
Hibiscus, Rose Mallow

Hosta species
Hosta Lily, Plantain Lily

Hymenocallis species
Spider Lily

Incarvillea delavayi
Chinese Foxglove

Kniphofia uvaria
Red Hot Poker, Torch Lily, Tritoma

Lilium species
Lilies

Lobelia cardinalis
Cardinal Flower Lobelia

Lycorus radiata
Autumn Crocus, Spider Lily, Surprise Lily

Malvaviscus drummondii
Turk's Cap

Penstemon species
Penstemon, Beardtongue

Physostegia virginiana
Fall Obedient Plant, False Dragonhead

Polianthes tuberorsa
Mexican Tuberose

Poliomintha longiflora
Mexican Oregano

Ruellia brittoniana
Ruellia, Mexican Petunia

Russelia equisetiformis
Firecracker Plant

Salvia 'Indigo Spires'
Indigo Spires Salvia

Salvia azurea var. grandiflora
Azure Sage, Pitcher Sage

Salvia coccinea
Scarlet Sage

Salvia greggii
Autumn Sage, Cherry Sage

Salvia guarantica
Anise Scented Sage

Salvia leucantha
Mexican Bush Sage

Salvia lyrata
Lyre Leaf Sage

Salvia penstemonoides
Penstemon Sage, Big Red Sage

Scutellaria suffrutescens
Pink Scullcap

Tecoma stans
Yellow Bells, Esperanza

SHRUBS, VINES, AND ROSES

Bignonia caprolata
Cross Vine

Caesalpinia species
Desert Bird of Paradise

Campsis radicans
Trumpet Vine

Chilopsis linearis
Desert willow

Clematis paniculata
Sweet Autumn Clematis

Gelsemium sempervirens
Carolina Jessamine

Hesperaloe species
Red Yucca

Lonicera sempervirens
Coral Honeysuckle

PLANTS FOR HUMMINGBIRDS

Hummingbirds favor flowers that are long and tubular. Their long, thin beaks are perfectly suited for retrieving nectar from these flowers where insects cannot reach. They are especially attracted to reds, oranges, and violets. In one of nature's many strokes of genius, most of these flowers bloom in late summer and fall when hummingbirds are at their peak in Texas.

PLANTS FOR BIRDS AND OTHER WILDLIFE

Providing food for birds and other wildlife is another consideration for the garden, especially in winter months. Plants with berries provide color as well as food. Cardinals and finches prefer thistle-type seeds that coneflowers (*Echinacea species*) and black-eyed Susans (*Rudbeckia species*) produce.

Plants for Birds and Other Wildlife

PERENNIALS

Achillea species
Yarrow, Milfoil

Aster species
Aster

Belamcanda chinensis
Blackberry Lily, Candy Lily

Chrysanthemum species
Ox-Eye Daisy, Shasta Daisy,
Chrysanthemum

Coreopsis species
Coreopsis

Echinacea purpurea
Purple Coneflower

Echinops ritro 'Vetch's Blue'
Globe Thistle

Foeniculum vulgare
Fennel

Gaillardia x grandiflora
Gaillardia, Indian Blanket

Helianthus maximiliani
Maximillian Sunflower

Heliopsis helianthoides
False Sunflower

Hibiscus species
Hibiscus

Malvaviscus drummondii
Turk's Cap

Rivina humilis
Pigeonberry

Rudbeckia species
Black-Eyed Susan, Rudbeckia

Sedum spectabile
Showy Sedum

Thalictrum aquilegifolium
Meadow Rue

SHRUBS, VINES, AND ROSES

Berberis thunbergii
Redleaf Barberry

Callicarpa americana
American Beautyberry

Hesperaloe species
Red Yucca

Ilex species
Holly

Mahonia bealei
Leatherleaf Mahonia

Myrica pusilla
Dwarf Wax Myrtle

Nandina domestica
Nandina

Opuntia species
Prickly Pear

Rosa species
Rose

Symphoricarpos orbiculatus
Coralberry

Vitex agnus-castus
Vitex, Chastetree

Yucca species
Adam's Needle, Yucca

Chapter Eleven
THE FIVE SEASONS OF CONTINUOUS COLOR

When planning a perennial border, plan for year-round color. Your garden will naturally go through peaks and valleys. Most gardens peak from midspring into early summer, slow down for the heat of summer, and then experience a healthy resurgence in autumn. However, you can always find some plant providing color, whether it's the sages and coneflowers in the heat of August, or the evergreen color from holly ferns and hellebores in the middle of winter. Since the growing period is long in Texas, the year can be divided into five major seasons. These seasons represent the stages that the perennial garden goes through and relate to changes in the climate and how the plants respond to them.

EARLY TO MIDSPRING: FEVER AND FLORA

Mid-February to Mid-April

This is the first time of the year when the garden comes alive. Spring starts with the first daffodils in mid-February in most parts of Texas. It peaks by mid-April when the dogwoods, azaleas, tulips, and bluebonnets are in full bloom.

"My personal endeavor is so to choose and combine any plants that at no time from early March to November shall the garden be without a number of lovely pictures. . . ."

LOUISE BEEBE WILDER
Colour in My Garden

Photo 11.2
Daffodils, *Narcissus species*, bloom in spring

Photo 11.3
Holly berries, *Ilex species*, adorn the branches in winter

Photo 11.4
Daffodils, *Narcissus species*, and cool-season annuals bloom in early spring

Early to Midspring

PERENNIALS

Anemone coronaria
Poppy Anemone, Windflower

Aquilegia species
Columbines

Crocus vernus
Crocus

Dianthus gratianopolitanus
Cheddar Pinks

Erysimum linifolium 'Bowles Mauve'
Wallflower

Helleborus orientalis
Lenten Rose

Hymenoxys scaposa
4 Nerve Daisy

Hyacinthoides hispanica
Woodland Bluebells

Iberis sempervirens
Candytuft

Ipeion uniflorum
Blue-Eyed Grass, Spring Star Flower

Iris hollandica
Dutch Iris

Leucojum aestivum
Summer Snowflake

Muscari species
Grape Hyacinth

Narcissus species
Daffodils, Jonquils, and Narcissus

Oxalis species
Pink Wood Sorrel, Shamrock

Phlox divaricata
Louisiana Phlox

Phlox pilosa
Prairie Phlox

Phlox subulata
Creeping Phlox

Scilla sibirica
Siberian Squill

Teucrium fruticans
Bush Germander

Tulipa species
Species or Wild Tulip

SHRUBS, VINES, AND ROSES

Bignonia caprolata
Cross Vine

Camellia species
Camellia

Clematis species
Clematis

Forsythia species
Forsythia

Gardenia jasminoides
Gardenia

Gelsemium sempervirens
Carolina Jessamine

Lonicera sempervirens
Coral Honeysuckle

Loropetalum chinensis rubrum
Fringe Flower

Magnolia stellata
Star Magnolia

Magnolia lilliflora
Saucer Magnolia

Mahonia bealei
Leatherleaf Mahonia

Pittosporum tobira
Mock Orange, Pittosporum

Raphiolepis indica
Indian Hawthorn

Rhododendron species
Azalea

Salvia lyrata
Lyre Leaf Sage

Sophora secundiflora
Texas Mountain Laurel

Spiraea species
Spirea

Trachelospermum jasminoides
Star Jasmine

Viburnum species
Viburnum

Weigela florida
Weigela

Wisteria sinensis
Wisteria

LATE SPRING TO EARLY SUMMER: PEAK OF THE PERENNIALS

Mid-April to Mid-June

This season starts when the daffodils and other spring bulbs fade in mid-April and continues to the peak of the perennial border in early June. Texas gardens become lush with iris, roses, daylilies, and the start of the summer flowers.

Photo 11.5
Purple coneflowers, *Echinacea purpurea*, gooseneck loosestrife, *Lysimachia clethroides*, and liatris, *Liatris spicata*, bloom in early summer

Perennials

Achillea species
Yarrow, Milfoil

Ajuga reptans
Ajuga, Bugleweed

Alchemilla mollis
Lady's Mantle

Allium species
Allium

Acanthus mollis
Bear's Breeches, Grecian
Leaf Plant

Agapanthus species
Lily of the Nile, Agapanthus

Baptisia australis
Blue False Indigo

Buddleia x davidii
Butterfly Bush, Summer Lilac

Bulbine frutescens
Bulbine

Callirhoe involucrata
Winecups, Poppy Mallow

Calyophus hartwegii
Sun Drops

Centranthus ruber
Red Valerian

Ceratostigma plumbaginoides
Creeping Plumbago

Chrysanthemum leucanthemum
Ox-Eye Daisy

Chrysanthemum maximum
Shasta Daisy

Colocasia esculenta
Elephant Ears

Coreopsis species
Tickseed, Coreopsis

Crinum species
Crinum Lily

Dianthus 'First Love'
Hardy Carnation

Echinacea purpurea
Purple Coneflower

Engelmannia pinnatifida
Engelmann Daisy

Foeniculum vulgare
Fennel

Gaillardia x grandiflora
Gaillardia, Indian Blanket

Geranium species
Hardy Geranium, Cranesbill

Gerbera species
Gerbera Daisy

Gladiolus species
Gladiolus

Guara lindhiemerii
Guara, Whirling Butterflies

Hemerocallis species
Daylily

Heuchera species
Coral Bells

Hippeastrum x johnsonii
Hardy Amaryllis

Hosta species
Hosta Lily, Plantain Lily

Hymenocallis species
Spider Lily

Incarvillea delavayi
Chinese Foxglove

Iris species
Iris

Kniphofia uvaria
Red Hot Poker, Torch Lily,
Tritoma

Lantana species
Lantana

Lavandula species
Lavender

Liatris spicata
Liatris, Kansas Gayfeather,
Blazing Star

Lilium species
Lilies

Lobelia cardinalis
Cardinal Flower Lobelia

Lythrum salicaria
Purple Loosestrife

Lysimachia clethroides
Gooseneck Loosestrife

Melampodium leucanthum
Blackfoot Daisy

Mentha species
Mint

Monarda species
Bee Balm, Bergamot

Morea species
African Iris, Fortnight Lily

Nepeta faassenii
Catmint

Nierembergia caerulea
Nierembergia, Cupflower

Oenothera species
Missouri Primrose, Ozark
Sundrop, Evening Primrose

Paeonia species
Peony

Penstemon species
Penstemon, Beardtongue

Perovskia atriplicifolia
Russian Sage

Phlomis russeliana
Jerusalem Sage

Phlox pilosa
Prairie Phlox

Platycodon gradiflorus
Balloon Flower

Polianthes tuberorsa
Mexican Tuberose

Ratibida columnifera
Mexican Hat

Rivina humilis
Pigeonberry

Rudbeckia hirta
Gloriosa Daisy, Rudbeckia

Rudbeckia maxima
Giant Rudbeckia,
Giant Coneflower

Salvia blepharophylla
Purple Leaf Sage

Salvia chamaedryoides
Gray Shrub Sage

Salvia coccinea
Scarlet Sage

Salvia farinacea
Mealy Cup Sage

Salvia greggii
Autumn Sage, Cherry Sage

Salvia lyrata
Lyre Leaf Sage

Salvia officinalis
Garden Sage

Salvia engelmanii
Engleman's Sage

Salvia guarantica
Anise Scented Sage

Salvia nemerosa 'Plumosa'
Plumosa Meadow Sage

Salvia x superba
Meadow Sage

Salvia uliginosa
Bog Sage

Salvia verticillata 'Purple Rain'
Purple Rain Salvia

Santolina species
Lavender Cotton, Santolina

Saxifrage stolonifera
Strawberry Geranium

Scabiosa caucasica
Pincushion Flower

Scilla peruviana
Peruvian Scilla

Scutellaria suffrutescens
Pink Scullcap

Sidalcea species
Prairie Mallow

Stachys species
Lamb's Ear, Woodland Betony

Stokesia laevis
Stokes Aster

Teucrium chaemedrys
Germander

Thalictrum aquilegifolium
Meadow Rue

Thymus species
Creeping Thyme

Tulbaghia violacea
Society Garlic

Verbena species
Verbena

**Veronica peduncularis
'Georgia Blue'**
Creeping Speedwell

Zantedeschia species
Calla Lily

Grasses

**Bouteloua curtipendula
var. caespitosa**
Sideoats Grama

Carex species
Sedge

Eragrostis curvula
Weeping Love Grass

Festuca ovina glauca
Blue Fescue

Panicum virgatum
Switch Grass

Sorghastrum nutans
Indian Grass

Typha latifolia
Cattail Reed

FERNS

All Ferns

SHRUBS, VINES, AND ROSES

Acer palmatum
Japanese Maple

Berberis thunbergii
Redleaf Barberry

Bignonia caprolata
Cross Vine

Campsis radicans
Trumpet Vine

Chilopsis linearis
Desert willow

Clematis species
Clematis

Cotinus coggygria
Smoke Tree

Cycas revoluta
Sago Palm

Gardenia jasminoides
Gardenia

Hesperaloe parviflora
Red Yucca

Hibiscus syriacus
Rose of Sharon, Althea

Hydrangea species
Hydrangea

Hypericum henryi
St. John's Wort

Lonicera sempervirens
Coral Honeysuckle

Magnolia grandiflora 'Little Gem'
Little Gem Magnolia

Nandina domestica
Nandina

Nerium oleander
Dwarf Oleander

Opuntia species
Prickly Pear

Rosa species
Rose

Spiraea x bumalda 'Anthony Waterer'
Anthony Waterer Spirea

Vitex agnus-castus
Vitex, Chastetree

Yucca species
Adam's Needle, Yucca

MIDSUMMER: SOME LIKE IT HOT

Mid-June to August

During this period of summer, the heat is turned up and many of the plants slow down. However, some heat-lovers are just getting started.

Photo 11.6
Russian sage, *Perovskia atriplicifolia*, tickseed, *Coreopsis species*, and purple coneflower, *Echinacea purpurea*, bloom in the heat of summer

PERENNIALS

Alpinia species
Ginger

**Aniscanthus quadrifidus
var. wrightii**
Hummingbird Bush,
Flame Acanthus

Asclepias tuberosa
Butterfly Weed

Agastache species
Hyssop, Hummingbird Mint

Agapanthus species
Lily of the Nile, Agapanthus

Beloperone guttata
Gold and Brown Shrimp Plant

Belamcanda chinensis
Blackberry Lily, Candy Lily

Berlandiera species
Greeneyes, Chocolate Daisy

Buddleia x davidii
Butterfly Bush, Summer Lilac

Bulbine frutescens
Bulbine

Calyophus hartwegii
Sun Drops

Canna x generalis
Canna Lily

Caryopteris x clandonensis
Caryopteris, Bluemist Spirea

Ceratostigma plumbaginoides
Creeping Plumbago

Colocasia esculenta
Elephant Ears

Coreopsis species
Tickseed, Coreopsis

Crinum species
Crinum Lily

Crocosmia x crocosmiflora
Crocosmia, Montbretia

Datura meteloides
Angel's Trumpet

Dianthus 'First Love'
Hardy Carnation

Echinacea purpurea
Purple Coneflower

Echinops ritro 'Vetch's Blue'
Globe Thistle

Foeniculum vulgare
Fennel

Gaillardia x grandiflora
Gaillardia, Indian Blanket

Gerbera species
Gerbera Daisy

Gladiolus species
Gladiolus

Guara lindhiemerii
Guara, Whirling Butterflies

Hedychium coronarium
Butterfly Ginger, Ginger Lily

Helianthus maximiliani
Maximillian Sunflower

Heliopsis helianthoides
False Sunflower

Hemerocallis species
Daylily

Hibiscus species
Hibiscus, Rose Mallow

Hosta species
Hosta Lily, Plantain Lily

Hymenocallis species
Spider Lily

Kniphofia uvaria
Red Hot Poker, Torch Lily,
Tritoma

Lantana camara
Lantana

Liatris spicata
Liatris, Kansas Gayfeather,
Blazing Star

Lilium species
Lilies

Lobelia cardinalis
Cardinal Flower Lobelia

Lythrum salicaria
Purple Loosestrife

Malvaviscus drummondii
Turk's Cap

Melampodium leucanthum
Blackfoot Daisy

Morea species
African Iris, Fortnight Lily

Nepeta faassenii
Catmint

Nierembergia species
Nierembergia, Cupflower

Pavonia species
Rock Rose

Penstemon species
Penstemon, Beardtongue

Perovskia atriplicifolia
Russian Sage

Phlomis russeliana
Jerusalem Sage

Phlox paniculata
Summer Phlox

Platycodon gradiflorus
Balloon Flower

Poliomintha longiflora
Mexican Oregano

Ratibida columnifera
Mexican Hat

Rivina humilis
Pigeonberry

Rudbeckia species
Black-Eyed Susan, Gloriosa
Daisy, Rudbeckia

Ruellia brittonia
Ruellia, Mexican Petunia

Russelia equisetiformis
Firecracker Plant

Salvia 'Indigo Spires'
Indigo Spires Salvia

Salvia azurea var. grandiflora
Azure Sage, Pitcher Sage

Salvia coccinea
Scarlet Sage

Salvia farinacea
Mealy Cup Sage

Salvia greggii
Autumn Sage, Cherry Sage

Salvia guarantica
Anise Scented Sage

Salvia nemerosa 'Plumosa'
Plumosa Meadow Sage

Salvia penstemonoides
Penstemon Sage, Big Red Sage

Salvia x superba
Meadow Sage

Salvia uliginosa
Bog Sage

Salvia verticillata 'Purple Rain'
Purple Rain Salvia

Salvia bicolor
Bicolor Sage, Cocoa
Sapphire Salvia

Salvia buchananii
Buchanan's Sage

Salvia Texana
Texas Sage

Scabiosa caucasica
Pincushion Flower

Scutellaria suffrutescens
Pink Scullcap

Stokesia laevis
Stokes Aster

Tecoma stans
Yellow Bells, Esperanza

Tradescantia virginiana
Spiderwort

Tulbaghia violacea
Society Garlic

Verbena species
Garden Verbena

Veronica species
Veronica, Speedwell

GRASSES

**Bouteloua curtipendula
var. caespitosa**
Sideoats Grama

**Calamagrostis arundinacea
'Karl Foerster'**
Karl Foerster Feather
Reed Grass

Chasmanthium latifolium
Inland Sea Oats

Elymus glaucus
Blue Wild Rye

Eragrostis curvula
Weeping Love Grass

Festuca ovina glauca
Blue Fescue

Hakonechloa macro 'Aureola'
Golden Japanese Forest Grass

Imperata cylindrica 'Red Baron'
Japanese Blood Grass

Miscanthus sinensis
Miscanthus, Maiden Grass,
Japanese Silver Grass

Muhlenbergia dumosa
Bamboo Muhly

Muhlenbergia rigens
Deer Grass, Deer Muhly

Nasella tenuissima
Mexican Feather Grass

Panicum virgatum
Switch Grass

Pennisetum species
Fountain Grass

Sorghastrum nutans
Indian Grass

Typha latifolia
Cattail Reed

FERNS	Berberis thunbergii Redleaf Barberry	Dasylerion species Desert Spoon, Sotol	Leucophyllum species Texas Sage, Texas Ranger
All ferns	Caesalpinia species Desert Bird of Paradise	Gardenia jasminoides Gardenia	Magnolia grandiflora 'Little Gem' Little Gem Magnolia
SHRUBS, VINES, AND ROSES	Campsis radicans Trumpet Vine	Hesperaloe species Red Yucca	Nerium oleander Dwarf Oleander
Abelia grandiflora Abelia	Chilopsis linearis Desert willow	Hibiscus syriacus Rose of Sharon, Althea	Rosa species Rose
Acer palmatum Japanese Maple	Cotinus coggygria Smoke Tree	Lagerstroemia indica Dwarf Crape Myrtle	Yucca species Adam's Needle, Yucca

LATE SUMMER TO MIDAUTUMN: LATE BLOOMERS

September to October

By the end of August, the temperatures start to drop and the moisture levels begin to rise. In September and October, the garden goes through another resurgence of blooms before the height of fall color. The temperatures are moderate with periods of sun and rain. This is also the peak season for monarch butterflies and hummingbirds in Texas.

Photo 11.7
Sages, *Salvia species*, and goldenrod, *Solidago sphacelata*, bloom at the end of summer and continue into fall

Late Summer to Midautumn

PERENNIALS

Anemone hupehensis
Japanese Anemone

Aniscanthus quadrifidus var. wrightii
Hummingbird Bush, Flame Acanthus

Artemisia ludoviciana abula 'Silver King'
Silver King Artemesia

Asclepias tuberosa
Butterfly Weed

Aster species
Aster

Agastache species
Hyssop, Hummingbird Mint

Beloperone species
Gold and Brown Shrimp Plant

Berlandiera species
Greeneyes, Chocolate Daisy

Buddleia x davidii
Butterfly Bush, Summer Lilac

Bulbine frutescens
Bulbine

Canna x generalis
Canna Lily

Caryopteris x clandonensis
Caryopteris, Bluemist Spirea

Ceratostigma plumbaginoides
Creeping Plumbago

Chrysanthemum x morifolium
Garden Mum

Chrysanthemum x 'Clara Curtis'
Clara Curtis Chrysanthemum

Datura meteloides
Angel's Trumpet

Dianthus 'First Love'
Hardy Carnation

Eupatorium species
Hardy Ageratum, Gregg's Mist Flower, Joe Pye Weed

Guara lindhiemerii
Guara, Whirling Butterflies

Hedychium coronarium
Butterfly Ginger, Ginger Lily

Helianthus maximiliani
Maximillian Sunflower

Heliopsis helianthoides
False Sunflower

Hibiscus species
Hibiscus, Rose Mallow

Kniphofia uvaria
Red Hot Poker, Torch Lily, Tritoma

Lantana species
Lantana

Lycorus radiata
Autumn Crocus, Spider Lily, Surprise Lily

Lythrum salicaria
Purple Loosestrife

Lysimachia clethroides
Gooseneck Loosestrife

Malvaviscus drummondii
Turk's Cap

Nierembergia caerulea
Nierembergia, Cupflower

Pavonia species
Rock Rose

Perovskia atriplicifolia
Russian Sage

Phlox paniculata
Summer Phlox

Physostegia virginiana
Fall Obedient Plant, False Dragonhead

Platycodon gradiflorus
Balloon Flower

Poliomintha longiflora
Mexican Oregano

Rivina humilis
Pigeonberry

Rudbeckia species
Black-Eyed Susan, Gloriosa Daisy

Ruellia brittoniana
Ruellia, Mexican Petunia

Russelia equisetiformis
Firecracker Plant

Salvia 'Indigo Spires'
Indigo Spires Salvia

Salvia azurea var. grandiflora
Azure Sage, Pitcher Sage

Salvia coccinea
Scarlet Sage

Salvia farinacea
Mealy Cup Sage

Salvia greggii
Autumn Sage, Cherry Sage

Salvia guarantica
Anise Scented Sage

Salvia leucantha
Mexican Bush Sage

Salvia x superba
Meadow Sage

Salvia uliginosa
Bog Sage

Salvia bicolor
Bicolor Sage, Cocoa Sapphire Salvia

Scabiosa caucasica
Pincushion Flower

Scutellaria suffrutescens
Pink Scullcap

Sedum spectabile
Showy Sedum

Solidago sphacelata
Goldenrod

Tagetes species
Copper Canyon Daisy, Mexican Mint Marigold

Tecoma stans
Yellow Bells, Esperanza

Tulbaghia violacea
Society Garlic

Verbena species
Verbena

Veronica species
Veronica, Speedwell

Zephyranthus species
Rain Lily

Zexmenia hispida
Zexmenia

GRASSES

Andropogon species
Bluestem Grasses

Calamagrostis arundinacea 'Karl Foerster'
Karl Foerster Feather Reed Grass

Chasmanthium latifolium
Inland Sea Oats

Imperata cylindrica 'Red Baron'
Japanese Blood Grass

Miscanthus sinensis
Miscanthus, Maiden Grass, Japanese Silver Grass

Muhlenbergia species
Muhly

Panicum virgatum
Switch Grass

Pennisetum species
Fountain Grass

Sorghastrum nutans
Indian Grass

SHRUBS, VINES, AND ROSES

Abelia grandiflora
Abelia

Acer palmatum
Japanese Maple

Berberis thunbergii
Redleaf Barberry

Caesalpinia species
Desert Bird of Paradise

Callicarpa americana
American Beautyberry

Campsis radicans
Trumpet Vine

Chilopsis linearis
Desert Willow

Euonymus alata
Burning Bush

Hesperaloe species
Red Yucca

Lagerstroemia indica
Dwarf Crape Myrtle

Leucophyllum species
Texas Sage, Texas Ranger

Nandina domestica
Nandina

Rosa species
Rose

Symphoricarpos orbiculatus
Coralberry

Yucca species
Adam's Needle, Yucca

Photo 11.8
In fall and early winter, dried grasses and evergreen perennials dominate the author's front walk

LATE AUTUMN TO WINTER: COLD BLOODED

November to Mid-February

This is the slowest period in the garden, and the evergreens and colorful fruiters are needed the most. However, a few bloomers exist. Some plants, mostly shrubs, have great fall color, too.

Winter Bloomers

PERENNIALS

Helleborus orientalis
Lenten Rose

Hymenoxys scaposa
4 Nerve Daisy

Ligularia tussilaginea 'Aureo-maculata'
Leopard Plant

Rosemarinus officinalis
Rosemary

SHRUBS AND VINES

Camellia species
Camellia

Loropetalum chinensis rubrum
Fringe Flower

Evergreen and Semievergreen Plants

PERENNIALS

Ajuga reptans
Ajuga, Bugleweed

Aquilegia chrysantha 'Hinckleyana'
Texas Gold Columbine

Artemisia species
Artemisia

Aspidistra elatior
Aspidistra, Cast Iron Plant

Acanthus mollis
Bear's Breeches, Grecian Leaf Plant

Agapanthus africanus
Lily of the Nile, Agapanthus

Bulbine frutescens
Bulbine

Erysismum linifolium 'Bowles Mauve'
Wallflower

Helleborus orientalis
Lenten Rose

Heuchera species
Coral Bells

Hymenoxys scaposa
4 Nerve Daisy

Iberis sempervirens
Candytuft

Kniphofia uvaria
Red Hot Poker, Torch Lily

Lavandula species
Lavender

Ligularia tussilaginea 'Aureo-maculata'
Leopard Plant

Liriope muscari and spicata
Liriope, Lilyturf

Morea species
African Iris, Fortnight Lily

Ophiopogon species
Ophiopogon, Mondo Grass

Oxalis species
Wood Sorrel, Shamrock

Phlox subulata
Creeping Phlox

Rosemarinus officinalis
Rosemary

Salvia chamaedryoides
Gray Shrub Sage

Salvia greggii
Autumn Sage, Cherry Sage

Salvia officinalis
Garden Sage

Salvia lyrata
Lyre Leaf Sage

Santolina species
Lavender Cotton, Santolina

Saxifrage stolonifera
Strawberry Geranium

Stachys lanata
Lamb's Ear

Teucrium species
Germander

Thymus species
Creeping Thyme

Viola species
Wood Violet, Sweet Violet

GRASSES

Acorus species
Sweet Flag

Carex species
Sedge

Equisetum hyemale
Horsetail Reed

Festuca ovina glauca
Blue Fescue

Muhlenbergia rigens
Deer Grass, Deer Muhly

FERNS

Cyrtomium falcatum
Holly Fern

Dryopteris erythrosora
Autumn Fern

SHRUBS, VINES, AND ROSES

Abelia grandiflora
Abelia

Acuba japonica
Acuba

Agave species
Agave, Century Plant

Bignonia caprolata
Cross Vine

Buxus species
Boxwood

Camellia species
Camellia

Clematis odorata
Evergreen Clematis

Cycas revoluta
Sago Palm

Dasylerion species
Desert Spoon, Sotol

Fatsia japonica
Japanese Fatsia

Ficus pumila
Fig Ivy

Gardenia jasminoides
Gardenia

Gelsemium sempervirens
Carolina Jessamine

Hesperaloe species
Red Yucca

Ilex species
Holly

Juniperus species
Junipers

Leucophyllum species
Texas Sage, Texas Ranger

Lonicera sempervirens
Coral Honeysuckle

Loropetalum chinensis
Fringe Flower

Magnolia grandiflora 'Little Gem'
Little Gem Magnolia

Mahonia bealei
Leatherleaf Mahonia

Myrica pusilla
Dwarf Wax Myrtle

Nandina domestica
Nandina

Nerium oleander
Dwarf Oleander

Norlina species
Bear Grass

Opuntia Species
Prickly Pear

Pittosporum tobira
Mock Orange, Pittosporum

Raphiolepis indica
Indian Hawthorn

Rhododendron species
Azalea

Sophora secundiflora
Texas Mountain Laurel

Trachelospermum jasminoides
Star Jasmine

Viburnum tinus
Spring Bouquet Viburnum

Viburnum x burkwoodii
Burkwood Viburnum

Yucca species
Adam's Needle, Yucca

PLANTS WITH COLORFUL FALL FOLIAGE

Lythrum salicaria
Purple Loosestrife

Berberis thunbergii
Redleaf Barberry

Euonymus alata
Burning Bush

Hydrangea quercifolia
Oakleaf Hydrangea

Lagerstroemia indica
Dwarf Crape Myrtle

Nandina domestica
Nandina

Spiraea species
Spirea

PLANTS WITH COLORFUL WINTER FRUIT

Malvaviscus drummondii
Turk's Cap

Callicarpa americana
American Beautyberry

Ilex species
Holly

Magnolia grandiflora 'Little Gem'
Little Gem Magnolia

Mahonia bealei
Leatherleaf Mahonia

Nandina domestica
Nandina

Rosa species
Rose

Symphoricarpos orbiculatus
Coralberry

Photo 12.1 (opposite page)
Yarrow, *Achillea millefolium* 'Cerise Queen'

Chapter Twelve
THE PERENNIALS: A TO Z

*P*erennials come in all shapes, sizes, colors, and textures. While many perennials are planted for their beautiful flowers, some are used for their bold and colorful foliage. Most perennials go dormant in winter and return from roots or bulbs in spring, but the few that are evergreen or semievergreen provide year-round color.

What's in a Name

Plants are listed here alphabetically by their botanical names instead of by their common names. Often, the same common name is used for many different plants. For example, the name "coneflower" is used for the purple coneflower (*Echinacea species*), the yellow coneflower, also known as the black-eyed Susan (*Rudbeckia species*), or the Mexican hat (*Ratibida species*). In addition, one plant will have many different common names. For example *Salvia greggii* may be called autumn sage, cherry sage, or Gregg's sage. Using the botanical name eliminates any confusion because every plant variety in the world has a unique botanical name, like a thumbprint, which can be identified in any garden center in the world.

"The earth laughs in flowers."

RALPH WALDO EMERSON

Understanding the botanical name is really quite easy. The first name is the genus name, which is like the plant's surname. It identifies a group of plants that are related or have similar characteristics and care requirements. For example, every type of iris has similarly shaped flowers in spring and long grass or swordlike foliage. The second name

Photo 12.2
Daffodils and narcissus,
Narcissus species

is the species name, which identifies the particular variety of the plant. Sometimes another name, appearing in single quotation marks, will follow the species name. This is called the cultivar name, which refers to a single species that has been bred for a special characteristic, such as unusual bloom color, size, shape, or hardiness. For example, a cultivar of the purple coneflower, *Echinacea purpurea 'White Swan,'* has white flowers instead of the standard lavender. Botanical name listings are consistent everywhere.

PLANT CHARACTERISTICS

For each plant listed in this section, information has been supplied referring to its zone, light, soil, size, color, and season.

Zone refers to the cold hardiness of the plant. The average low temperatures a plant can survive in winter determine its cold hardiness. The zones in Texas range from zone 6 (–10° to 0°) to zone 9 (20° to 30°).

Photo 12.3
Zexmenia detail,
Zexmenia hispida

Photo 12.4
Bed of early summer
perennials in bloom

Light refers to the amount of shade or sun a plant needs to grow well.

Soil refers to the soil type and moisture level that a plant needs to thrive (such as, dry, moist, or well-drained).

Size refers to the height of the plant. Low plants, growing from 0 to 18 inches high, should be planted in the front of the border. Medium plants, growing from 18 to 36 inches, should be planted in the middle of the border. Tall plants, growing from 36 inches or more, should be planted at the back of the border.

Color generally refers to flower colors but includes foliage color when noted.

Season refers to the time of year a particular plant is at its peak.

A

Achillea filipendulina,
Achillea millefolium

Photo 12.5
Yarrow, *Achillea millefolium*
'Summer Pastels'

Yarrow, Milfoil

- ◆ **Zones:** 2–9
- ◆ **Light:** full sun to light shade
- ◆ **Soil:** well-drained
- ◆ **Size:** medium
- ◆ **Color:** yellow, white, pink, red
- ◆ **Season:** early to midsummer

Yarrow is a group of easy-care perennials that have feathery and fernlike foliage and large groups of tiny flowers that are closely packed on flat clusters. The flowers last a long time and can

Photo 12.6
Coronation gold yarrow,
Achillea x 'Coronation Gold'

POPULAR VARIETIES

'Apple Blossom' has pale pink flowers and is 24 inches tall.

'Cerise Queen' has darker rosy red flowers and reaches only 18 inches tall.

'Paprika' has darker scarlet flowers and is 24 inches tall.

'Summer Pastels' bloom in a range of pastel colors from white to pink, to yellow and orange; they reach 24 inches tall.

'Snow Sport' has white flowers and reach 24 inches high.

be cut and dried in permanent flower arrangements. Some yarrow, like *Achillea millefolium*, spread underground by rhizomes and can be invasive. Other yarrow, such as the fernleaf yarrow (*A. filipendulina*), spreads by clumps and is better behaved. Yarrow is moderately drought tolerant but needs a regular water supply in the hottest parts of summer. High humidity and heavy soils can result in problems with disease fungus.

Full sun is best for yarrow, but light afternoon shade in summer may be preferred. If the flowers do not get enough sun, they can get weak stems, which will flop over with heavy heads and require support and staking. Cut back the faded blooms to produce more throughout the summer and into fall. You may want to leave the last blooms of fall; they will dry nicely in the beds for winter interest. In winter, the foliage forms low evergreen mats.

Many varieties and hybrids exist in the nursery trade. Below are some of the most popular.

Photo 12.7 *(far right)*
Bugleweed, *Ajuga reptans*
'Bronze Beauty'

A. x 'Anthea' has light yellow flowers with gray-green foliage and grows to 18 inches high.

A. x 'Coronation Gold' has mounding foliage with gray-green leaves and flowers that are mustard yellow. The flower heads are 3 to 4 inches across and grow to 36 inches tall and wide. Yarrow is hardy to zone 6.

A. x 'Moonshine' has silvery-gray foliage and reaches only about 24 inches high. The flower color is bright sulfur yellow. The color is vibrant and works well with a "hot" summer border. It shows up at night when the moon is bright, hence the name. It is hardy to zone 7.

A. millefolium has green foliage and is hardy to zone 2.

Ajuga reptans
Ajuga, Bugleweed

◆ **Zones:** 4–8

◆ **Light:** shade

◆ **Soil:** moist, well-drained

◆ **Size:** low

◆ **Color:** blue (flower); bronze, burgundy, green (foliage)

◆ **Season:** midspring

Ajuga is commonly grown as an evergreen ground cover in the United States in the Northeast and Midwest. Because it is not as tolerant of heavy soils and hot summers, it does not make a vigorous ground cover in Texas. Depending on the variety, it has low-growing, 3 to 6 inch high, shiny foliage and blue flower spikes in April that reach 9 inches high. Keep it moist in the heat of summer. Plant it at the front of the border, between stepping-stones, and as a ground cover under large shrubs and trees.

r. 'Bronze Beauty' has metallic bronze foliage with short spikes.

r. 'Burgundy Glow' has variegated foliage with pink highlights on the new growth.

Alchemilla mollis
Lady's Mantle

◆ **Zones:** 3–8

◆ **Light:** shade to part shade

◆ **Soil:** moist

◆ **Size:** medium

◆ **Color:** yellow-green

◆ **Season:** late spring

Lady's mantle is a low-growing plant for the shade garden. The leaves are large with rounded lobes and a silvery sheen. They bloom in masses of tiny yellow-green and chartreuse flowers above the foliage in May and June. The plant forms clumpy mounds that reach 24 inches tall and wide. Continual moisture is necessary, especially during hot, dry weather. Lady's mantle works best in eastern parts of the state.

Allium sphaerocephalum
Drumstick Allium

◆ **Zones:** 1–9

◆ **Light:** full sun to light shade

◆ **Soil:** well-drained

◆ **Size:** medium

◆ **Color:** lavender pink

◆ **Season:** early summer

The many types of alliums available have strap-like foliage and produce balls of tiny flowers on the tops of slender stems. They grow from bulbs that should be planted in fall or early spring for the following summer's blooms. The drumstick allium is one of the more dependable repeat bloomers. It has very fine-bladed foliage and forms lavender, oval-shaped flower heads about 3 inches in diameter on top of stems 24 to 36 inches high. Once planted, it is drought tolerant and very dependable.

The foliage dies away as the summer wears on, so place the bulbs behind plants with good foliage that will mask the dying leaves. Like all bulbs, the foliage produces energy for next year's bloom, so don't trim it away until it's dry. Even as it browns out, the foliage holds its shape and provides an interesting texture. It mixes well with other early-summer bloomers, like purple coneflower, liatris, lavender, and meadow sage. If it does not get enough sun, it will flop over as it starts to bloom. If the foliage is bruised, it has a distinct onion scent.

Other alliums include:

A. 'Purple Sensation' which grows to 36 inches high with globular purple flowers.

A. Caeruleum, blue allium, has powder blue globular flowers and grows to 20 inches tall.

A. moly, golden garlic, has yellow flowers in a loose head and grows to only 12 inches tall.

Anemone coronaria
Poppy Anemone, Windflower

◆ **Zones:** 7–10

◆ **Light:** full sun to light shade

◆ **Soil:** moist, well-drained

Photo 12.9
Drumstick allium,
Allium sphaerocephalum

Photo 12.8 *(far left)*
Lady's mantle,
Alchemilla mollis

- ◆ **Size:** low to medium
- ◆ **Color:** white, pink, red, blue, violet
- ◆ **Season:** early to midspring

Anemones have large buttercuplike flowers and are popular as cut flowers in bouquets and arrangements. The poppy anemone sprouts from tubers that should be planted in fall or late winter. The foliage is medium green and finely dissected. The large flowers can be single, semi-double, or double on tall, single stems in spring. They grow to 12 to 18 inches tall. The foliage is spare, so plant them behind lower foliage plants. As soon as the temperature rises, the plants will fade. Soak the tubers in water overnight prior to planting, and set them 1 inch deep. They may work best as a spring annual because they do not always return after the heat of summer.

Anemone hupehensis
Japanese Anemone

- ◆ **Zones:** 6–8
- ◆ **Light:** shade to light shade
- ◆ **Soil:** moist, humus rich
- ◆ **Size:** medium to tall
- ◆ **Color:** white and pink
- ◆ **Season:** early to midfall

This is a fibrous rooted anemone that doesn't bloom until fall and grows 24 inches to 36 inches high. Plant Japanese anemones in humus-rich, moist soil, in shade and semishade, and avoid hot afternoon sun. Flowers range in colors of white, pink, and rose and form in singles, doubles, and semidoubles. The foliage is large, dark

green, lobed, and hairy. The plant is slow to establish but will fill in with age. The texture is delicate and makes an elegant plant. Heat and drought are its biggest problems, so keep it moist in summer. Better to limit it to the eastern parts of Texas.

Japanese anemone is a middle or back-of-the-border plant for the shady garden. Plant it behind ferns, hostas, Lenten rose, and coral bells. Divide every 3 or 4 years to keep it vigorous. The grapeleaf anemone (*Anemone vitifolia* and *Anemone x hybrida*) is bred from several types of Japanese anemones. It's a spreading perennial with grape-leaf-shaped leaves that turn bronze and bloom in autumn.

POPULAR VARIETIES

A. 'Prince Heinrich' has deep rose flowers and grows 2 to 3 feet tall.

A. 'Honorine Jobert' has white flowers and grows to 24 inches tall.

Flame Acanthus
Hummingbird Bush

- ◆ **Zones:** 7–10
- ◆ **Light:** full sun
- ◆ **Soil:** dry, well-drained
- ◆ **Size:** medium to tall
- ◆ **Color:** red-orange
- ◆ **Season:** late summer to fall

Hummingbird bush is a subshrub native to southern Texas. In the southern regions it's evergreen, but in North Texas, it's deciduous and should be treated as a perennial that's cut back close to the ground in winter. It quickly grows back in summer, forming a large bush. The foliage is thin and medium green. The flowers are

orange-red and tubular shaped, therefore perfect food for hummingbirds. They bloom from July until the first frosts in fall. The shape of the plant is loose, shrubby, and open. This plant is good for the back of a sunny border and is great if you want to attract hummingbirds. It mixes well with salvias, especially autumn sage, and black-eyed Susan.

Aquilegia chrysantha 'Hinckleyana'
Texas Gold Columbine

- ◆ **Zones:** 3–9
- ◆ **Light:** shade to part shade
- ◆ **Soil:** dry, well-drained
- ◆ **Size:** medium
- ◆ **Color:** yellow-gold
- ◆ **Season:** midspring

This native is by far the best columbine for Texas. Like all columbines, it has composite flowers with long spurs. It blooms in March and April with bright yellow flowers. The blue-green, airy foliage dies back quite a bit during the heat of summer. However, by winter it comes back to life, and it is full and lush by the time the plant starts to bloom in spring. The plant grows 24 to 30 inches high and wide. Unlike most shade loving plants, columbine prefers drier, well-drained soils. This makes it perfect for our dry hot summers. In fact, it can develop fungal problems with too much irrigation. It will reseed easily as well. Plant columbine with other dry shade plants, like lyre leaf sage and some ferns.

Other columbines, such as wild columbine (*A. canadensis*) and dwarf columbines (*A. x hybrida 'Bierdermiere'),* should be grown in the same conditions and will bloom around the same time. However, in Texas these are short-lived plants. Both grow to about 12 to 18 inches high and wide. The wild columbine has yellow petals with red spurs. The dwarf and other hybrid types have mixed pastel colors with long spurs. Unlike Texas gold columbine, these types need to be kept evenly moist, but not wet, and are not as drought tolerant.

Artemisia x 'Powis Castle'
Powis Castle Artemisia

- ◆ **Zones:** 6–10
- ◆ **Light:** full sun to light shade
- ◆ **Soil:** dry, well-drained
- ◆ **Size:** medium-tall
- ◆ **Color:** silver gray
- ◆ **Season:** year-round

Artemisia is a group of long-lived, easy-to-grow perennials with silver evergreen or semievergreen foliage. Powis Castle grows 24 to 30 inches

Photo 12.12 *(far left)*
Hummingbird bush, *Aniscanthus quadrifidus var. wrightii*

Photo 12.13 *(far left)*
Texas Gold columbine, *Aquilegia chrysantha 'Hinckleyana'*

Photo 12.14 *(left)*
Powis Castle artemisia, *Artemisia x 'Powis Castle'*

Photo 12.15 *(far right)*
Butterfly weed,
Asclepias tuberosa

tall and 24 to 36 inches wide with silvery foliage that is finely dissected and semievergreen. It dies back some with cold weather. Prune back damaged foliage in early spring, and it will flush back fully. In fact, if not pruned regularly, the plant can become gangly with thick woody stems. This artemisia does not bloom.

Like all artemisias, Powis Castle needs good drainage because it can develop root rot in the heat and humidity of summer. However, it will bounce back quickly after it dries out. Once established, it is very drought tolerant. The foliage is extremely fragrant when cut or bruised. Plant artemisia in sunny locations with other drought-tolerant plants. It makes a nice backdrop to purple flowers, like lavender and verbena.

OTHER POPULAR VARIETIES

Artemisia ludoviciana abula 'Silver King,' or silver king artemisia, has coarser foliage than Powis Castle and grows to 4 feet tall. The yellow flowers are not showy and bloom in midsummer. This plant spreads by underground roots and can be aggressive.

A. l. 'Valerie Finnis' is less invasive and more compact, growing to only 12 inches tall and wide.

A. schmidtiana 'Silver Mound,' or silver mound artemisia, is a short-lived perennial that grows to only 12 inches by 12 inches. It must have good drainage to survive.

Asclepias tuberosa
Butterfly Weed

◆ **Zones:** 3–10

◆ **Light:** full sun to light shade

◆ **Soil:** well-drained

◆ **Size:** tall

◆ **Color:** orange

◆ **Season:** midsummer to fall

Butterfly weed is part of the milkweed family. The orange flowers are attractive to butterflies of every variety, especially monarch butterflies, who lay their eggs on milkweeds. Monarch caterpillars are one of the few that can eat the poisonous milkweed leaves. The toxins in the milkweed are taken in by caterpillars, which make them and the mature butterflies unsavory to birds and other insect eaters. Butterfly weeds grow to 24 to 33 inches tall. The plant forms stems with long, green lancelet leaves. Atop the stems are tiny orange or yellow/orange/red flowers in flat clusters, which start blooming in June and continue through the autumn. If the flowers are left to seed, pods form which open to fuzzy seeds that blow in the wind.

Butterfly weed is native to the sandy soils of East Texas and should be planted in well-drained soils. If grown in good conditions, it will stay long-lived. The roots are deep and tuberous, so leave them undisturbed for longevity. Wet winters can cause the plant to rot. If it does not return in spring, new plants grow fast and fill in quickly. Plant butterfly weed in the back of the sunny border with other hot-colored plants, like gaillardias, hummingbird bush, and coreopsis.

RELATED VARIETY

A. incarnata, or pink milkweed, is similar with dusky pink flowers, but it prefers wetter soils.

Aspidistra elatior
Aspidistra, Cast Iron Plant

◆ **Zones:** 7–10

◆ **Light:** shade

◆ **Soil:** moist

◆ **Size:** medium

◆ **Color:** green foliage

◆ **Season:** all year

Aspidistra is a clump-forming evergreen plant that grows best in the shade. The leaves are 4 to 5 inches wide and 24 inches tall. Plant it in rich, moist soil with a lot of humus, and apply

nitrogen-rich fertilizer during the growing season. Leaves can become ragged and torn if exposed to too much wind and dry heat, and too much sun can scorch the leaves. Remove damaged leaves, especially in late winter or early spring. Aspidistra is commonly planted in Southern landscapes, especially at the bases of live oaks and magnolias, where light levels are low. Use aspidistra as a backdrop plant for most of the year and a source of green for winter.

Aster oblongifolia

Fall Aster

- ◆ **Zones:** 3–9
- ◆ **Light:** full sun to light shade
- ◆ **Soil:** well-drained
- ◆ **Size:** medium
- ◆ **Color:** lavender, blue
- ◆ **Season:** late summer to fall

A Texas native, fall aster blooms in August and September and has a 1-inch diameter lavender daisy-type flower with a yellow-green eye. It grows 24 to 30 inches tall and just as wide. The leaves are light green and pointed. Once established, the asters are drought tolerant. Trim off faded flowers to keep it in bloom. Pinch it back during summer to keep it full and bushy.

Asters are an essential part of the fall landscape and, along with chrysanthemums, complete the year's colors. Plant them with other sun lovers that bloom late, like butterfly weed and goldenrod. The lavender color works well in both pastel and darker colored borders.

OTHER VARIETIES

Aster x frikartii has a range of vibrant colors in purple, pink, and blue. It grows 24 to 30 inches tall. Not as durable, it is often planted as an autumn annual.

A. ke Viking' has raspberry flowers and grows 12 to 18 inches high.

A. 'Professor Kippenberg' has clear blue flowers on 18-inch stems.

Astilbe x arendsii

Astilbe, False Spirea

- ◆ **Zones:** 4–9
- ◆ **Light:** shade
- ◆ **Soil:** moist, acidic
- ◆ **Size:** medium
- ◆ **Color:** whites, pinks, reds, violets
- ◆ **Season:** early summer

Astilbe is a shade-loving plant that blooms in May and June. It has finely dissected green foliage topped with spikes of fine, fluffy flowers. Its flowers retain their color and form long after they have stopped blooming. It prefers acidic, well-drained soil that should be kept evenly moist during the growing season. In fact, astilbe will suffer in the hottest, driest parts of the summer and must be kept moist. However, it is not a bog plant, and wet soil in winter will cause it to rot. The plant grows 24 to 36 inches tall and clumps up to 24 inches wide. Plant it in the middle of the border with other shade-loving plants, like azaleas, ferns, and hostas. It works best in East Texas where drought and heat aren't as excessive.

Photo 12.18 *(right)*
Astilbe, *Astilbe x arendsii*

Photo 12.19 *(far right)*
Anise hyssop, *Agastache foeniculum 'Blue Fortune'*

POPULAR VARIETIES

'Fanal' has deep red flowers.

'Cattleya' has rose-pink flowers.

'Deutschland' has white flowers.

'Peach Blossom' has peachy pink flowers.

'Rheinland' has lavender pink flowers and only grows to 24 inches tall.

'Purple Lance' has rose-purple flowers and grows 3 to 4 feet high. The leaves are thicker and glossier, and it is said to be more drought-tolerant.

A. chinensis 'Visions' has raspberry pink plumes and grows 24 to 30 inches tall. It also is said to be more drought tolerant.

A. simplicifolia 'Sprite' is a dwarf astilbe that grows to only 15 inches high. The foliage is bronzy green, and it has pink flower plumes. It was selected "1994 Perennial of the Year."

Agastache foeniculum 'Blue Fortune'

Anise Hyssop, Hummingbird Mint, Agastache

- ◆ **Zones:** 6–10
- ◆ **Light:** full sun to light shade
- ◆ **Soil:** well-drained, dry
- ◆ **Size:** medium
- ◆ **Color:** blue
- ◆ **Season:** summer to fall

'Blue Fortune' hyssop is an easy-care plant with lavender-blue flower spikes in midsummer into autumn. Once established, it does well in dry, poor soils and heat. The puffy, blue flowers are very attractive to bees, butterflies, and hummingbirds. The foliage is medium-sized, slightly fuzzy, and fragrant when touched. In fact, the fragrance smells like anise or licorice. Agastache is in the mint family and makes a good cut flower.

It grows 24 to 36 inches high and 15 to 20 inches wide. It is suited for the middle of the border with other sun-loving late summer perennials, like pincushion flower, black-eyed Susan, sages, and hummingbird bush. Remove the spent flowers to keep it in bloom.

OTHER POPULAR VARIETIES

A. 'Pink Panther' has rosy pink flower spikes and grows to 36 inches high.

A. 'Golden Jubilee' has bright, golden-chartreuse foliage with blue flowers and grows to 20 inches high.

A. 'Tutti-Frutti' has bright pink flowers and grows 24 to 30 inches high.

Acanthus mollis

Bear's Breech, Grecian Leaf Plant

- ◆ **Zones:** 8–9
- ◆ **Light:** shade to partial shade
- ◆ **Soil:** well-drained to dry
- ◆ **Size:** medium to tall
- ◆ **Color:** white, purple
- ◆ **Season:** early summer

Bear's breech is an evergreen plant with large, shiny, deeply cut leaves. It is so large that it can reach 2 feet long. This gives the plant a bold, course texture that looks almost tropical. In late April to early May, the plant starts sending up flower spikes that can reach 4 feet tall. The plant itself grows to 4 feet tall by 4 feet wide. The spikes have white flowers with purplish bracts.

Plant bear's breech with other shade lovers, like ferns and columbine. Unlike most shade-loving plants, bear's breech is fairly drought tolerant once established, although it will need regular water during hot months to keep from wilting. Plant it in the middle to back of a shady border. Trim off the flower spikes when they have finished blooming.

Agapanthus africanus
Lily of the Nile, Agapanthus

- ◆ **Zones:** 8–10
- ◆ **Light:** sun to light shade
- ◆ **Soil:** well-drained
- ◆ **Size:** medium to tall
- ◆ **Color:** blue, white
- ◆ **Season:** early to late summer

Lily of the Nile is an evergreen, semitropical perennial. It has long, straplike leaves growing in clumps as grass does and mounding to 18 inches high. In summer, it sends up tall, thin stems, topped with round clusters of dark blue flowers. The bell-shaped flowers form loose 6-inch diameter balls on stems, growing 36 to 48

inches high. Agapanthus is a semitropical plant that does well in the southern parts of Texas. It does not survive well over winter in Dallas, so it should be planted in the zones 8b and lower or as a pot plant or annual in more northern zones. The dark blue flowers look great next to bright yellow flowers, such as daylilies.

POPULAR VARIETIES

'Albus' has white flowers.

'Peter Pan' is a dwarf variety with foliage that resembles liriope and flowers that grow to only 18 inches high.

A. *'Elaine'* is a vigorous growing, 4- to 5-foot tall variety, with dark blue flowers and evergreen foliage. It is hardy to zone 8.

A. x *'Headbourne Hybrids'* is a smaller growing agapanthus (to only 3 feet high) with dark blue flowers. It is hardy to zone 6 and is not evergreen.

A. x *'Midnight Blue'* is also hardy to zone 6 and has dark blue flowers atop 36 inch stems.

Alpinia zerumbet 'Variegata'
Variegated Shell Ginger

- ◆ **Zones:** 9–10
- ◆ **Light:** light shade to shade
- ◆ **Soil:** moist

Photo 12.20 *(far left)*
Bear's breech,
Acanthus mollis

Photo 12.21
Dwarf Lily of the Nile,
Agapanthus africanus
'Peter Pan'

Photo 12.22
Vareigated shell ginger,
Alpinia zerumbet 'Variegata'

- **Size:** medium to tall
- **Color:** white, pink flowers, yellow variegated foliage
- **Season:** year-round

Variegated shell ginger is grown chiefly for its foliage, which is large and striped with yellow and green. Like all gingers, it grows from fleshy rhizomes. In spring, its white, fragrant clusters will bloom in frost-free areas , but it is grown mostly for the foliage. Plant it in a shady border for a tropical look and protect it from cold weather, or use it as a potted plant or an annual. It will grow 4 feet tall and wide, and it will remain evergreen unless hit with a freeze. Keep it moist, or it will dry out.

B

Baptisia australis
Blue False Indigo

- **Zones:** 3–10
- **Light:** full sun to light shade
- **Soil:** well-drained
- **Size:** medium
- **Color:** blue
- **Season:** late spring

Blue false indigo is a little-used perennial gem. It has lovely blue-green leaves that spring from

the ground early in spring to form a large, rounded bush. In April and May, it sends up indigo-blue flower spikes with large, pea-like flowers. Following the flowers, large green pods form, which quickly turn black and become nearly as decorative as the flowers. Be patient with this one; it is slow to establish but fills out nicely after a couple of years and is drought tolerant. It grows to 3 feet high and wide. Even though it blooms early, the foliage is attractive all summer and makes a nice backdrop to other perennials. Plant it with shasta and ox-eye daisies, lilies, and daylilies.

POPULAR VARIETIES

B. alba is similar with white flowers.

B. 'Purple Smoke' is a cross between the *B. alba* and *B. australis* and smoky purple flowers.

Belamcanda chinensis
Blackberry Lily, Candy Lily

- **Zones:** 5–10
- **Light:** sun to light shade
- **Soil:** well-drained
- **Size:** medium
- **Color:** white, yellow, orange, red, pink, purple
- **Season:** midsummer

Photo 12.23 *(right)*
Blue false indigo,
Baptisia australis

Photo 12.24 *(far right)*
Candy lily,
Belamcanda chinensis

Blackberry lily is an easy-to-grow perennial with leaves that look like that of an iris. The straplike leaves arise from rhizomes to 24 to 36 inches tall. In midsummer, it blooms with sprays of small flowers. The original flower has yellow petals with red dots, but new varieties include ranges in red, pink, white, and purple.

Remove dead flowers to keep it in bloom. If you don't, seedpods will develop that have little black seeds. Plant it in the middle of the border with summer bloomers, like purple coneflowers, black-eyed Susans, and balloon flowers.

Berlandiera texana

Greeneyes

- ◆ **Zones:** 6–9
- ◆ **Light:** sun to light shade
- ◆ **Soil:** well-drained
- ◆ **Size:** medium to tall
- ◆ **Color:** yellow
- ◆ **Season:** early summer to fall

This Texas native is a yellow daisy that begins blooming in May and continues through fall. The flowers are similar to tickseed with one exception: the centers are bright green. The flowers are supposed to smell like chocolate. The foliage is light green and fuzzy. It is very drought tolerant and requires little care once established. It will go completely dormant in winter, so trim back foliage once it has frozen. Plant it among similar sun lovers, like yarrow, lamb's ear, asters, grasses, and yuccas. In fact, it normally grows among grasses in meadows.

Berlandiera lyrata, or chocolate daisy, is a similar flower. It has small yellow daisies on more delicate stems and chocolate brown to maroon centers. This one really smells like chocolate. It grows only 12 inches high, but can reach up to 4 feet with extra moisture.

Buddleia x davidii

Butterfly Bush, Summer Lilac

- ◆ **Zones:** 5–9
- ◆ **Light:** sun to light shade
- ◆ **Soil:** well-drained
- ◆ **Size:** tall
- ◆ **Color:** white, yellow, blue, pink, purple
- ◆ **Season:** early summer to fall

Butterfly bush should be on everyone's list for the perennial border. It is actually a deciduous, flowering shrub often treated as a perennial. It has fragrant flowers, born profusely in spikes all summer from May to October. Even though it grows 6 to 8 feet tall and 4 to 5 feet wide, it should be pruned severely in late winter as with perennials. The flowers are born on the new summer's growth. Cutting the stems down forces the new growth to be full and bloom heavily. The lanceolate, pointed leaves are green on the top and silvery on the bottom. The overall effect is wispy and loose. As the name implies, it is especially attractive to butterflies and other insects. Size and flower depend on the variety.

Photo 12.26
Butterfly bush, *Buddleia x davidii 'Pink Delight'*

Photo 12.25 *(far left)*
Greeneyes,
Berlandiera texana

Photo 12.27
Butterfly bush flower detail,
Buddleia x davidii 'White Profusion'

Photo 12.28
Yellow butterfly bush
flower detail, *Buddleia x
wyeriana 'Honeycomb'*

B. x wyeriana 'Honeycomb' is a large-growing hybrid that has a unique golden color resembling a honeycomb. It grows 6 to 8 feet tall and 4 to 6 feet wide. It seems to wilt more easily than the *B. davidii.*

OTHER Bs

Beloperone guttata (Justicia brandegeana), or gold and brown shrimp plant, is a semitropical shrub that dies down in winter and returns in spring. It grows mounding to 3 to 4 feet tall and wide. The flowers are actually white with purple spots encased in spikes of tubular coppery-bronze bracts; they bloom early summer through fall. The bracts resemble shrimp, hence the name. It does best in shade or morning sun. Keep the soil moist, but not wet. Only hardy to zone 8, it does quite well in pots, especially if you need to move it inside in winter.

Bulbine, *Bulbine frutescens,* is a low-growing evergreen perennial succulent. The light green foliage is long, pointed, and fleshy and resembles aloe vera foliage. It grows in clumps that reach 12 to 15 inches high and eventually as wide. The flowers start to bloom in May and continue through November or until the first freeze. The flower spikes are made up of tiny bright orange and yellow blooms that rise 12 inches above the foliage on thin stems. Bulbine has few needs other than sun and good drainage. It will take light shade, but it will not bloom as heavily, and the flower spikes tend to flop over. Like all succulents, very well-drained soils are necessary, and it will rot if the base stays wet. Since heat and drought are preferred, it works very well in raised beds and pots in full, hot sun. It is supposed to be hardy to zone 8, but in Dallas/Ft. Worth cold snaps will kill it. Protect it from deep-freezing temperatures. The variety *'Lemon Drop'* has bright yellow flowers.

Once established, it is fairly drought tolerant, but a little irrigation in the hottest months will keep it from wilting, and it does best when it gets a little relief from the hot sun. Conversely, it does not like wet feet and will develop root rot and fungus if the soil does not drain. Cut the stems to 6 to 12 inches above the soil in winter and early spring to promote vigor. Trim off faded blooms in summer to promote blooming and keep a tidy appearance. Plant butterfly bush in the back of the border with lower, fuller plants to mask its leggy bottoms. Plant it with other tall summer bloomers, like English rose, Herbestonne rudbeckia, bog and indigo spires sages.

POPULAR VARIETIES

'Black Knight' has dark violet-purple flowers.

'Pink Delight' has long medium pink flower spikes.

'Mongo,' or petite indigo, is a compact grower to 5 feet with looser, lilac pink flowers.

'Monum,' or petite plum, is a compact grower with plum-violet flowers.

'Nanho Blue' has medium blue flowers and grows only 3 to 4 feet tall and wide.

'White Profusion' has long, white flower spikes.

'Harlequin' has reddish purple flowers and variegated leaves. This one grows to only 4 to 5 feet tall and is not as vigorous. It suffers more from fungal problems, too.

'Santana' has jeweled reddish violet flowers and variegated leaves of bright gold and green leaves. This one is a newer introduction and out performs *'Harlequin.'* The violet flowers stand out nicely against the vibrant golden foliage.

C

Callirhoe involucrata
Winecups, Poppy Mallow

- ◆ **Zones:** 3–10
- ◆ **Light:** full sun to light shade
- ◆ **Soil:** dry, well-drained
- ◆ **Size:** low
- ◆ **Color:** wine red, magenta
- ◆ **Season:** late spring

This Texas native blooms along the roadsides in late April through late May. In the wild, it goes dormant in summer, but in your garden, it may bloom all summer if you give it ample water. The flowers are large, wine red or magenta buttercup-type blossoms on lacy, low-growing foliage 6 to 12 inches high. It is low and rambling and looks good sprawled across stone pathways or cascading over walls. It grows from tubers where the energy is stored when it is dormant.

Calyophus hartwegii

Sun Drops

◆ **Zones:** 7–10

◆ **Light:** sun

◆ **Soil:** dry, well-drained

◆ **Size:** low

◆ **Color:** yellow

◆ **Season:** early summer to fall

Sun drops are a Texas native growing throughout the state and up into Oklahoma. Its foliage is light gray-green and very fine with needlelike

leaves. It's habit is open, bushy, and sprawling, growing 12 to 15 inches high and twice as wide. It blooms with 1-inch lemon yellow flowers starting in April and sporadically on through October, but the biggest flush of flowers will be from April to June. Sun drops look best when planted at the front of the border and allowed to ramble across paths and cascade over walls. Plant them with other natives and low-water using plants, like lavenders, sages, and thymes. This flower should be used more. Unlike winecups, sun drops are not overly aggressive and plays well with other plants.

Canna x generalis

Canna Lily

◆ **Zones:** 7–10

◆ **Light:** sun to light shade

◆ **Soil:** moist, wet

◆ **Size:** medium to tall

◆ **Color:** yellow, orange, red, burgundy

◆ **Season:** early summer to early fall

Canna is a subtropical plant that grows from large tubers. The leaves are very large, up to 3 feet long, and the plants can grow 4 to 6 feet high. The flowers are large, vivid, and colorful. Typically, the leaves are green, but some varieties are bronze, red, purple, or striped with two colors. Dwarf varieties are available that grow only 12 to 24 inches high.

The canna tubers multiply rapidly in moist conditions, including boggy soils and lake edges, and they can become aggressive if left untended. You can plant canna from pots or tubers

Photo 12.29 *(far left)*
Winecups, *Callirhoe involucrata*

BULLY ALERT

Winecups are a native wildflower and will quickly run wild in your garden if the conditions are right. It works best in native settings, with grasses, or as a ground cover to larger shrubs that won't get swallowed up by it.

Photo 12.31
Canna lily, *Canna x generalis*

Photo 12.30 *(far left)*
Sun drops, *Calyophus hartwegii*

Photo 12.33 (far right)
Caryopteris detail,
Caryopteris x clandonensis
'Worcester Gold'

in late spring; plant 6 inches deep. In climates where the soil freezes deeply, it must be dug up after the first freeze, and the foliage should be trimmed off. Let the tubers dry out in a cool dry place stored in sawdust. Plant canna anywhere you want a bold, tropical looking affect. It works well in pots and shallow ponds, as well.

POPULAR VARIETIES

'Bengal Tiger' has orange flowers with striped foliage.

'Black Knight' is a dwarf with deep red flowers and burgundy foliage.

'Crimson Beauty Dwarf' is a dwarf with crimson flowers and green foliage.

'King City Gold' has yellow and orange flowers with green foliage.

'King Humbert' has red flowers with bronze foliage.

'Pink Starburst' is a dwarf with pink flowers with stripped foliage.

'Salmon Pink' is a dwarf with salmon pink flowers and green foliage.

'Stadt Feltback' has pink-orange flowers and green foliage.

'Tropical Rose' is a dwarf with pink flowers and green foliage.

'Striped Beauty' is a dwarf with yellow flowers and striped foliage.

Caryopteris x clandonensis

Caryopteris, Bluemist Spirea

- ◆ **Zones:** 5–9
- ◆ **Light:** sun to light shade
- ◆ **Soil:** well-drained
- ◆ **Size:** medium
- ◆ **Color:** blue
- ◆ **Season:** midsummer to fall

Photo 12.32
Caryopteris,
Caryopteris x clandonensis

Caryopteris is a shrub or subshrub that can be treated like a perennial. It has fine, delicate stems and foliage that grows 2 to 3 feet high and wide. The flowers start to bloom on the new year's growth in midsummer and continue through fall. The flower color is powdery blue in small, fluffy, flat-topped clusters. The effect is soft and misty. It goes dormant and dies down partially in winter. For this reason, you can prune it heavily.

Once established, caryopteris is heat and drought tolerant. In late summer and early fall, the blue flowers look good with other pastels, like black-eyed Susans, Mexican sage, *'Nearly Wild'* rose, and guara.

POPULAR VARIETIES

'Blue Mist' is more compact with silvery foliage, and it blooms heavily with powdery blue flowers.

'Dark Knight' has darker green leaves, is more compact, and has deeper, purple-blue foliage.

'Longwood Blue' features dark blue flowers atop longer, sturdier stems that reach 3 feet high. It is named for the long alleé that it lines at Longwood Gardens.

'Worcester Gold' has golden chartreuse foliage and powdery blue flowers. It is less vigorous but beautiful in sunny gardens where the foliage is radiant.

Centranthus ruber

Red Valerian

- ◆ **Zones:** 5–9
- ◆ **Light:** sun to light shade
- ◆ **Soil:** well-drained
- ◆ **Size:** medium to tall
- ◆ **Color:** red
- ◆ **Season:** early summer to fall

Red valerian is an easy growing perennial that does well in sunny and dry conditions. It forms a bushy clump with upright stems that grow to 3 feet tall. The blue-green foliage is lanceolate and pointed. Beginning in June and continuing throughout summer, it blooms if the faded flowers are cut back. The flowers are dense clusters of tiny crimson to rosy pink blooms. Its only problems seem to arise from wet soils or heavy shade.

POPULAR VARIETY

'Albus' has white flowers.

CHRYSANTHEMUMS

Chrysanthemums include some 160 different species mostly native to Japan, China, and Europe. The most well known is *C. morifolium*,

the common mum, a fall bloomer grown by florists in a myriad of colors and shapes. These and several others are useful for the perennial garden.

Chrysanthemum leucanthemum

Ox-Eye Daisy

- ◆ **Zones:** 5–9
- ◆ **Light:** sun to light shade
- ◆ **Soil:** well-drained
- ◆ **Size:** medium
- ◆ **Color:** white
- ◆ **Season:** late spring to early summer

Although not native, the common ox-eye daisy is the quintessential white daisy for Texas. It grows to 24 to 30 inches high and 6 to 12 inches wide. The white 4-inch daisies have yellow centers and are born on long, thin stems in late April through early June. After the first flush, it blooms sporadically throughout summer if you remove the flowers when they fade. However, if you leave it to seed, it may multiply and come up in larger clumps. Keep the new flowers you want, and pull out those you don't. The leaves are dark green and thin. Although it dies down in winter, it leaves a low, evergreen rosette of flowers all winter.

If ox-eye is too shaded, the stems will flop over. It is drought tolerant once established and doesn't survive winter well if the soil is too heavy or moist. Plant it with other flowers that like the same conditions in late spring and early summer. It looks especially good with bearded iris, penstemon, and dianthus.

Photo 12.34 *(far left)*
Red and white valerian, *Centranthus ruber* and *C. r. 'Albus'*

Photo 12.36
Ox-eye daisy, *Chrysanthemum leucanthemum*

Photo 12.35 *(far left)*
Shasta daisies, *Chrysanthemum maximum*, brighten this walk in late spring

Chrysanthemum x morifolium

Garden Mum

- ◆ **Zones:** 5–9
- ◆ **Light:** sun to light shade
- ◆ **Soil:** well-drained
- ◆ **Size:** medium
- ◆ **Color:** white, yellow, pink, red, maroon, bronze, lavender, purple
- ◆ **Season:** late summer to fall

The garden mum is the standard flower for autumn, and it comes in a wide range of colors and shapes. It is most often used as an annual for color beds in September. The standard form is a low, mounding shrublike plant that begins to bloom in mid-September, but it will bloom in late May and June, too. Pinch the flowers back heavily after early blooming to promote fuller, heavier flowers in fall. The flowers come in a variety of shapes from the standard daisy, to spoon petals, to pompoms.

Plant it with other fall bloomers, like black-eyed Susan, aster, and sages. You may want to plant it with spring bulbs because by the time they die back, the mums emerge and mask the withering foliage. The colors can be quite bold, which is why it is used as an annual. Mix in the right color for your garden, so it does not overpower the rest of the plants.

Chrysanthemum maximum (Leucanthemum x superbum)

Shasta Daisy

- ◆ **Zones:** 5–9
- ◆ **Light:** sun to light shade
- ◆ **Soil:** well-drained
- ◆ **Size:** medium
- ◆ **Color:** white
- ◆ **Season:** early summer to late summer

Shasta daisy is the big, white daisy that everyone knows. Like the ox-eye daisy, the flowers are large and white, with yellow centers. It has 3- to 4-inch daisies on long stems that grow up to 3 to 4 feet high. It blooms in midsummer and reseeds easily in well-drained soils. It does well in Austin, but in Dallas, where the soils are heavy clay and summers are humid, it doesn't do as well. In heavy soils, ox-eye is a better choice.

Plant shasta daisy with other flowers that bloom in midsummer, like meadow sage, lavender, and roses.

POPULAR VARIETIES

'Becky' is lower growing (to 18 to 30 inches high) with large flowers.

'Crazy Daisy' has double flowers and petals that grow in all directions.

'Marconi' has larger, long-lasting flowers.

'Snow Cap' is a tough, dwarf variety that grows to 12 inches high.

Chrysanthemum x 'Clara Curtis'

Clara Curtis Chrysanthemum

- ◆ **Zones:** 5–9
- ◆ **Light:** sun to light shade
- ◆ **Soil:** well-drained
- ◆ **Size:** medium
- ◆ **Color:** pink
- ◆ **Season:** late summer to fall

Clara Curtis mum is a carefree daisy that blooms at the end of summer. The foliage looks very similar to that of garden mums. It makes a nice

Photo 12.38 *(far right)*
Shasta daisy,
Chrysanthemum maximum

Photo 12.37 *(right)*
Garden mums,
Chrysanthemum x morifolium

pastel alternative to the intense, hot colors you usually find at the end of summer.

Other chrysanthemums include *C. coccinieum*, pyrethrum or painted daisy. It has feathery foliage and large pink, red, or white daisies on long stems. It grows to 24 to 30 inches high but will not do well in heavy soils and high humidity.

Colocasia esculenta

Elephant Ear

- ◆ **Zones:** 8–10
- ◆ **Light:** partial sun to shade
- ◆ **Soil:** moist
- ◆ **Size:** large
- ◆ **Color:** green foliage
- ◆ **Season:** summer to fall

This tropical-looking plant has huge, heart-shaped green leaves 18 to 30 inches long. It originates in the tropics and makes a bold statement. It can grow 6 feet tall, but normally will reach only about 3 to 4 feet. Elephant ear prefers consistently moist soil that is rich in humus. In fact, it grows happily along the edges of ponds and streams, but in such a wet environment, it will reproduce quickly.

It is commonly planted as large tubers in spring. In areas where the ground does not freeze, like zone 8, it can be left in the ground. Further north, it must be removed in fall and stored in a cool, dry spot for winter. It does flower, but the calla lily-type bloom usually develops only in more tropical regions. Unless you are planting it in wet soil, elephant ear should be in shade or part shade because it burns easily in full sun and dry conditions. Plant it for tropical effects along ponds and in shady nooks.

POPULAR VARIETIES

'Black Magic,' the black elephant ear, has smoky purple leaves but is not as hardy.

C. antiqorum, the black taro, has blackish red leaves. It, too, is not as hardy and is most often grown in lily ponds.

COREOPSIS SPECIES

Coreopsis is a group of easy-care perennials in the sunflower family. Most are short to medium-tall, drought tolerant, and sun loving. The most common types have a small yellow daisy, but they come in shades of orange, maroon, and red, not to mention other shapes, like doubles. Usually they require good drainage, but the pink coreopsis actually prefers moist soils.

Coreopsis grandiflora

Coreopsis, Tickseed

- ◆ **Zones:** 5–9
- ◆ **Light:** sun to light shade
- ◆ **Soil:** well-drained, dry
- ◆ **Size:** medium
- ◆ **Color:** golden yellow
- ◆ **Season:** summer to fall

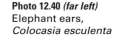

Photo 12.39 *(far left)*
Clara Curtis chrysanthemum, *Chrysanthemum x 'Clara Curtis'*

Photo 12.40 *(far left)*
Elephant ears, *Colocasia esculenta*

Photo 12.41
Tickseed, *Coreopsis grandiflora*

Tickseed is a short-lived perennial that has become widely popular. It has larger foliage than the other coreopsis, growing in low clumps. The flowers are large golden yellow 2- to 3-inch daisies that rise high above the foliage on long stems. Tickseed blooms in April and May, but sporadically reblooms in summer if the faded flowers are removed. Even though it is short-lived, it reseeds easily and is often used in natural settings like wildflower meadows and along roadsides. The foliage grows in dark green clumps with thin, lanceolate leaves. It grows 18 to 24 inches high and 12 to 18 inches wide. Plant it in the middle of the border. It is drought tolerant once established and will fall apart if the soils stay wet too long.

POPULAR VARIETIES

'Sunburst' has large, yellow semidouble flowers.

'Early Sunrise' has double flowers and blooms earlier than the standard variety.

Coreopsis rosea
Pink Coreopsis

- ◆ **Zones:** 5–9
- ◆ **Light:** sun to light shade
- ◆ **Soil:** moist to well-drained
- ◆ **Size:** medium
- ◆ **Color:** pink, red
- ◆ **Season:** summer to fall

Photo 12.43 (far right)
Moonbeam coreopsis,
Coreopsis verticillata
'Moonbeam'

Photo 12.42
Pink coreopsis, *Coreopsis rosea* 'Lime Rock Ruby'

Pink coreopsis has fine, delicate foliage. It grows to 18 to 24 inches high. The flowers are 1- to 2-inch pink daisies with yellow centers that start blooming in June and continue through fall. Unlike the other coreopsis varieties, pink coreopsis likes moist soils and does well with wetter conditions. Keep it evenly moist the first couple of years to get it established.

POPULAR VARIETIES

'American Dream' has light pink flowers, grows 24 to 30 inches high, and is more drought tolerant.

'Lime Rock Ruby' has darker, ruby red flowers and blooms heavily.

'Sweet Dreams' has white outer petals with darker pink centers.

Coreopsis verticillata
Thread Leaf Coreopsis

- ◆ **Zones:** 4–9
- ◆ **Light:** sun to light shade
- ◆ **Soil:** well-drained, dry
- ◆ **Size:** medium
- ◆ **Color:** yellow
- ◆ **Season:** summer to fall

Thread leaf coreopsis is a delicate-looking, finely textured member of the coreopsis family. It grows to 24 to 30 inches tall and half as wide. The stems are airy, and the leaves are extremely long and thin, giving it a light and wispy effect. Atop the stems are bright yellow 1- to 2-inch daisies, which start blooming in June and continue through fall. Remove the faded flowers to keep it blooming all summer. It will tolerate moist soils in summer when it is blooming and growing, but needs to be high and dry in winter. For this reason, it does best in pots and raised beds in parts of Texas where the soils are heavy.

Thread leaf coreopsis blends well with other flowers because of its light foliage.

POPULAR VARIETIES

'Moonbeam' has bright lemon yellow flowers, blooms heavily all summer, and grows 18 to 24 inches tall. This is the "1992 Perennial Plant of the Year."

'Zagreb' is similar but with light yellow flowers.

Coreopsis auriculata 'Nana,' or dwarf coreopsis (also known as mouse ear coreopsis), is a low-growing ground-cover-type perennial that spreads by underground stolons. The flowers are bright yellow-orange daisies that grow only 6 to 8 inches high. Plant it in the front of the border. Care for it as you would other coreopsis. It first blooms in late spring and repeats through the rest of the summer and into fall. Once established, it is drought tolerant, and it is hardy to zone 5.

Crinum species

Crinum Lily

- ◆ **Zones:** 7–10
- ◆ **Light:** full sun to light shade
- ◆ **Soil:** moist
- ◆ **Size:** medium to tall
- ◆ **Color:** white, pink
- ◆ **Season:** early to late summer

Crinum lilies are tropical-looking, old-fashioned favorites that grow from bulbs. The foliage consists of long, evergreen, straplike leaves from clumps, which tend to flop over. They grow 3 to 4 feet high, depending on the variety. In summer, flowers emerge atop long stems with large trumpet-shaped lilies. The most common color is white, but pinks and striped varieties are becoming available. The effect is bold, tropical, and a bit coarse. They can be found growing in older neighborhoods and abandoned homesites. However, their popularity is making resurgence and many new varieties are being developed with new colors and with foliage that is less coarse. Plant crinums from bulbs or potted plants in soils that are rich in organic matter and kept evenly moist. Most grow naturally in swampy areas and perform well in wet conditions.

Crocosmia x crocosmiflora

Crocosmia, Montbretia

- ◆ **Zones:** 5–8
- ◆ **Light:** sun to light shade
- ◆ **Soil:** well-drained
- ◆ **Size:** medium
- ◆ **Color:** red, orange, yellow
- ◆ **Season:** midsummer

Crocosmia is a perennial corm (tuber) that produces red and orange flowers in June to August. The foliage is long and swordlike and looks sim-

Photo 12.45
Crocosmia, *Crocosmia x crocosmiflora*

ilar to a gladiola or iris. The leaves reach up to 24 to 30 inches tall and are 1 inch wide, spraying out in a fan. The orange and red tubular flowers are born on thin stalks above the foliage. Plant the tubers 3 to 4 inches deep in spring in beds or in pots. Be sure to keep crocosmia evenly moist during the growing season with good drainage

Photo 12.44 *(far left)*
Crinum lily, *Crinum species*

for winter. The foliage dies down to the ground with the first freeze. North of zone 5, mulch the ground heavily in winter or dig the tubers up as you would gladiolas. While the standard flower color is red, varieties are available in orange and yellow.

POPULAR VARIETIES

'Lucifer' is a popular long-lasting variety that has flame red flowers.

Crocus vernus

Crocus

- ◆ **Zones:** 3–8
- ◆ **Light:** sun to shade
- ◆ **Soil:** well-drained
- ◆ **Size:** low
- ◆ **Color:** white, yellow, pink, blue, purple
- ◆ **Season:** early spring

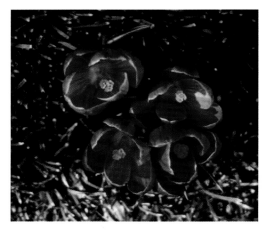

Photo 12.46
Crocus, *Crocus vernus*

Crocus is a tiny bulb that begins blooming in February and into March. In northern zones, crocus is the first sign of spring and often blooms in the snow. The foliage is thin and grasslike, with white stripes, growing to 3 inches high. The flowers are cup shaped in a range of colors, including stripes.

The bulbs are widely available in garden centers and nurseries or wherever you find daffodils and tulips. Plant the bulbs in the fall, 2 to 3 inches deep, several inches apart and in informal drifts among other perennials that will rise out of the ground after they bloom. Leave the foliage to provide food for next year's flower. As the other plants grow out, the foliage will be hidden. It looks particularly good among mondo grass where the foliage blends right in. It can handle shady conditions because it blooms before the trees leaf out.

OTHER Cs

Creeping plumbago, *Ceratostigma plumbaginoides,* is a sprawling perennial growing 6 to 10 inches high. It spreads by underground stems and can be used as a ground cover. Its dark green leaves turn reddish in fall. It dies back to the ground in colder areas but may be semievergreen in lower zones. Cut the foliage back in early spring even if it does not die back. The cobalt blue flowers are small and bloom from July to October. Plant creeping plumbago as a ground cover or let it intertwine with other low-growing perennials. It works very well in planters and along walls where it can drape over. It is hardy to zone 8 and grows in shade to partial sun.

D

Datura meteloides (Brugmansia)

Angel's Trumpet

- ◆ **Zones:** 7–10
- ◆ **Light:** full sun to light shade
- ◆ **Soil:** well-drained
- ◆ **Size:** tall
- ◆ **Color:** white
- ◆ **Season:** early summer to fall

Angel's trumpet is a large, shrubby perennial native to parts of Texas. It has large, wooly leaves and grows 4 to 5 feet tall and nearly as wide. Starting in May and June, it begins to bloom with huge, white, fragrant, trumpet-shaped flowers, 6 to 8 inches long, which open in the after-

Photo 12.47
Crocus, *Crocus vernus*, planted in dwarf mondo grass

noon and stay open all night perfuming the air. The large white flowers and heavy fragrance attract large moths, which pollinate them.

Angel's trumpet dies to the ground in winter but quickly recovers the next spring. In southern parts of the state, it may stay semievergreen. It grows in fairly dense shade but will be leggy and may not bloom as much. Plant it where you have room and can smell it at night. Other angel's trumpets are available including double purple, yellow, and pink varieties.

Dianthus species

Pinks

Dianthus is a large group of plants, popular with gardeners and florists, typified by spicy-fragrant flowers in shades of pink, red, white, and purple. Some of the most common include carnations, pinks, and Sweet William. While most of these do not grow well in the South, a few will grow in Texas provided that they have good drainage and protection from intense summer sun.

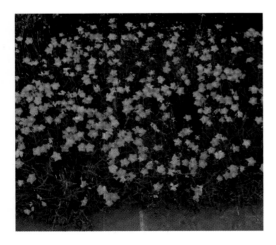

Dianthus gratianopolitanus

Cheddar Pinks

- ◆ **Zones:** 4–8
- ◆ **Light:** sun to light shade
- ◆ **Soil:** well-drained
- ◆ **Size:** low
- ◆ **Color:** pink
- ◆ **Season:** midspring

Cheddar pink is a low-growing, mat-forming, evergreen perennial. The foliage is grayish green and waxy, with long, thin, pointed leaves. It grows 6 to 12 inches high and spreads out twice as much. In April, it blooms with clear pink flowers that have a spicy carnation fragrance. Even though it tends to be short lived, this is probably the best dianthus for Texas. Drainage and good light are its main requirements. The soil can be medium to dry, and the light should be sunny with respite from hot afternoon sun. Plant it in the front of the border, in rock gardens, and in raised planters because it sprawls nicely over walls and rocks. Cheddar pinks grow well with other low spring bloomers, like creeping phlox and candytuft.

POPULAR VARIETIES

'Bath's Pink' has bright pink flowers with fringed ends that bloom heavily in spring and then sporadically in summer. The foliage is more blue-green.
'Firewitch' has magenta flowers.

Dianthus 'First Love'

Hardy Carnation First Love

- ◆ **Zones:** 5–8
- ◆ **Light:** sun to light shade
- ◆ **Soil:** well-drained
- ◆ **Size:** medium
- ◆ **Color:** white to pink to dark pink
- ◆ **Season:** early to late summer

Hardy carnation is an easy growing hybrid that grows 18 to 24 inches high and 8 to 12 inches wide. The small single and semidouble fringed flowers are born atop long, thin stems. The bluish green foliage is extremely fine. The flowers start in May and will keep blooming through summer and fall if deadheaded regularly. The

Photo 12.48 (far left)
Angel's Trumpet,
Datura meteloides

WARNING

All parts of the angle's trumpet plant are poisonous. Even touching the leaves can cause skin rash.

Photo 12.49 (far left)
Cheddar pinks, *Dianthus gratianopolitanus* 'Bath's Pink'

blossoms range from white to dark pink on the same plant. Hardy carnation is fragrant but not as intense as other dianthus. The overall effect is delicate and airy.

Plant hardy carnations in the middle of the border among other spring bloomers, like iris, guara, and ox-eye daisy. A little shade in the hot afternoon sun is probably best. It seems to prefer a little more moisture and shade than Bath's pinks.

E

Echinacea purpurea
Purple Coneflower

- ◆ **Zones:** 4–9
- ◆ **Light:** full sun to light shade
- ◆ **Soil:** well-drained
- ◆ **Size:** medium
- ◆ **Color:** pink to lavender
- ◆ **Season:** early summer to fall

Purple coneflower is one of the most popular native perennials and wildflowers because it is easy to grow and extremely showy. It grows 24 to 36 inches tall and half as wide from clumps. The stems are long, and the leaves are long, pointed, medium green and rough textured. It dies completely to the ground in winter and is slow to return in spring, so be patient. It begins blooming early to mid-June with large rosy pink to lavender daisies up to 5 inches across. The centers are rust to orange, coned, and prickly. It continues to bloom all through summer and well into fall. Remove faded blooms to promote repeat blooming, but leave the last blooms at the end of fall. The centers turn into thistle-type seeds, which become food for birds wintering in Texas. In summer, purple coneflower is a favorite source of nectar for insects, especially butterflies, because it has a large landing pad to rest on.

Purple coneflower is drought tolerant once established, but it doesn't mind a bit of extra moisture in the heat of summer. It has few pest or disease problems as long as its roots don't stay wet. In fact, wet soil in winter when it is dormant is probably its worst enemy. It naturalizes well and can self-sow but never becomes overly aggressive. Plant it in the middle of the border with other easy-care sun lovers, like aster, guara, iris, and black-eyed Susan. A great lavender combination consists of purple coneflower with lavender, liatris, and drumstick allium.

POPULAR VARIETIES

'Magnus' is the most well-known cultivar and has large lavender pink flowers. It grows up to 3 feet tall, and the petals grow straight and horizontal. It was the "1996 Perennial of the Year."

'Bright Star' has rosy pink petals that droop.

'Ruby Star' has carmine red flowers and grows 36 to 40 inches tall.

'White Swan' and *'White Luster'* have white petals and yellow-orange centers.

Echinacea pallida
Prairie Coneflower, Pale Coneflower

- ◆ **Zones:** 4–9
- ◆ **Light:** full sun to light shade
- ◆ **Soil:** well-drained
- ◆ **Size:** medium
- ◆ **Color:** pink to lavender
- ◆ **Season:** early to midsummer

Prairie coneflower has the same lavender pink petals as the purple coneflower, but they are narrower and droop down. The foliage is a low, clumping, and narrow. The flowers rise 12 to 18 inches above the foliage clump. Prairie cornflower does not bloom nearly as long as *E. purpurea*, nor is it as vigorous, but it is quite attractive, and the effect is more delicate.

Echinops ritro 'Vetch's Blue'

Globe Thistle

◆ **Zones:** 4–8

◆ **Light:** full sun to light shade

◆ **Soil:** well-drained

◆ **Size:** medium to tall

◆ **Color:** metallic blue

◆ **Season:** midsummer to fall

Globe thistle is a tall thistle that never gets invasive or out of control. It grows 24 to 36 inches high and half as wide. The foliage is metallic blue and prickly. The flowers are also metallic blue, spherical, 1 inch in diameter, and prickly like a pincushion. It starts blooming in June and continues into fall. The biggest problems for globe thistle are heavy soils and heavy humidity, which can cause rot and fungus. It especially needs good drainage in winter. Globe thistle looks great with whites, silvers, and other blues, like aster, artemisia, ox-eye daisy, and guara. The flowers also dry nicely.

POPULAR VARIETY

'Taplow Blue' is a larger form that grows to 4 feet tall and has larger flowers.

Erysismum linifolium 'Bowles Mauve'

Wallflower

◆ **Zones:** 7–10

◆ **Light:** sun to light shade

◆ **Soil:** well-drained

◆ **Size:** medium

◆ **Color:** mauve, lavender

◆ **Season:** early to late spring

Wallflower is a short-lived, evergreen perennial that grows low and bushy. The foliage is gray-

Photo 12.52 *(far left)*
Prairie coneflower,
Echinacea pallida

Photo 12.54 *(left)*
Wallflower, *Erysismum
linifolium 'Bowles Mauve'*

Photo 12.53 *(far left)*
Globe thistle, *Echinops
ritro 'Vetch's Blue'*

green with long, thin, waxy leaves. It grows 18 to 24 inches high and wide. Starting in late February, it sends up spikes with lavender mauve flowers that have a sweet fragrance. Its overall effect is similar to that of lavender, and it mixes well with them. It stays in bloom until the beginning of May when temperatures start getting too warm. Trim off the spent flower spikes to keep it in bloom. If it does not survive the heat and humidity of summer, plant more in fall when temperatures cool because it will provide winter evergreen color and very early spring flowers.

POPULAR VARIETY

'*Variegated*' has yellow-green variegated foliage with the same mauve flowers. It does not seem to be as durable or as vigorous.

Eupatorium coelestinum

Hardy Ageratum

- ◆ **Zones:** 7–10
- ◆ **Light:** sun to light shade
- ◆ **Soil:** well-drained to moist
- ◆ **Size:** medium
- ◆ **Color:** lavender blue
- ◆ **Season:** midsummer to fall

Photo 12.55
Hardy ageratum,
Eupatorium coelestinum

Hardy ageratum is a Texas native that grows freely and spreads quickly. The foliage is dark green and fine toothed, and it grows 24 to 36 inches high, spreading quickly as wide. The flowers begin to bloom in late June and are clusters of small, lavender blue, puffy blossoms. If you keep the blossoms trimmed when they fade, it will keep flowering. It grows naturally and spreads rapidly in sites that are seasonally wet, and it tends not to grow nearly as well in drier sites. The foliage dies down completely in winter and is slow to return in spring.

Eupatorium greggii

Gregg's Mist Flower, Palmleaf

- ◆ **Zones:** 5–10
- ◆ **Light:** sun to light shade
- ◆ **Soil:** well-drained to dry
- ◆ **Size:** medium
- ◆ **Color:** lavender blue
- ◆ **Season:** midsummer to fall

Gregg's mist flower looks very similar to hardy ageratum. The foliage is thinner and more chartreuse. The flowers are a medium, powdery blue and are quite fluffy. Gregg's mist is quite a draw to butterflies and other insects. It is native to more western parts of Texas where the soils are drier, and it spreads by underground roots that take over an area quickly. Even though it spreads quickly, the roots are shallow and easy to pull out.

Gregg's mist flower should be planted around larger, sturdier plants that can compete. It is very good for butterflies and produces a nice pastel flower in late summer and fall. Plant it with rudbeckias and sages.

*Eupatorium maculatum '*Gateway*'*

Joe Pye Weed

- ◆ **Zones:** 7–10
- ◆ **Light:** sun to light shade
- ◆ **Soil:** moist to well-drained
- ◆ **Size:** tall
- ◆ **Color:** purple
- ◆ **Season:** midsummer to fall

Photo 12.56 (far right)
Gregg's mist flower,
Eupatorium greggii

This native grows 3 to 5 feet in moist areas of meadows and woodlands. With long, rough leaves, it is topped with dusky purple, powder-puff flowers in a dome-shaped cluster. Joe Pye weed typically grows where the soils are seasonally moist. It is large and bold and best suited for the back of the border and for natural gardens.

Eupatorium rugosum 'Chocolate'

Chocolate Mist Flower

- ◆ **Zones:** 3–7
- ◆ **Light:** light shade
- ◆ **Soil:** dry to well-drained
- ◆ **Size:** medium to tall
- ◆ **Color:** white flowers, purple foliage
- ◆ **Season:** midsummer to fall

This mist flower is distinctive for its chocolaty brown foliage that has a purplish hue. It grows 3 to 4 feet tall and half as wide, and it can take drought and heat. The flowers are white, fluffy, and attractive to butterflies. Plant it with other dry, shade-loving plants, like columbine and Turk's cap.

OTHER Es

Engelmannia pinnatifida, Engelman's daisy, is a native, daisy-type wildflower that begins

blooming in March and continues through summer in meadows and along roadsides throughout Texas. It peaks in May and early June and will grow in almost any type of soil, as long as it is well drained and in full sun. The foliage is fine and cutleaf, and the stems are long and thin with small lemon yellow daisies. It is very drought tolerant once established and will reseed. It looks best in native plantings and in meadows. It is hardy to zone 4, and grows 3 to 4 feet tall.

F

Foeniculum vulgare

Fennel

- ◆ **Zones:** 4–9
- ◆ **Light:** full sun to light shade
- ◆ **Soil:** well-drained
- ◆ **Size:** medium to tall
- ◆ **Color:** yellow flowers, bronze foliage
- ◆ **Season:** midsummer

Perennial fennel is an herb typically grown for its licorice-flavored seeds and young leaves, which are used as seasoning. Large yellow and black striped swallowtail butterflies are also attracted to fennel and lay their eggs on it. Once the eggs hatch, the caterpillars eat the foliage, which is yellow-green, lacy, and fern-like, growing on thick, upright stems 3 to 4 feet tall. In June and July, it blooms with delicate, flat, clusters of yellow flowers that look similar to dill. The overall effect is a colorful and airy texture. After it blooms, birds eat the seeds. It may die down in winter but will remerge in spring.

Photo 12.57 *(far left)*
Joe Pye weed, *Eupatorium maculatum 'Gateway'*

Photo 12.58 *(far left)*
Chocolate mist flower, *Eupatorium rugosum 'Chocolate'*

Photo 12.59
Fennel, *Foeniculum vulgare,* with Gregg's mist flower

'*Purpurascens*' and '*Smokey*' have bronzy purple foliage and grow up to 6 feet high.

G

Gaillardia x grandiflora

Gaillardia, Indian Blanket

- ◆ **Zones:** 3–9
- ◆ **Light:** full sun to light shade
- ◆ **Soil:** well-drained to dry
- ◆ **Size:** medium
- ◆ **Color:** yellow, orange, red
- ◆ **Season:** summer to fall

Photo 12.60 *(right)*
Gaillardia, *Gaillardia x grandiflora*

Photo 12.61 *(far right)*
Hardy geranium, *Geranium x 'Johnson's Blue'*

Gaillardia x grandiflora is a hybrid cross with natives *Gaillardia aristata* and *Gaillardia pulchella*. It has mounding, gray-green, fuzzy foliage and goes into flower at the end of April, continuing into fall if dead flowers are removed. It grows 18 to 24 inches high and wide. In nature, gaillardia grows well in full sun among the grasses in meadows and along roadsides. The flowers are large daisies up to 3 inches wide and come in yellow, orange, red, and maroon, often on the same petal.

Gaillardia is drought and heat tolerant, but it appreciates a little water in the hot, dry months. It can be short lived but will reseed easily and is useful in native plantings and wildflower meadows.

POPULAR VARIETIES

'*Burgundy*' has wine red flowers.

'*Goblin*' is a lower growing variety with maroon daisies edged in yellow. These flowers grow only to 12 inches high and wide.

'*Monarch*' has yellow and red flowers.

Geranium species

Hardy Geranium, Cranesbill

- ◆ **Zones:** 3–7
- ◆ **Light:** partial sun to light shade
- ◆ **Soil:** well-drained
- ◆ **Size:** low
- ◆ **Color:** blue, purple, lavender, pink
- ◆ **Season:** late spring

The true geranium is a hardy, sprawling perennial, not the annual with huge red and pink flowers. It has small leaves and tiny flowers that bloom in April and May. Geranium grows only 12 to 18 inches high and wide. It grows best in morning sun or light shade and in well-drained soils that should be kept evenly moist in the heat of summer. Plant it in lots of humus and organic matter. Heat and drought will destroy it, so plant it only in the eastern parts of the state.

POPULAR VARIETIES

G. sanguineum, or bloody cranesbill, has lacy foliage with magenta flowers in early summer. The petals are often striped with darker shades. Bloody cranesbill has many cultivars in shades of white, pink, and violet.

G. x 'Johnson Blue' has bright, clear blue flowers in May and early June. This is one of the most common and popular varieties.

Gerbera species

Gerbera Daisy

- ◆ **Zones:** 7–9
- ◆ **Light:** partial sun to light shade
- ◆ **Soil:** well-drained, moist
- ◆ **Size:** low
- ◆ **Color:** white, yellow, pink, red, orange
- ◆ **Season:** late spring to fall

Gerbera daisy is a bright, candy-colored flower often seen in florists' shops. It is not very dependable in the garden but will survive if given the right conditions. It does not tolerate excessive heat or cold. Gerbera daisy has large, lettuce leaf foliage, and large 4- to 5-inch daisy flowers on pencil-thick stems. Plant it in raised beds with rich, acidic soil that gets morning sun. It comes into bloom in April through June and stops in the heat of summer but will start up again in fall when the temperatures drop. Plant it in areas protected from the cold.

Gladiolus species

Gladiolus

- ◆ **Zones:** 7–9
- ◆ **Light:** sun to light shade
- ◆ **Soil:** well-drained
- ◆ **Size:** medium to tall
- ◆ **Color:** all colors
- ◆ **Season:** summer

A gladiolus is a large, ruffled flower that blooms in a variety of vibrant colors on long stalks in summer. Plant it from corms (bulbs) 3 to 4 inches deep in well-drained soil. The foliage is first to emerge with long, swordlike leaves. After the flowers bloom in midsummer, the foliage begins to turn brown and wither. Leave it until it is completely dry, because it is storing food for next year's blooms. North of zone 7, the corms should be dug up and stored in a cool, dry place for winter, or just treat them as annuals and replant new ones each year.

POPULAR VARIETY

G. byzintinus, or dwarf gladiolus, is smaller with leaves that grow only to 12 inches high. The flower spikes are magenta-pink and bloom in late spring and early summer. Heavy soils are detrimental. Plant it from corms in early summer.

Guara lindhiemerii

Guara, Whirling Butterflies

- ◆ **Zones:** 5–9
- ◆ **Light:** sun to light shade
- ◆ **Soil:** well-drained to dry
- ◆ **Size:** medium
- ◆ **Color:** white, pink
- ◆ **Season:** summer to fall

Guara is a Texas native that grows wild in meadows across the state. The foliage emerges late in spring but quickly forms tufts with thin, willowy leaves. The flowers soon follow in late April, emerging as pink buds and opening into delicate, white flowers with airy petals atop long, very fine stems. The flowers grow 18 to 30 inches tall and half as wide. Plant it in wildflower meadows or among other perennials. It

Photo 12.63
Dwarf gladiolus,
Gladiolus byzintinus

Photo 12.62 *(far left)*
Gerbera daisy, *Gerbera species*

Photo 12.64 *(right)*
Whirling butterflies,
Guara lindheimeri

Photo 12.65 *(far right)*
Butterfly ginger,
Hedychium coronarium

works well with many plants because the foliage is so light and lacy. It tolerates a wide range of conditions from moist and humid to dry and is very drought tolerant once established. Remove the faded flowers to keep it blooming all summer. Guara looks especially good with other pastel-colored flowers, like iris, pincushion flower, purple coneflower, and grasses.

POPULAR VARIETIES

'Corries Gold' has variegated green and gold foliage with white flowers.

'Siskiyou Pink' has bright pink flowers. Mix it with the white flowered variety for a colorful effect.

H

Hedychium coronarium
Butterfly Ginger, Ginger Lily

- ◆ **Zones:** 7–10
- ◆ **Light:** light shade to shade
- ◆ **Soil:** moist
- ◆ **Size:** tall
- ◆ **Color:** white
- ◆ **Season:** late summer to early fall

Butterfly ginger is a tropical-looking plant that grows from fleshy roots. In early summer, it sends up stalks that grow 5 to 6 feet high, with large, long leaves. By July and August, it blooms with cones of fragrant, jasmine-scented flowers. The cones send out large white bracts that resemble butterflies. Plant it in the shady garden, in humus-rich soil that stays evenly moist. Protect it from hot winds, which will dry it out and tatter the leaves. It will die down in freezing temperatures. Mulch it heavily to protect it in zone 7.

POPULAR VARIETIES

'Elizabeth' has pink flowers with orange highlights.

'Anne' has yellow flowers.

Helianthus maximiliani
Maximillian Sunflower

- ◆ **Zones:** 3–10
- ◆ **Light:** full sun to light shade
- ◆ **Soil:** moist, well-drained
- ◆ **Size:** tall
- ◆ **Color:** yellow
- ◆ **Season:** late summer to fall

Photo 12.66 *(far right)*
Maximillian sunflower,
Helianthus maximiliani

Maximillian sunflower is a native that grows in moist meadows and ditches throughout the prairies of Texas. It has large 4- to 6-inch bright yellow flowers with green centers. The foliage looks grasslike with long, thin, gray-green leaves, and the stems are long and thin. Although it grows naturally in moist soils, it will withstand fairly dry soils. Too much shade will cause it to get leggy and flop over, so provide good sun. It is deciduous and dies down completely in winter and is slow to return each spring. It can grow 4 to 6+ feet tall with regular irrigation, so plant it at the back of the border. Maximillian sunflower looks best planted among grasses and other natives.

Heliopsis helianthoides

False Sunflower, Heliopsis

- ◆ **Zones:** 4–10
- ◆ **Light:** full sun to light shade
- ◆ **Soil:** well-drained, dry
- ◆ **Size:** medium
- ◆ **Color:** yellow
- ◆ **Season:** midsummer to fall

Heliopsis is an easy-growing, sun-loving perennial with sunny yellow flowers, which resemble the closely related sunflower. It grows 24 to 30 inches high and half as wide. The flowers begin blooming in July and continue into fall. The foliage is dark green and rough textured. It has 4-inch-wide yellow daisies with golden centers. Once established, it is heat and drought tolerant. In fact, too much water can be detrimental, although it appreciates extra moisture in the heat of summer. Plant it with other sun lovers in the middle of the border where you want bright yellow in midsummer. It mixes with other hot sum-

mer colors, like hummingbird bush, gaillardia, orange daylily, and black-eyed Susan.

POPULAR VARIETIES

'Ballerina' has semidouble yellow flowers on 3-foot stems.
'Summer Sun' grows 3 to 4 feet high with bright, golden 4-inch daisies.

Helleborus orientalis

Lenten Rose

- ◆ **Zones:** 5–10
- ◆ **Light:** shade to light shade
- ◆ **Soil:** moist, well-drained
- ◆ **Size:** low
- ◆ **Color:** white, rose, mauve, purple
- ◆ **Season:** late winter to early spring

Lenten rose is a terrific, durable, evergreen perennial that serves as a ground cover in woodland and shady conditions. It grows 15 to 18 inches high and wide, and it slowly multiplies from the base. It has large, glossy, dark green leaves that fan out from the base. The flowers begin blooming in mid-February through April. The flowers are large 1- to 2-inch buttercup-shaped blossoms that bunch in nodding clusters. Since they often face downward, you may not even realize that they have come into bloom. Lenten rose adds nice color to the winter landscape and provides a good companion to spring bulbs.

Plant Lenten rose in moist soils with a lot of organic matter. Be sure to keep it evenly moist all year long. It prefers shady conditions but will do well with a little direct morning sun, and is perfect for a woodland garden. It grows well with

BULLY ALERT

Maximillian sunflower spreads vigorously by underground rhizomes, or root structures, and can get very aggressive, especially if the moisture level is good. If it spreads too much, it is easy to yank out.

Photo 12.68 *(left)*
Lenten rose, *Helleborus orientalis*

Photo 12.67 *(far left)*
Heliopsis, *Heliopsis helianthoides*

Photo 12.69
Mass of daylilies,
Hemerocallis species

other shade lovers like ferns, hostas, and coral bells, as well as spring bulbs like daffodils and snowflakes.

Hemerocallis species

Daylily

◆ **Zones:** 4–10

◆ **Light:** full sun to light shade

◆ **Soil:** moist, well-drained

◆ **Size:** low to medium

◆ **Color:** yellow, peach, pink, orange, red, purple

◆ **Season:** late spring to fall

Photo 12.70
Stella O'doro daylily,
Hemerocallis 'Stella O'doro'

Along with iris, purple coneflower, and black-eyed Susan, daylilies are one of the most durable and heavily used perennials. They develop from fleshy roots called tubers that send up clumps of long, green, swordlike foliage, which arches over like grass. In Texas, the flowers typically begin blooming in late April and continue into June. The flowers are large lilies produced on the ends of long, thin stems that rise high above the foliage. The flowers are formed in clusters, and each blooms for only a day.

Photo 12.71 (far right)
Little business daylily,
Hemerocallis 'Little Business'

The original daylily has flowers in orange and red. Because it is so easy to grow, thousands have been hybridized to produce hundreds of colors, shapes, and sizes. The colors now come in shades of yellow, orange, pink, salmon, red, rust, and purple. Some even have a different color throat, or center, than petals. The flowers' shapes vary from wide, ruffled petals to thin, spider lily-like petals. They vary in heights from 12 inches to 5 feet tall. Most are deciduous, but evergreen and semievergreen varieties are available, although they do not seem to be ever-green north of zone 8. Dwarf varieties are available and make a nice leafy edge at the front of the border. They mix well with liriope, which has similar foliage but is evergreen. Many of the dwarf varieties have a heavy bloom period in April and May, but will continue blooming periodically into fall.

For the best results, add humus and organic matter to the bed preparation for daylilies. They prefer mostly full sun; however they do quite well in fairly heavy shade, although they may not bloom as well. They can be quite drought tolerant once established, but they prefer regular moisture and work well with irrigation systems. Not only do they work in borders, but they also work well as ground cover planted in large, blooming masses. Feed them in spring and summer and keep faded blooms trimmed off to promote continual flower production and to eliminate the growth of large seedpods. Cut the stems off once all the flowers have bloomed. Divide the clumps in fall every couple of years to keep them healthy.

Literally hundreds of varieties are available. Purple and red varieties fade with the Texas sun, so give them a little afternoon shade. Generally,

the dwarf varieties grow only 18 to 24 inches high and have low, grassy foliage.

POPULAR VARIETIES

'Aztec Gold' is a dwarf with thin golden orange petals, and it reblooms.

'Barbara Mitchell' is a low semievergreen with pink flowers and a green throat.

'Bitsy' is a dwarf with small, lemon yellow flowers.

'Black-Eyed Stella,' similar to *'Stella O'doro,'* has yellow-gold flowers with a brownish rust throat and is a repeat bloomer.

'Fairy Tale' is a dwarf with pink flowers and a green throat.

'Happy Returns' is a dwarf, semievergreen, with bright lemon yellow flowers that will rebloom.

'Hyperion' is a taller variety that reaches 36 to 42 inches high. Its blooms are bright yellow flowers with thin petals in summer, and it has a sweet fragrance.

'Irish Limerick' is a medium daylily that reaches up to 30 to 36 inches high and has yellow flowers that have almost a chartreuse green cast to them.

'Lemon Lollipop' is a dwarf with small, lemon yellow flowers with green throats, and it is a repeat bloomer.

'Little Business' is a dwarf with semievergreen foliage and raspberry red flowers with green throats.

'Little Dandy' is a semievergreen dwarf with purple flowers with green throats.

'Little Grapette' is a dwarf with purple flowers, and it will rebloom.

'Mary Todd' has large yellow, ruffled petals and is very showy.

'Pardon Me' is a dwarf with red flowers with green throats.

'Plum Perfect' is a medium grower to 30 inches high with plum purple flowers that are small and rebloom.

'Prairie Blue Eyes' is a medium grower to 30 inches high with lavender blue flowers and yellow throats, and the foliage is semievergreen.

'Stella O'doro' is probably the most well known and the most used. It is dwarf variety with lush, low, green foliage and bright golden yellow flowers. It reblooms well from April into fall.

Photo 12.72
Purple coral bells, *Heuchera americana 'Palace Purple'*

Heuchera americana 'Palace Purple'
Palace Purple Coral Bells

- ◆ **Zones:** 5–10
- ◆ **Light:** shade to partial shade
- ◆ **Soil:** moist, well-drained
- ◆ **Size:** low
- ◆ **Color:** white flowers, purple foliage
- ◆ **Season:** late spring to early summer

Coral bells is a low-growing perennial with clumps of evergreen foliage. The leaves are generally large and rounded with ruffled or scalloped edges. Beginning in late April, sprays of tiny flowers arise from the foliage on thin stems. Palace purple has bronze-purple leaves that grow 12 to 18 inches high and wide. The tiny flowers are white and are born on stalks 12 to 18 inches above the foliage.

Plant coral bells in the front of the border in shade and semishade. The soils should be moist, well drained, and full of organic matter. Be sure to provide ample irrigation in the heat of summer. Plant it with ferns, Lenten rose, and golden Japanese forest grass. It was the "1991 Perennial Plant of the Year."

Photo 12.74 *(far right)*
Texas Star hibiscus,
Hibiscus coccineus

Heuchera sanquinea

Coral Bells

- ◆ **Zones:** 5–10
- ◆ **Light:** shade to partial shade
- ◆ **Soil:** moist, well-drained
- ◆ **Size:** low
- ◆ **Color:** red
- ◆ **Season:** late spring to early summer

Photo 12.73
Coral bells,
Heuchera sanquinea
'Bressingham Hybrids'

- ◆ **Size:** tall
- ◆ **Color:** red
- ◆ **Season:** late summer to fall

Several species of hibiscus are available in the nursery trade, and all have similar flowers. Many hibiscus species are easy growing perennials with large vibrant flowers. Texas Star hibiscus is a native that grows 4 to 5 feet tall and almost as wide. The foliage is medium green and thinner than most hibiscuses. It dies down to the ground as soon as the first frost hits, but it shoots up quickly in late spring. By July, it begins to bloom with large 5- to 6-inch cherry red flowers. The petals are thin and star shaped.

Provide ample water in the hottest months for this hibiscus. It grows naturally in marshy areas, so it does well in wet soils. It gets very tall, so plant it at the back of the border with grasses, shrubs, and hummingbird bush. The red flowers are especially attractive to butterflies and other insects.

The coral bells plant has low, ruffled, green foliage and grows to only 12 to 18 inches high and wide. In April and May, delicate stalks rise above the foliage with tiny red and coral pink flowers that continue blooming through most of June. The flower color and leaf shape is different based on the cultivar. Planting and care is the same as *'Palace Purple'* coral bells. Plant it with ferns, columbine, and hostas.

Popular Variety

'Bressingham Hybrids' is a popular variety with white to crimson red flowers and mottled green leaves.

Hibiscus coccineus

Texas Star Hibiscus

- ◆ **Zones:** 8–10
- ◆ **Light:** full sun to light shade
- ◆ **Soil:** wet, moist, well-drained

Hibiscus moscheutos

Hibiscus, Rose Mallow

- ◆ **Zones:** 5–10
- ◆ **Light:** full sun to light shade
- ◆ **Soil:** moist, well-drained
- ◆ **Size:** medium to tall
- ◆ **Color:** white, pink, red
- ◆ **Season:** midsummer to fall

Hibiscus, or rose mallow, is a popular species grown mostly for its huge flowers, which can reach up to 12 inches in diameter. It is a bushy perennial with large fuzzy leaves that can grow anywhere from 30 inches to 6 feet tall. Most of

Amaryllis is a large lily-type flower. The hardy amaryllis has long, straplike leaves that emerge in spring, grows 18 to 24 inches high, and in May produces large scarlet flowers with white stripes down the center of the petals. Bulbs should be planted so the tops stick out of the soil. Trim back the foliage after it dies down and divide clumps in fall when they get too large.

the cultivars have more compact shapes and very large flowers. The flowers last only a day but are replaced quickly by another one the following day. Remove faded flowers to promote continual bloom.

Plant hibiscus in loose, well-drained soil with a lot of organic matter and ample irrigation in hot summer months. Feed it during the growing season. The stems die quickly to the ground in winter but return in early summer. The shorter varieties need to be in the middle of the border, while the large ones should be at the back with the tall summer grasses. The texture is bold and coarse, which gives the appearance of a Southern or tropical garden. Flower color and size depend on the variety.

POPULAR VARIETIES

'Southern Bell' series grows 4 feet tall with large red, pink, and white flowers.

'Dixie Belle' and *'Frisbee'* series grow only 24 to 36 inches high with enormous flowers in reds, pinks, and white. Some of the flower centers will be a different colors.

'Lord Baltimore' grows to 6 feet tall with 10-inch red flowers. *'Lady Baltimore'* is similar, but the flowers are pink with red centers.

Hippeastrum x johnsonii
Hardy Amaryllis

- ◆ **Zones:** 7–10
- ◆ **Light:** full sun to light shade
- ◆ **Soil:** moist, well-drained
- ◆ **Size:** medium
- ◆ **Color:** red
- ◆ **Season:** late spring to early summer

RELATED SPECIES

The related species, **spider lily,** *Hymenocallis species*, has long, evergreen, straplike leaves growing from clumps to 3 feet high. In June, flowers emerge atop long stems with white daffodil-like flowers surrounded by long, 5-inch spidery segments. It provides a bold tropical effect, especially in moist or boggy soils. *H. 'Tropical Giant'* has large 6-inch flowers. The native spider lily, *H. liriosme*, grows in moist areas including the edges of ponds and ditches. It has 7-inch flowers with an overall height of 18 to 30 inches. It is hardy to zone 8 and grows in full sun to light shade.

Hosta species
Hosta Lily, Plantain Lily

- ◆ **Zones:** 5–9
- ◆ **Light:** shade to partial shade
- ◆ **Soil:** moist, well-drained
- ◆ **Size:** low to medium
- ◆ **Color:** white, lavender flowers, green, gold, blue, or white variegated foliage
- ◆ **Season:** early summer to fall

Hosta lily is grown largely for its bold leafy foliage. Depending on the variety, the leaves

grow from 12 to 30 inches high and wide. As a rule, the smaller-leaved varieties do better in the Texas climate. The leaves come in shades of green, yellow-green, blue, and variegated with white or creamy edges. The leaves die down completely in winter but return mid-spring. In summer, flowers with small spikes on thin stems appear, usually in shades of white and lavender.

Plant hostas in deep soil full of rich organic matter and humus. Make sure the soil stays evenly moist, especially in the hotter months. Once they dry out, they die quickly. Hostas struggle when temperatures go up and the humidity goes down, so they do best in the northern and eastern sections of the state. They do not like heavy, alkaline soils either. Their other great enemies are slugs and snails, which will dine happily on the lush, moist leaves. Provide snail bait where pets and children can't come into contact with it. Outside East Texas, plant them only if you can provide regular irrigation. Fertilize them in spring as the leaves begin to unfold. Like ferns, hostas make good companions with spring blooming bulbs whose foliage disappears as the hostas emerge in spring.

Hundreds of cultivars and varieties exist in the trade.

POPULAR VARIETIES

'Albo marginata' has green leaves with white edges and lavender flowers. It grows 18 to 24 inches high and wide.

'Antioch' has spear-shaped leaves with creamy white margins and grows 24 inches high and wide.

'Aureo marginata' has yellow variegated leaves and lavender flowers and grows 18 to 24 inches high and wide.

'Blue Cadet' has short blue-green leaves with dark-lavender flowers and grows 12 to 18 inches high and wide.

'Elegans' has round, blue-green leaves with light-lavender flowers. It grows 24 to 30 inches high and wide, and it burns easily in sun.

'Frances Williams' has large leaves with yellow variegation and lavender flowers. It grows 18 to 24 inches high and wide.

'Honey Bells' is a vigorous grower with bright green foliage and light-lavender flowers. It grows to 24 feet high and wide and is said to be the best hosta for Texas.

'Krossa Regal' has frosty blue-green foliage with lance-shaped foliage. The flowers are lavender, and it grows to 18 inches high and wide.

'Royal Standard' is a vigorous grower with bright green foliage and white flowers. It grows to 24 inches high and wide.

'Sugar and Cream' has white variegated foliage with lavender flowers. It has vigorous growing leaves to 24 inches high and wide.

Hyacinthoides hispanica (Scilla campandulata)

Spanish Bluebell, Woodland Bluebell

◆ **Zones:** 4–10

◆ **Light:** partial shade

◆ **Soil:** well-drained, moist

◆ **Size:** low

- ◆ **Color:** blue, white, purple, pink
- ◆ **Season:** midspring

Spanish bluebell grows from small bulbs. It sends up 12-inch long, straplike leaves in early spring followed by 12- to 15-inch flower spikes with small, nodding, bell-shaped flowers in April. Plant the bulbs in fall when you plant daffodils and tulips. They are small and can be quite soft. Since bluebells prefer moist, semishady conditions, they work well under trees with early blooming daffodils and summer snowflakes. Trim off the stalks once the flowers have faded, and leave the foliage until it has completely dried up. It looks similar to Siberian squill but is more dependable in mild-winter areas.

Hymenoxys scaposa
4 Nerve Daisy

- ◆ **Zones:** 5–10
- ◆ **Light:** full sun
- ◆ **Soil:** well-drained, dry
- ◆ **Size:** low
- ◆ **Color:** yellow
- ◆ **Season:** fall to winter, spring to early summer

Native to West Texas, 4 nerve daisy grows in low clumps with thin, gray-green foliage. The foliage is evergreen, and the flowers begin to bloom in the warmer times of winter and into spring. As summer starts, the flowers slow down but begin again in fall when the temperatures drop. These cheerful small yellow daisies with yellow centers seem to be in bloom when others are not. The 4 nerve daisy plant is drought tolerant once established and has few problems if it doesn't get too much water or too little drainage.

I

Iberis sempervirens
Candytuft

- ◆ **Zones:** 4–10
- ◆ **Light:** full sun to light shade
- ◆ **Soil:** well-drained
- ◆ **Size:** low
- ◆ **Color:** white
- ◆ **Season:** early to midspring

Photo 12.80
Candytuft, *Iberis sempervirens*

Candytuft is a low-growing, mat-forming evergreen perennial that mounds and trails over rocks, walks, and walls. It is perfect for the front of the border and rock garden, and it grows 6 to 8 inches high and spreads to 12 to 15 inches wide. It has tiny dark green leaves. And in March and April, it is covered with tiny fragrant, white flowers. Candytuft likes rich, well-drained soil, and some afternoon shade may be preferable in hot locations. Shear it after flowering to keep the shape from getting too leggy. Candytuft makes a nice complement to creeping phlox and as a foreground to early bulbs like daffodils and tulips.

Photo 12.79 *(far left)*
4 nerve daisy,
Hymenoxys scaposa

Ipeion uniflorum
Blue-Eyed Grass, Spring Star Flower

- ◆ **Zones:** 4–10
- ◆ **Light:** full sun to light shade
- ◆ **Soil:** moist, well-drained
- ◆ **Size:** low
- ◆ **Color:** blue
- ◆ **Season:** mid- to late spring

Blue-eyed grass has grasslike leaves that emerge from bulbs in early spring and produces small star-shaped flowers in pale blue for about two months in March and April. The overall height is only 6 to 8 inches high. Plant the bulbs in rich, moist well-drained soil in fall or pots in early spring. Because it is a low-growing plant, place it at the front of the border among summer blooming perennials that will grow in around it. After blooming, the foliage will wither and die. Do not remove the foliage until it is dry because it is storing food for next year's bloom. As the summer perennials grow, they will mask the drying foliage. Feed it as you would all bulbs.

Iris species

Iris

The iris family is one of the largest and most popular groups of plants in the perennial garden. Irises feature swordlike and grasslike foliage and an array of flower colors in spring. In fact, the word "iris" means rainbow in Latin. Irises grow in nearly every color except true red. All flowers have similar shapes with three upturned petals called tepals, and three downturned petals called falls. Irises are extremely hardy and easy to take care of. They can be found growing in most old

neighborhoods and farmsteads around Texas, the Midwest, and the South. Some are very drought tolerant while others prefer moist, boggy soils. All are bloomers from mid- to late spring and arise from bulbs or fleshy rhizomes.

Plant irises in the fall and let them root out over winter. Unfortunately, they are usually available only in spring right before they are going to bloom. Don't expect them to bloom much the first year or two. Even healthy plants that are full and blooming in the nursery take a couple years to get acclimated to their site once planted, so be patient. Once established, you will be rewarded every year. As clumps get large, dig them up and divide them in the fall.

Irises fall into many categories according to the American Iris Society:

1. Bearded irises comprise the largest group, growing from rhizomes and preferring well-drained soil. They have beards or hairs in the center of the falls.

2. Aril irises are a bearded variety that goes dormant in summer.

3. Beardless irises produce more flowers and generally prefer rich, moist soils. This group includes Siberian, Spuria, Japanese, and Louisiana irises.

4. Crested irises, so named for the ridge or crest on each fall, prefer moist soils.

5. Bulbous irises, like the Dutch irises, go completely dormant in summer.

Literally hundreds of colors and sizes are available through catalog nurseries, mail order, or online. In addition, almost every city has an Iris Society where enthusiasts meet and swap plants.

Iris fulva, Iris giganticaerulea, Iris foliosa

Louisiana Iris

- ◆ **Zones:** 5–10
- ◆ **Light:** full sun to light shade
- ◆ **Soil:** wet, moist, well-drained
- ◆ **Size:** tall
- ◆ **Color:** white, yellow, pink, rust, blue, purple, burgundy
- ◆ **Season:** midspring

The Louisiana iris is a group of swamp-dwelling irises native to Louisiana and East Texas. It is a

Photo 12.83 *(far left)*
Louisiana iris varieties

fast growing, tall, beardless iris that is available in an array of colors. The gray-green, swordlike foliage grows to 2 to 3 feet tall and even taller if it gets ample moisture. In April the flowers bloom successively on stems from a single stalk. The flower stalks can range from 1 to 5 feet tall. Although it typically grows under swampy conditions, Louisiana iris does well in any rich, well-drained soil. Keeping it moist is best, but normal conditions will work. It needs good moisture in spring prior to blooming and in autumn when it begins to regenerate after a summer dormancy. A half-day of sun is necessary for good flower production.

Louisiana iris is a heavy feeder and should be fertilized regularly with organics. Mix in a general fertilizer, like 8-8-8 or 10-20-10, when preparing a bed. Add a top dressing of fertilizer to old clumps in late summer or early fall. An acid-type liquid or slow-release fertilizer is good. Superphosphate in late winter will promote better blooms and stronger stalks. Lack of fertilizer results in small rhizomes and smaller stalks with fewer blooms. Yellowing of the foliage, or chlorosis, is caused from alkaline soils. If you plant in alkaline soils, add 2 or 3 pounds of soil sulfur per 100 square feet. Also, dig in peat moss, compost, and/or rotted manure to loosen soil and hold moisture. Sharp sand will improve heavy clay soil, but a clay subsoil helps hold water.

Cut spent bloom stalks to prevent the seedpods from forming. Remove dead leaves only after they are ready to fall away from the rhizomes. Some varieties stay green all summer and some go completely dormant. Most, if kept well mulched and watered, will remain green all summer. Provide shade over rhizomes in summer to cut down on sunscald that reduces future blooms. Plant the Louisiana iris in the middle to the back of the border, depending on the variety. It is perfectly suited for planting alongside ponds and streams. The foliage makes a nice grassy accent and backdrop in summer.

POPULAR VARIETIES

'Bayou Classic' has purple, lavender, and yellow flowers and grows 42 inches high.

'Black Gamecock' has dark, velvety purple-black flowers and grows 24 inches high.

'Bryce Lee' has light pink flowers and grows 30 inches high.

'Clara Gould' has white flowers and grows 42 inches high.

'Delta Star' has blue-violet flowers and grows 42 inches high.

'Nuevo Blue' has light blue and yellow flowers and grows 42 inches high.

'Red Echo' has rusty red flowers and grows 30 inches high.

'Sloan's Yellow' has yellow flowers and grows 42 inches high.

Photo 12.84 *(far left)*
Dark purple Louisiana iris, *Iris 'Black Gamecock'*

Iris germanica

German Bearded Iris

- ◆ **Zones:** 3–10
- ◆ **Light:** full sun to light shade
- ◆ **Soil:** well-drained, dry
- ◆ **Size:** medium
- ◆ **Color:** white, yellow, pink, rust, blue, purple, burgundy
- ◆ **Season:** midspring

Photo 12.85
German bearded iris,
Iris germanica

German bearded iris is the large flowering type that you see everywhere from your grandmother's garden to Monet's paintings. It is also the variety that has the beard, or hairs, prominently on its falls. German bearded iris comes in almost any color except true red. Many have

Photo 12.86
Flower detail German
bearded iris, *Iris germanica*
'Cranberry Ice'

several colors or are two-toned, with the upper petals and the falls different colors. The semievergreen leaves are swordlike and arise 2 feet from thick rhizomes. The flowers appear at the end of spring and the beginning of summer around mid-April and early May. However, some old clumps around Dallas begin to bloom as soon as it warms up in the end of February. Some varieties even have a repeat blooming cycle in autumn, although it is not as spectacular. Dwarf varieties are available that reach only 6 inches high.

Ideal growing conditions for German bearded iris include almost any soil as long as it is well drained. The rhizomes are planted at the top of the soil and will rot if drainage is not good, so plant them in mounded or raised beds with well-composted organic matter, sand, agricultural gypsum, and an all-purpose fertilizer (10–10–10) worked into the soil. Transplant this iris in early fall allowing the roots to grow before winter. It is available already planted in 1-gallon grow pots or as dried, bare roots. Either way, it should develop nicely.

Water it well to get established, but it doesn't need heavy watering once it is growing. Avoid watering it from overhead in the heat of summer. Apply a high superphosphate or a good quality general fertilizer in mid-September and in early March for good flower production. Avoid fertilizers with high nitrogen because they cause vigorous leaf growth with little or no bloom and can cause root rot. Remove leaves as they turn brown, and treat fungal leaf spot with fungicide. If root rot occurs due to overwatering or too much nitrogen, dig the rhizome, scrape out the rot, apply a cleansing agent (such as Comet), and sundry the rhizome before replanting it. After 3 to 5 years, you may need to dig up big clumps. Remove the old centers and replant the active outer rhizomes or give some to a friend.

Plant German bearded iris in the middle of the border with lavender, coneflower, and ox-eye daisy. Hundreds of colors and sizes are available for sale. The fan-shaped, swordlike foliage makes a nice accent to the daisy-shaped flowers in summer.

POPULAR VARIETIES

'Beverly Sills' has light pink flowers.
'Bold Look' has bright golden flowers.

'Cranberry Ice' has light red flowers.

'Feminine Charm' has light pink and white petals.

'Dover Beach' has light lavender tepals and dark lavender falls.

'Ringo' has white tepals and purple falls.

'Royal Knight' and **'Dark Knight'** have rich, velvety purple flowers.

'Royal Touch' has cobalt blue-purple flowers.

'Red at Night' has dark, velvety burgundy flowers.

'Superstition' has velvety black-purple flowers.

'Titan's Glory' has cobalt blue-purple flowers, and it reblooms in fall.

'Victoria Falls' has sky blue flowers.

I. pumila, dwarf bearded iris, is similar looking but grows only 6 to 12 inches high with yellow, blue, and purple flowers.

Iris pseudacorus

Yellow Flag Iris

- ◆ **Zones:** 6–10
- ◆ **Light:** full sun to light shade
- ◆ **Soil:** wet, moist, well-drained
- ◆ **Size:** tall
- ◆ **Color:** yellow
- ◆ **Season:** midspring

Yellow flag Iris is a beardless Iris that grows naturally in bogs and waterside conditions. It has gray-green foliage that can reach 4 to 5 feet tall and half as wide. The large, bright yellow flowers bloom in April and May. Yellow flag tolerates drier soils but prefers wet conditions and can be quite aggressive alongside ponds or lakes. Planting and care requirements are similar to that of the Louisiana iris.

Iris pallida 'Argentea Variegata'

Zebra Iris

- ◆ **Zones:** 6–10
- ◆ **Light:** full sun to light shade
- ◆ **Soil:** well-drained, dry
- ◆ **Size:** medium
- ◆ **Color:** lavender, blue, purple
- ◆ **Season:** midspring

Photo 12.88
Zebra iris, *Iris pallida 'Argentea Variegata'*

The zebra iris is a bearded variety whose leaves are striped with green and silvery white. The flowers are generally blue to purple, and the overall height is 2 to 3 feet. Culture for this iris is similar to that of the German bearded iris. Good drainage is even more necessary, and it is quite drought tolerant once established.

Iris sibirica

Siberian Iris

- ◆ **Zones:** 4–9
- ◆ **Light:** full sun to light shade
- ◆ **Soil:** wet, moist, well-drained
- ◆ **Size:** medium
- ◆ **Color:** white, yellow, pink, rust, blue, purple, burgundy
- ◆ **Season:** midspring

Photo 12.87 (far left)
Yellow flag iris,
Iris pseudacorus

Photo 12.89
Siberian iris, *Iris sibirica*
'Caesar's Brother'

Iris spuria, Iris orientalis,
Iris graminea

Spuria Iris

◆ **Zones:** 5–10

◆ **Light:** full sun to light shade

◆ **Soil:** well-drained, dry

◆ **Size:** middle to tall

◆ **Color:** yellow, white, blue, purple

◆ **Season:** midspring

Photo 12.90 *(far right)*
Spuria iris, *Iris spuria*

Siberian iris is a beautiful plant that is not difficult to grow. It is a more delicate looking member of the iris family. The slender, dark green, grassy leaves grow 2 feet tall in clumps. The flowers are beardless and smaller than most of the previously mentioned varieties, but are more graceful. Siberian iris prefers rich, moist, acidic soil. Like the Louisianan iris, it is a heavy feeder and grows well in bog and wetland conditions. However, it does not outgrow its area as quickly as some of the larger irises can. The flowers bloom in April. In Southern climates they prefer morning sun with some afternoon shade. Keep it well watered in summer, and feed it in spring and fall. Plant Siberian by ponds or in the middle of the border with purple loosestrife, lobelia, and acorus grass.

Japanese iris, *Iris ensata*, is a similar looking crested iris found commonly in Japanese and European water gardens. It is larger and just as elegant, but it is less tolerant of the summer heat and alkaline soils that we have in Texas. The Siberian or Louisiana iris should be used unless you absolutely have to plant the real Japanese iris.

Popular Varieties

'Butter & Sugar' has white and yellow flowers.

'Bennerup Blue' has cobalt blue flowers.

'Caesar's Brother' has cobalt bluish purple flowers.

'Illini Charm' has lavender with white flowers.

'King of Kings' has white flowers.

'Ruffled Velvet' has dark purple-red flowers.

'Snow Queen' has white flowers.

Spuria iris is graceful, tall, and slender with very upright foliage that reaches 3 to 5 feet tall. The flowers are similar to those of the Dutch iris. Spuria iris adapts well to neutral or alkaline soils and prefers full sun, but tolerates some shade, especially in the hottest parts of summer. It typically has a late summer dormant period, and a drying off period during July and August is beneficial. Too much moisture combined with summer heat causes a rot that damages the new growth. In established clumps, water should be withheld until fall growth begins. Foliage of the summer dormant types can be cut back to the ground for garden neatness after the foliage dies down about the first of August. Like most other irises, it is a heavy feeder and will keep blooming well if you fertilize it annually with a general garden fertilizer (10–10–10) or manure.

Once established, it is drought tolerant, but good irrigation in springtime promotes growth. Transplanting it in autumn is best, but it can be transplanted almost any time of year as long as the rhizomes are kept moist. Plant it 1 inch deep in heavy soils, 2 inches deep in sandy soils. Spuria iris will not bloom much the first year or two after planting, but should do well by the third year. It takes very little care and blooms well in sun and fairly heavy shade.

Iris hybride

Dutch Iris

- ◆ **Zones:** 3–10
- ◆ **Light:** full sun to light shade
- ◆ **Soil:** moist, well-drained
- ◆ **Size:** medium
- ◆ **Color:** white, yellow, blue, purple
- ◆ **Season:** midspring

Dutch iris is a bulbous, beardless iris that has been bred from several parents and has very narrow, upright foliage reaching 18 to 24 inches high. Plant Dutch iris in fall with other spring bulbs, like daffodils and tulips. It blooms in early spring and, like other bulbs, the foliage dies away after blooming. It is very showy in bloom, but may not be that dependable for re-blooming year after year. Fertilize as you would other spring bulbs. Plant it 4 inches deep in groupings and clumps. It works well planted in containers and with other spring bulbs or as un-derplanting to winter or spring annuals. Dwarf varieties that grow to only 6 inches high are also available.

POPULAR VARIETIES

'Golden Harvest' has bright yellow-gold flowers.

'Imperator' has dark blue flowers with yellow spots.

'Purple Sensation' has purple flowers with yellow spots.

OTHER IS

Incarvillea delavayi, **Chinese foxglove,** has bright purplish pink flowers that start bloom-ing in midsummer and continue through the end of fall. The foliage is leafy, medium green, and rough textured. The large, trumpet-shaped flowers are bright pink and are born on stalks that reach 12 inches high. Chinese foxglove does best with morning sun, but prefers after-noon shade in the heat of summer. It prefers rich, well-drained soil and does well among the ferns, hostas, and coral bells. In the moist shady garden, it adds excellent summer color. It is hardy to zone 6.

K

Kniphofia uvaria

Red Hot Poker, Torch Lily, Tritoma

- ◆ **Zones:** 5–10
- ◆ **Light:** full sun to light shade
- ◆ **Soil:** well-drained, dry
- ◆ **Size:** medium to tall
- ◆ **Color:** yellow, orange, red
- ◆ **Season:** late spring to midsummer

Red hot poker is a succulent with spiky foliage that resembles yucca with long, evergreen, fleshy leaves. It is evergreen, gray-green, and ta-pered to a point. The foliage grows in clumps to 3 feet high and wide. Starting in April, it sends up thick flower spikes 3 to 4 feet in the air. The

Photo 12.91 *(far left)*
Dutch iris, *Iris hybride*

Photo 12.92
Red hot poker,
Kniphofia uvaria

Photo 12.93 (far right)
Lantana, *Lantana camara*

spikes are topped by a cone-shaped cluster of small, tubular flowers, which are yellow on the bottom of the cluster and graduate from orange to red on the top. It usually flowers through June and may revive a bit in fall. Keep the faded spikes trimmed off to promote blooming. This hot, fiery coloration and shape gives it the names torch lily and red hot poker. The overall effect is extremely striking and sculptural. It is also attractive to butterflies and bees.

Plant red hot poker in the middle of the border for a nice, spiky texture. It prefers medium to alkaline soils but will tolerate some acidity. It is drought tolerant and should be planted in very well-drained soil. In fact, the combination of moisture and humidity with heavy soils can cause it to develop rot and die out.

Even though the standard variety has yellow to red flowers, you can buy varieties that are more red or yellow. They look great with other hot colored flowers, like the yellow sun drops, the orange Aztec Gold daylily, and the red autumn sage.

POPULAR VARIETIES

'Pfizer' is more compact and has the standard yellow-orange-red flower color.

'Bressingham Comet' is a hybrid with thin, grassy foliage and smaller spikes in yellow and orange that blooms in late summer and fall. It grows to 24 inches high and wide, and it tolerates more shade and moisture than the others.

'Flamenco' is a hybrid with tall orange-red flowers on 4-foot spikes.

L

Lantana camara

Lantana

- ◆ **Zones:** 8–10
- ◆ **Light:** full sun to light shade
- ◆ **Soil:** moist, well-drained, dry
- ◆ **Size:** medium
- ◆ **Color:** yellow, orange, red, pink, white
- ◆ **Season:** late spring to fall

Lantana is commonly used as an annual, but in southern parts of Texas it is reliable as a perennial. Many cultivars and varieties are available

in the trade. *Lantana camara* can make a large shrub but dies to the ground when freezing temperatures hit. Lantana begins blooming in late spring and continues through fall with flat clusters of small flowers usually ranging from yellow to red on the same cluster. Some have yellow to pink.

Lantana is very tolerant of heat, humidity, and multiple soil types. It will tolerate moist to dry soils and needs full sun. Apparently, deer don't eat it, but butterflies love it. Cut it to the ground after it freezes, and mulch it heavily in winter in zones 8 and farther north. Lantana has become invasive in Southern states.

POPULAR VARIETIES

'New Gold' is a popular ground cover that blooms heavily all season with golden yellow flowers.

'Silver Mound' is similar to **'New Gold'** but has white flowers.

L. montevidensis is a trailing lantana with purple flowers that bloom in all but the hottest of summer days. It is commonly used to spill over baskets and retaining walls.

Photo 12.94 (far right)
Trailing lantana,
Lantana montevidensis

Lavandula angustifolia

English Lavender

- ◆ **Zones:** 6–10
- ◆ **Light:** full sun to light shade
- ◆ **Soil:** well-drained, dry
- ◆ **Size:** medium
- ◆ **Color:** lavender, pink, blue
- ◆ **Season:** late spring to early summer

The lavenders are a group of aromatic, shrubby herbs that are very fragrant and grown for the production of essential oils in the perfume industry. Lavender fragrance is said to promote calmness and restfulness. The most common species grown for gardens is English lavender, which has soft, velvety gray-green foliage that is extremely fragrant when touched and bruised. In May through July, it grows to 24 inches high and wide sending up finely textured, lavender-colored flower stalks. Over time, it becomes woody and leggy and should be pruned after it flowers in summer to encourage a fuller shape.

English lavender suffers when temperatures get hot and humid in the middle of summer, and it tends to rot. It is the most winter hardy but may die out with sudden cold snaps especially when wet. Do not overwater. Drainage is the number one priority. In many parts of Texas, it may serve only as an annual, fading in July and August.

Plant lavender with other herbs and perennials that like similar sunny, dry conditions. German bearded iris, wallflower, creeping thyme, and alliums bloom around the same time as lavender, and many sages, yarrow, liatris, and coneflowers grow well with it. Once established, lavender provides a nice low to medium evergreen border in English and Mediterranean in-

spired landscapes. Keep it planted near walks so you can enjoy the fragrance when you brush up against it.

POPULAR VARIETIES

'Hidcote Blue' has blue-violet flowers and is a common English garden perennial. It does not do well with humid summers.

'Munstead' is smaller, growing to only 12 to 15 inches high, with silvery foliage and delicate flower spikes in summer.

French lavender, *Lavender dentata,* is similar to English lavender with softer foliage and more luxuriant flowers. It is hardy only to the lower parts of zone 8 and is an annual in Dallas and north. However, it may be more tolerant of humidity and a better option for Southern coastal regions. *'Goodwin Creek'* is the most tolerant of heat and humidity. The foliage is gray, and the flower color is darker purple.

Lavandula stoechas

Spanish Lavender

- ◆ **Zones:** 7–10
- ◆ **Light:** full sun to light shade
- ◆ **Soil:** well-drained, dry
- ◆ **Size:** medium
- ◆ **Color:** lavender
- ◆ **Season:** late spring to early summer

The best lavender for Texas gardens, Spanish lavender, handles extremes in heat, humidity, and heavy soils. It is woodier than other lavenders and should be pruned after blooming to promote fuller growth and additional flowers. It blooms in early April and continues through the beginning of June. The flowers have square-shaped heads with fanciful petals flaring out like

Photo 12.95 *(far left)*
English lavender,
Lavandula angustifolia

Photo 12.96
Spanish lavender,
Lavandula stoechas

wings from the tops. Although not as delicate as the other varieties, it is very attractive, fragrant, and durable. Spanish lavender typically grows to about 3 feet tall and wide if not pruned out regularly. The care and culture is similar to that for English lavender.

Photo 12.98 (far right)
Liatris, *Liatris spicata 'Kolbold'*

POPULAR VARIETIES

'Otto Quest' is a stouter, fuller lavender with light, deep purple flowers and blue-gray foliage. It grows to 24 inches tall and wide.

'Rosea' is similar to *'Otto Quest'* but with pink flower heads.

Leucojum aestivum
Summer Snowflake

- ◆ **Zones:** 6–10
- ◆ **Light:** full sun to light shade
- ◆ **Soil:** well-drained, dry
- ◆ **Size:** low
- ◆ **Color:** white
- ◆ **Season:** early to midspring

Photo 12.97
Summer snowflake,
Leucojum aestivum

Summer snowflake is a spring flowering bulb that is easy to grow and naturalizes well. The flowers bloom in March and April with drooping, white, bell-shaped petals with green spots. The foliage consists of slender, dark green, grassy leaves similar to those of daffodils. It grows 12 to 18 inches high and eventually as wide. Plant the small bulbs in fall/winter when you plant daffodil bulbs. Eventually, it multiplies and forms large drifts. Plant with other spring bloomers, like daffodils, grape hyacinths, and Lenten rose. Once planted, it requires little care. The foliage dies to the ground after it blooms. Don't remove the foliage until it is completely brown because it is supplying the bulb

with food for next year's flower. As summer perennials sprout and grow, the withering foliage will disappear behind it. Fertilize as you would other spring bulbs.

Liatris spicata
Liatris, Kansas Gayfeather, Blazing Star

- ◆ **Zones:** 4–10
- ◆ **Light:** full sun to light shade
- ◆ **Soil:** well-drained, dry
- ◆ **Size:** medium
- ◆ **Color:** lavender
- ◆ **Season:** late spring to early summer

Liatris is a group of perennials native to Texas and the Great Plains states. On a whole, the group consists of tall, spiky plants with fluffy lavender and pink flowers atop stems with grassy foliage. The most common is *liatris spicata,* whose roots grow from small bulbs or corms. The grassy foliage forms clumps that grow 6 to 8 inches high. The flowery spikes shoot up 24 to 36 inches high in May and June. The fluffy, fringelike lavender pink petals begin blooming at the bottom of the spike and work their way to the top. Liatris attracts all nectar loving insects, especially butterflies. Trim the spikes off when they are finished blooming. By the end of summer, it has pretty much gone dormant. Don't trim the foliage until it has completely dried out.

Plant liatris in the middle of the border from pots in spring or bulbs in fall and winter. The bulbs should be 2 inches deep and spaced 4 to 6 inches apart. Although liatris likes moisture when it is growing, it becomes drought tolerant and prefers to stay on the dry side after it is finished blooming. It tolerates heavy soils, but prefers looser, sandier soils. Too much moisture causes the bulbs to rot. The texture is fine, but spiky. It looks good with bee balm, ox-eye and shasta daisies, lavenders, and purple coneflower.

POPULAR VARIETIES

'Floristan White' and *'White Spires'* have white flowers. *'Floristan White'* grows 24 to 30 inches high. *'White Spires'* grows to 36 inches high.

'Kolbold' has mauve-lavender flowers and grows to only 18 to 24 inches high.

Ligularia tussilaginea 'Aureo-maculata'

Leopard Plant

- ◆ **Zones:** 7–10
- ◆ **Light:** partial shade to shade
- ◆ **Soil:** moist, well-drained
- ◆ **Size:** low
- ◆ **Color:** yellow flowers, yellow variegated foliage
- ◆ **Season:** fall to winter, foliage year-round

Ligularia features a group of plants that has large leaves and yellow and orange flowers and grows in moist, shady areas. Usually, they do not tolerate heat or drought. However, the leopard plant is quite durable and tolerant of conditions in the northern and eastern parts of Texas. It has large round leaves up to 6 to 10 inches in diameter that are glossy, thick, and leathery. The foliage grows in a clump, 15 to 18 inches high and wide. The leaves are scattered with yellow or creamy spots. Leopard plant is evergreen if the temperature remains above 20 degrees but will die back if it gets colder, and it will releaf quickly in spring. The flowers are bright yellow daisies that are 2 inches in diameter and are borne in clusters 6 to 12 inches above the

leaves in late fall and winter. Sudden cold snaps may freeze the flowers back.

Plant leopard plant in the front of the shady border. Include a generous amount of humus and organic matter in the soils as you would with ferns or hostas. It does well near ponds and other semiwet areas. Although it prefers some shade, it does not get the nice, spotty coloration in full shade. Morning sun with afternoon shade is best. Provide ample irrigation in the heat of summer. Plant it where you will see the flowers in winter when you are not in the garden as much.

POPULAR VARIETY

'Crespata' has large curled and ruffled leaves.

Lilium species

Lilies—Asian, Oriental, Trumpet

- ◆ **Zones:** 5–9
- ◆ **Light:** full sun to light shade
- ◆ **Soil:** well-drained
- ◆ **Size:** medium to tall
- ◆ **Color:** all colors
- ◆ **Season:** late spring to midsummer

Photo 12.100
Lilies, *Lilium species*, are perennials that grow from bulbs

Photo 12.101
Yellow Asiatic hybrid lily,
Lillium 'Connecticut King'

Lilies have large, trumpet-shaped flowers that are extremely fragrant. They all grow from large bulbs and bloom in all colors with different shapes and sizes. Their only requirements are rich, well-drained soils and protection from the hot summer afternoon sun. Plant the bulbs in late winter and early spring 4 to 6 inches deep and 6 to 12 inches apart. The soil must be amended so it is rich with organic matter and humus and more on the neutral to acidic side. They do best in raised planters or pots with good morning sun and afternoon shade.

Keep the stems dry, but mulch the base so the bulbs stay cool. After they bloom, remove the spent flowers, or they will start to develop seeds. They will also develop bulblets (tiny bulbs) on the leaves that can be planted to develop into full-scale bulbs. Provide ample moisture and fertilizer while the flowers develop. The stems appear midspring, growing and blooming quickly in late spring. Plant different varieties to keep the blooming season going from late spring to late summer. Once flowering ends, the foliage begins to whither and should be allowed to dry out. After a few years, the clump of bulbs will multiply and should be lifted and divided in fall.

Hundreds of varieties and colors are available in nurseries, garden centers, catalogs, and on-line, in fall and early spring.

POPULAR VARIETIES

L. candidum, the Madonna lily, is the classic large white, fragrant lily. In the garden it blooms in May and June on 3-foot stems. The original plant grows 4 to 6 feet high.

L. lancifolium (L. tigrinum), tiger lily, is one of the easiest lilies to grow. Tolerant of soils, it does well with afternoon shade and grows 3 to 5 feet tall in colors ranging from white, red, yellow, orange, and pink. The flowers face downward, and the petals recurve upward. Many have black or dark brown spots on the petals. It blooms in late summer and early fall.

L. longiflorum is the white Easter lily that is available in every grocery store in the spring. It is very fragrant, with long, white trumpet-shaped flowers. It grows on 2-foot stems and blooms in June. It is not as hardy as other varieties.

The Asiatic hybrids are the easiest to grow and find in stores. They have stouter stems and most have upward-facing flowers. A full range of colors including white, yellow, orange, pink, red, blue, and purple is available. Some even have multiple colors on the same flower. Depending on the variety, they grow from 12 to 48 inches high. They bloom in May and June. The shorter varieties are particularly good for pots and containers.

The Oriental hybrids have more elegant looking flowers in shades of white, pink, red, and violet. They have long, graceful stems and will grow from 12 inches to 5 feet tall and are topped with large, nodding flowers. They are very fragrant and bloom in June and July. *'Stargazer,'* probably the best known lily, has red petals with white edges.

Liriope muscari, Liriope spicata

Liriope, Lilyturf

- ◆ **Zones:** 6–10
- ◆ **Light:** full sun to shade
- ◆ **Soil:** moist, well-drained
- ◆ **Size:** low
- ◆ **Color:** lavender, white
- ◆ **Season:** flowers midsummer, foliage year-round

Photo 12.102
Tiger lily, *Lillium lancifolium*

Liriope is an evergreen ground cover with clumping, grassy foliage that grows well in many conditions. It can be used in the front of the border and will provide green color all year. The flowers, which resemble grape hyacinths, are small spikes that rise above the foliage and bloom in July and August. *L. muscari* has dark green 2-foot long leaves and violet flowers. *L. spicata* has a more yellow-green blade that is 10 to 12 inches high with lavender flower spikes. Liriope is drought tolerant once established but prefers ample moisture, especially in full sun. It tolerates most soils, but prefers a rich, deep soil. Cut back the foliage in late winter before the new foliage emerges in spring.

POPULAR VARIETIES

L. m. 'Big Blue' has large blue-green foliage with blue-violet flowers.

L. m. 'Majestic' has 2-foot leaves and violet, crested flower spikes.

L. m. 'Silvery Sunproof' has gold stripes along the leaves and lilac flowers.

L. m. 'Variegata' has long, thin leaves with golden edges and violet flower spikes.

L. m. 'White' has white flower spikes.

L. s. 'Silver Dragon' has green leaves with silvery white stripes and purple flowers.

L. gigantea, giant liriope, has longer, dark green leaves that grow 24 to 30 inches tall. It is evergreen and resembles a large tuft of grass. It has blue-violet flower spikes in midsummer.

Lobelia cardinalis

Cardinal Flower, Lobelia

- ◆ **Zones:** 5–10
- ◆ **Light:** full sun to light shade
- ◆ **Soil:** wet, moist, well-drained
- ◆ **Size:** medium
- ◆ **Color:** red
- ◆ **Season:** early to midsummer

Lobelia is usually found growing in wet soils and bogs. It has long, thin foliage, and stems that grow 24 to 36 inches tall and half as wide. In mid- to late summer, it blooms with long, scarlet red trumpet flowers on top of long spikes. A bog plant, it needs rich, deep soils that are continually moist during the growing season, especially in the heat of summer. It is attractive to hummingbirds and insects.

POPULAR VARIETIES

'Queen Victoria' and *'Royal Robe'* have purple-red foliage and scarlet flowers.

'Heather Pink' has soft pink flowers.

'Cinnabar Rose' has rosy pink flowers.

Lycorus radiata

Autumn Crocus, Spider Lily, Surprise Lily

- ◆ **Zones:** 7–10
- ◆ **Light:** full sun to light shade
- ◆ **Soil:** well-drained, dry
- ◆ **Size:** medium
- ◆ **Color:** red
- ◆ **Season:** late summer to early fall

Photo 12.103 *(far left)*
Lilyturf, *Liriope muscari* 'Big Blue'

Photo 12.104
Cardinal flower lobelia, *Lobelia cardinalis*

Purple loosestrife is a free-flowering perennial that loves moisture. Its foliage is medium green with long, thin leaves. It grows in clumps and sends up long spikes of tiny lavender pink flowers from May until September. Purple loosestrife will grow in any soil type, but it normally grows in wet, boggy soils.

Spider lily is an old-fashion favorite that pops up in old neighborhoods and farmyards around Texas in August and September. It is a large spider-shaped lily with cherry red flowers, and it quite literally appears out of the ground and blooms within a couple of days. The flowers reach 18 to 24 inches high. The foliage does not appear until the flowers are gone in fall. It forms a grassy clump that resembles liriope and grows to 15 inches high. It stays around until midspring and then disappears again until the next fall. Plant from bulbs in late summer or spring for a bit of color late in summer or among low ground covers. Divide clumps of bulbs every 5 to 10 years when they get too crowded.

POPULAR VARIETIES

L. x albiflora has creamy white flowers.

L. aurea has yellow flowers.

L. squamigera, belladonna lily, sends up clusters of large trumpet-lily-like pink flowers with yellow centers to 18 inches high in July and August. It provides a nice surprise of color in summer.

Lythrum salicaria
Purple Loosestrife

- ◆ **Zones:** 3–10
- ◆ **Light:** full sun to light shade
- ◆ **Soil:** wet, moist, well-drained
- ◆ **Size:** medium to tall
- ◆ **Color:** lavender pink
- ◆ **Season:** early to late summer

POPULAR VARIETIES

'Morden's Pink' is the most common hybrid and grows 30 to 36 inches high. It blooms all summer and actually has great fall color in October and November.

'Dropmore Purple' has lavender flowers on 3-foot stems.

'Morden's Gleam' has rosy red flowers on 3-foot stems.

Lysimachia clethroides, or gooseneck loosestrife, although not related, grows in similar conditions of moist soils and sun to partial sun. It grows to 3 feet tall, has similar narrow leaves, and produces white flower spikes that bend like a goose's neck.

M

Malvaviscus drummondii
Turk's Cap

- ◆ **Zones:** 7–10
- ◆ **Light:** sun to shade
- ◆ **Soil:** well-drained, dry
- ◆ **Size:** tall
- ◆ **Color:** red
- ◆ **Season:** midsummer to fall

Turk's cap is an old-fashioned native plant that has been grown for decades in Texas. Although it dies completely to the ground in winter, it

BULLY ALERT

Plant hybrid varieties of loosestrife only. They are said to be sterile and don't reseed as easily. However, do not plant them next to any body of water because they will multiply quickly. Plant only in gardens or ponds that are not located where they can go wild.

quickly returns in spring and forms a large, loose shrub by the beginning of summer. It grows 4 to 5 feet tall and nearly as wide. The leaves are large, round and quite attractive. By mid-July, it goes into bloom and continues through fall. The flowers have red petals wound together tightly around the stamens resembling a Turk's cap. Because it begins to bloom in time for the hummingbird's migration, it is quite popular with them as well as with butterflies.

Place it in the back of a border that gets some shade and has well-drained soils. It makes a welcome addition to the midsummer garden when conditions are too hot and dry for most other flowers.

POPULAR VARIETY

'*Fiesta*' has creamy white variegations to the leaves and provides accents of color in shady gardens. Pruning it back a couple of times a year apparently prevents it from reverting to solid green. It does not seem to be as tough as the parent.

Melampodium leucanthum
Blackfoot Daisy

◆ **Zones:** 5–10

◆ **Light:** full sun to light shade

◆ **Soil:** well-drained, dry

◆ **Size:** low

◆ **Color:** white

◆ **Season:** late spring to fall

Blackfoot daisy, an easy care perennial native throughout Texas, is a low-growing plant for the front of a sunny border and does well where it can spill over rocks and paths. It grows 12 inches tall and 12 to 18 inches wide. In late spring, it starts to bloom with small, white daisies with yellow centers, and it continues until fall. It grows naturally in poor soils, so any well-prepared bed will be sufficient. Once established, it is drought tolerant. In fact, wet soils seem to be its worst enemy, so good drainage is necessary. Shear off faded blooms to promote more flowers. It may be short-lived, especially in gardens where it receives too much moisture but is easy to reestablish.

Monarda didmyma
Bee Balm

◆ **Zones:** 4–9

◆ **Light:** full sun to light shade

◆ **Soil:** well-drained, moist

◆ **Size:** medium

◆ **Color:** red, pink, white, violet

◆ **Season:** late spring to midsummer

Photo 12.107 *(far left)*
Turk's Cap, *Malvaviscus drummondii*

Photo 12.108
Blackfoot daisy, *Melampodium leucanthum*

Photo 12.109
Bee balm, *Monarda didmyma*

Photo 12.110 *(far right)*
African iris, *Morea iridiodes*

Bee balm is a showy perennial that grows 24 to 30 inches high and wide. It spreads easily by underground roots and can be invasive in ideal conditions. A relative to the mint family, the foliage is fragrant when crushed. In late April and May, it comes into bloom with showy bracts that whorl around the central flower. Flower color depends on the variety, but it usually comes in shades of reds and pinks. It is very popular with hummingbirds and butterflies. Remove faded flowers to promote continual bloom. It will slow down in the heat of summer but may rebloom a bit in fall.

Plant bee balm in the middle of any moist, well-drained garden where you want butterflies and insects. It will droop in the hottest and driest weather, so be sure to provide ample moisture in summer. Mildew can be a problem in wet areas.

POPULAR VARIETIES

'Cambridge Scarlet' and *'Grandview Scarlet'* have large, showy, scarlet red flowers.

'Croftway Pink' has bright pink flowers.

'Marshall's Delight' has lavender pink flowers and is mildew resistant.

'Snow Queen' and *'Snow White'* have white flowers.

'Violet Queen' has violet flowers and is mildew resistant.

M. fistulosa, or bergamot, is a native bee balm and grows naturally in moist, sunny meadows. It has lavender pink flowers from May to October if faded flowers are removed. It can be quite invasive, so it should be used in meadows and native plantings. It works well with gaillardia.

Morea iridiodes (Dietes vegeta)
African Iris, Fortnight Lily

- ◆ **Zones:** 8–10
- ◆ **Light:** full sun to light shade
- ◆ **Soil:** well-drained
- ◆ **Size:** medium
- ◆ **Color:** white
- ◆ **Season:** late spring to fall

African iris is so named because the foliage and the flowers resemble that of the iris. The foliage is long, straplike, pointed, and grows in clumps that remain evergreen in areas with warm winters. It grows 3 to 4 feet tall and half as wide.

Photo 12.111 *(far right)*
Grape hyacinth,
Muscari armeniacum

Starting in late spring, it begins to bloom with small iris-like, white flowers with yellow and purple-blue blotches. The flowers each bloom only a day but others follow. The blooming cycle is every two weeks, which is why it is called fortnight lily. Remove the faded flowers and seedpods but don't cut off the flower stalks. New flowers develop from these stalks. It is hardy to zone 8 but needs protection in cold snaps.

RELATED SPECIES

M. bicolor, butterfly iris, grows to only 2 feet wide and high, and it has light yellow flowers with maroon blotches.

Muscari armeniacum
Grape Hyacinth

- ◆ **Zones:** 4–9
- ◆ **Light:** full sun to light shade
- ◆ **Soil:** well-drained
- ◆ **Size:** low
- ◆ **Color:** blue, purple
- ◆ **Season:** early to midspring

Narcissus species

Daffodils, Jonquils, and Narcissus

- ◆ **Zones:** 4–10
- ◆ **Light:** sun to partial shade
- ◆ **Soil:** well-drained
- ◆ **Size:** low
- ◆ **Color:** yellow, white, pink, red, orange
- ◆ **Season:** early to late spring

Photo 12.112 *(far left)*
White grape hyacinth,
Muscari botryoides 'Album'

Photo 12.113
White and yellow large-
cupped daffodils,
Narcissus species

Grape hyacinth is a low perennial that springs from bulbs. In autumn, grassy, liriope-like foliage springs up and remains all through winter. The foliage grows in 6 to 8-inch-high clumps in late fall. In March and April, it sends up small spikes of bright blue flowers. Trim off the faded flowers so they save the energy for next year's bloom instead of going to seed. The foliage dies down after it blooms. Plant the bulbs 2 inches deep in fall when you plant daffodils. Provide bone meal and fertilizer in fall as you would for other bulbs. Take care not to damage the bulbs in summer when you're digging around in the garden. Eventually, they will naturalize nicely. Dig up clumps and divide them when they become too crowded.

The narcissus family includes all the spring flowering bulbs known as daffodils, jonquils, and paper whites. In general, they have long, strap-like leaves that spring from the ground in late winter and announce the springtime with bright, cheery flowers. The most common daffodils have large cups or trumpets, known as coronas, which are surrounded by a ring of petals at the base. The flowers are divided into classes that define their shapes. Flower color varies from golden yellow, the most common, to shades of white, pink, salmon, orange, and red, as well as multiple colors on one flower. The different va-

POPULAR VARIETIES

'Fantasy Creation' has double lavender flowers.

M. botryoides 'Album' has small white flower spikes.

M. comosum 'Plumosum' has fuzzy, lavender flowers.

M. latifolium has larger blue flower spikes, which grow to 12 inches, and a single large leaf.

Photo 12.114
Jonquil, *Narcissus 'Suzy'*

rieties bloom at different times, so select several types to extend the blooming season. Early-season varieties bloom in mid-February to early March, midseason varieties bloom throughout March, and late-season varieties bloom in April to early May. They are also animal proof as well; squirrels will not eat the bulbs and deer won't eat the foliage. Many are quite fragrant, too.

The culture for narcissus is easy. Plant them in well-drained soils in autumn. November to December is best for most of Texas. Buy the largest No. 1 grade bulbs for the best flowers. Plant them 6 inches deep (4 inches for smaller jonquils) with bone meal and bulb fertilizer. They

look best in loose drifts, so naturalize them or plant them randomly in loose groups. Plant large groups of the same variety together. They will start to reproduce and form big natural clumps on their own. The blooms face the sun, so plant them where they will get at least half-day sun. Narcissus can be planted under deciduous trees and shrubs because they will receive light before the canopy above leafs out. Remove flowers after blooming. The foliage will

begin to fade after blooming, but do not cut it off until it has completely turned brown and dried. It is storing food in the bulb for next year's flowers.

In summer, narcissus bulbs are completely dormant and can handle the heat and drought that may come. For this reason, they are great with summer perennials. As the leaves begin to fade, the summer flowers grow up around them and mask the fading foliage. Be careful when planting new plants around them not to injure the bulbs. Use bone meal and bulb fertilizer to fertilize the beds in late autumn or winter before the leaves start to reemerge. Plant daffodils and jonquils with other spring bulbs, like Dutch iris, snowflakes, and grape hyacinths. Below is a list of the different classes of narcissus.

CLASSES AND POPULAR VARIETIES

Trumpet daffodils have large cups that are as long as or longer than the surrounding petals.

'King Alfred' is a bloomer with bright, golden yellow petals.

'Mount Hood' is a bloomer with white petals.

'Music Hall' has golden cups with white petals and blooms midseason.

'Sensation' has yellow trumpets and white petals and blooms late season.

'Spellbinder' is a bloomer with a yellow cup and white petals.

'Unsurpassable' is a bloomer with bright yellow petals.

Large-cupped daffodils have cups more than ⅓ the length of the surrounding petals, but not as long.

'Accent' has pink cups with white petals and blooms early.

'Carlton' has bright yellow flowers and blooms heavily.

'Easter Bonnet' has a frilly pink cup with white petals and blooms late-season.

'Fortissimo' has orange cups and yellow petals and blooms late season.

'Ice Follies' has white flowers and blooms midseason.

'Las Vegas' has bright lemon yellow cups with white petals and blooms midseason.

'Mrs. R. O. Backhouse' is a pale salmon pink cup with white petals and blooms late season.

'St. Patrick's Day' has yellow-green flowers and blooms late season.

'Salome' has light pink cups that fade to creamy white with white petals and bloom midseason.

'Touch of Lemon' has frilly white cups edged in yellow with white petals and bloom mid-season.

Small-cupped daffodils have cups less than ⅓ the length of the surrounding petals

Double daffodils have frilly, double cups.

'White Lion' has creamy white and yellow petals and resembles a lion's mane.

Triandrus hybrids have clusters of small, nodding blossoms on each stem with cups at least ⅔ the length of the petals.

'Thalia' has white flower clusters and is a midseason bloomer.

Cyclamineus hybrids are small daffodils with petals that curve backward that resemble cyclamen flowers.

'February Gold' has bright golden yellow flowers and is an early bloomer.

Jonquilla hybrids have small flowers in clusters of two to four and are very fragrant.

'Suzy' has yellow petals with orange cups.

Tazetta hybrids have small clusters of fragrant flowers and are not as hardy as other daffodils. Paper whites and others used for indoor forcing are part of this group.

'Cheerfulness' has white flowers.

'Golden Cheerfulness' has bright yellow flowers.

'Geranium' has orange cups and white petals.

'Grand Soleil d'Or' has golden yellow flowers.

Poeticus narcissus have shallow cups.

'Actaea' has tiny yellow cups edged in red, with white petals, and it blooms midseason.

'Sempre Avanti' has yellow and orange cups with white petals.

Others include miniature varieties that grow only to 6 inches tall. These include *N. cyclamineus,* which have backward-curved petals; *N. jonquilla* with round, rushlike leaves and clusters of early yellow flowers and short cups; and *N. bubocodium,* which have wide cups with tiny petals. They are perfect for pots and small gardens.

'Golden Bells' is a hoopskirt-type early bloomer with golden yellow flowers and grassy foliage.

'Jack Snipe' is a miniature with yellow cups and white petals.

'Jet Fire' is a miniature with yellow-orange cups and yellow petals; it blooms early season.

'Tête-À-Tête' is a miniature with golden yellow flowers.

Split corona varieties have the cups split into six equal sections that lay flat against the petals.

'Lemon Beauty' has yellow and white split cups against white petals; it blooms midseason.

'Orangery' has frilly, orange cups that lie against white petals; it blooms late season.

Nepeta faassenii

Catmint

- ◆ **Zones:** 3–8
- ◆ **Light:** full sun to light shade
- ◆ **Soil:** well-drained, dry
- ◆ **Size:** low to medium
- ◆ **Color:** lavender blue
- ◆ **Season:** late spring to fall

Photo 12.117
Catmint, *Nepeta faassenii*
'Walker's Low'

Catmint is a low-growing, sprawling herb with fragrant gray-green leaves. Closely related to catnip, it is attractive to cats as well. It spreads vigorously by underground stems and roots and is drought tolerant once established. The foliage grows to 12 to 18 inches high depending on variety. In May and June, sprays of fragrant lavender blue flowers emerge. Keep the faded flowers and the foliage trimmed back for better blooming and a neater appearance.

Photo 12.118
Evening primrose,
Oenothera speciosa

POPULAR VARIETIES

'Six Hills Giant' grows 24 to 36 inches tall.
'Walker's Low' grows to only 12 inches high and wide with light blue flowers.

RELATED SPECIES

Mentha species, mint, is an herb, which can be planted as an attractive, low-growing, ground cover that comes into bloom in late spring and early summer. Mint, of course, is grown mainly for its leaves, which are extremely fragrant and used to flavor food and drinks. Mints have different flavors including spearmint, peppermint, and lemon mint. They are hardy to zone 5.

OTHER Ns

Cupflower, *Nierembergia caerulea,* is a low-growing, sprawling perennial with finely textured leaves and small cup-shaped flowers. It grows 6 to 8 inches high and spreads to 12 inches wide and comes into bloom in early summer with dime-sized flowers. *'Purple Robe'* has purple flowers, and *'Mont Blanc'* has white flowers. Cupflower is drought tolerant once established and will not tolerate wet soils. Plant in full sun to light shade at the front of the border and in pots and planters where it can spill over the edges. It is a short-lived perennial and is hardy to zone 5.

O

Oenothera speciosa
Evening Primrose

- ◆ **Zones:** 4–10
- ◆ **Light:** full sun to light shade
- ◆ **Soil:** well-drained, dry
- ◆ **Size:** low
- ◆ **Color:** pink, magenta
- ◆ **Season:** late spring to early summer

Evening primrose is a native commonly seen in grasslands and along roadsides in Texas. In spring, it sends up low, sprawling green foliage and comes into bloom in April through June. The flowers are 2-inch diameter buttercup-type blooms in shades of magenta and pink. White and lighter pink varieties are also available. By the heat of summer, the plants generally die back. Little care is required.

RELATED SPECIES

Oenothera missouriensis, or Missouri primrose (also known as Ozark sundrop), is a native that grows throughout the grasslands of Texas and into the Midwest. It grows in dry, limestone soils and has low thin, green, sprawling foliage that rambles and spills over rocks and walks. In April through June, the large 4-inch yellow buttercup-type flowers open at the end of the day. After the bloom period, the plant shrinks to about 6 inches high and goes dormant in fall. In well-tended beds with added moisture, it may last longer. A Texas native, it needs little care or extra moisture and is ideal for a Xeriscape. It is hardy to zone 5.

Ophiopogon japonicas
Ophiopogon, Mondo Grass

- ◆ **Zones:** 7–10
- ◆ **Light:** partial to full shade
- ◆ **Soil:** well-drained, moist
- ◆ **Size:** low
- ◆ **Color:** evergreen foliage, lavender flowers
- ◆ **Season:** year-round

Mondo grass is an evergreen perennial typically used as a ground cover in shady areas. The thin, dark green clumping foliage resembles grass and is often used as a grass substitute under trees. The foliage grows 8 to 12 inches high and spreads reasonably well once established. In summer, small lavender or white spikes appear similar to those of liriope. Plant mondo grass at the front of the bed to keep it looking neat year-round. You will have to prevent it from spreading too far into your beds, but it is not terribly aggressive. It also looks attractive planted under larger, deciduous plants, like shrubs or ferns, to provide an evergreen ground plane when the other plants go dormant. Bulbs such as daffodils,

crocus, and rain lilies mix in well, especially with the dwarf variety.

Be sure to provide irrigation in the hotter parts of the year, although, it can be quite drought tolerant in shade once established. Mondo grass may burn a bit if it dries out too much or gets too much sun. Trim back the foliage in early spring, or you can even mow large areas.

POPULAR VARIETIES

'Nana,' dwarf mondo grass, grass grows only about 3 to 4 inches high and is ideal for planting with bulbs, ferns, and in between stepping-stones.

O. planiscapus 'Nigrescens' and **'Ebknizam,'** black and ebony knight mondo grass, have dark purple-black foliage and grow 5 to 6 inches high. They are less aggressive than regular mondo.

O. jaburan. Aztec grass, is a creamy white variegated mondo grass that grows up to 18 to 24 inches high and wide in neat clumps. It makes an attractive accent in shady areas, but may not be as cold hardy.

Oxalis crassipes
Pink Wood Sorrel

◆ **Zones:** 7–9

◆ **Light:** partial to light shade

◆ **Soil:** well-drained

◆ **Size:** low

◆ **Color:** pink

◆ **Season:** winter to midspring

Oxalis is a low-growing plant with clumps of cloverlike leaves that arise from small bulbs to 12 inches high and wide. Covered with small pink flowers in late winter and spring, it stops blooming and may go dormant as temperatures

rise. It reemerges in fall and may even rebloom in November and December. Plant oxalis in shady gardens at the front of the border or under deciduous shrubs where it can be seen in winter. It grows best in deep, well-drained soils and is drought tolerant once established. Turk's cap and Texas Gold columbine prefer similar conditions.

Oxalis triangularis
Purple Shamrock

◆ **Zones:** 7–9

◆ **Light:** partial to light shade

◆ **Soil:** well-drained, moist

◆ **Size:** low

◆ **Color:** pink flowers, purple foliage

◆ **Season:** spring to early summer

Purple shamrock is similar to pink wood sorrel, but it has dark purple foliage. In early spring, it blooms with light pink flowers, which may reoccur throughout summer. A bit of moisture helps in the heat of summer.

Photo 12.119 *(far left)*
Mondo grass,
Ophiopogon japonicas

Photo 12.120
Pink wood sorrel,
Oxalis crassipes

Photo 12.121
Purple Shamrock,
Oxalis triangularis

P

Paeonia species

Peony

- ◆ **Zones:** 3–8
- ◆ **Light:** sun to partial shade
- ◆ **Soil:** well-drained
- ◆ **Size:** medium
- ◆ **Color:** white, pink, red, violet
- ◆ **Season:** late spring

Photo 12.122
Peony, *Paeonia species*

Peonies are old-fashioned favorites for the perennial garden. They grow in large clumps with leaves that are large, glossy on top of thin, erect stems. The leaves are red when they unfurl in spring and quickly shoot up to 24 to 36 inches high and 24 to 30 inches wide. In late April and May, they bloom with very large flowers (4 to 6 inches in diameter), in single, semidouble, and double forms. Flower color and form depend on

Photo 12.123
Peony detail, *Paeonia species*
'Sarah Bernhardt'

the cultivar. The blossoms are fragrant, and the petals are luminescent.

Plant peonies in fall or early spring before they begin to leaf out. Take care not to plant them too deep, or they will not bloom well. Soil that is deep and rich with organic matter and very well-drained will help prevent fungal problems and root rot. In Texas, morning sun with afternoon shade is desirable to avoid scalding or burning in summer. Herbaceous peonies require a cold period and will only grow and bloom well in the most northern parts of Texas. Be patient: Peonies take a minimum of 2 to 3 years before they really start to bloom after they have been planted. For this reason, don't dig up clumps unless necessary. In autumn, trim away the leaves and stems after they have died to the ground. Keep a thin layer of mulch around the roots in winter, but don't bury them too deep.

POPULAR VARIETIES

'Felix Crousse' has red double flowers.

'Festiva Maxima' has white double flowers.

'Karl Rosenfield' has red-violet double flowers.

'Sarah Bernhardt' has bright pink double flowers.

Tree peonies are shrubs that develop woody stems that do not die to the ground in winter. They are not as winter hardy as the herbaceous varieties, but they do not require as much cold weather. They are becoming more available in nurseries because they now are grafted onto the more vigorous root stalks of the herbaceous peonies. They bloom in late March to early April and may need to be protected from late cold snaps. Plant tree peonies in rich, well-drained soils with morning sun and afternoon shade. The flower colors are similar with the addition of yellows, oranges, and purples.

Pavonia lasiopetala

Rock Rose

- ◆ **Zones:** 7–10
- ◆ **Light:** full sun to light shade
- ◆ **Soil:** well-drained, dry
- ◆ **Size:** medium
- ◆ **Color:** pink
- ◆ **Season:** early summer to fall

Rock rose, a Texas native perennial that is extremely easy to grow, goes completely dormant in winter but emerges quickly in spring forming an open, bushy-type plant that grows 24 to 36 inches high and wide. The foliage is small, light green, and a bit fuzzy. Starting in May, 1-inch medium pink flowers bloom into fall. Once established, it is drought tolerant and may reseed.

RELATED VARIETIES

P. hastata (brazilliensis), Brazilian rock rose, grows in similar conditions with larger white flowers that have dark pink splotches called eyes. It also dies to the ground in winter in all but the warmest zones.

Penstemon species

Penstemon, Beardtongue

◆ **Zones:** 5–10

◆ **Light:** full sun to light shade

◆ **Soil:** well-drained, dry

◆ **Size:** medium

◆ **Color:** white, pink, red, blue, purple

◆ **Season:** late spring to fall depending on variety

Penstemon is a group of free blooming perennials, most of which are native to the Southwest, with long stalks of tubular flowers that are extremely popular with hummingbirds and butterflies. They require very well-drained soils and will die if the roots sit in water or heavy soils too long. Cut back the faded flowers to encourage more blooms. They bloom in late spring through summer and tend to be short lived. Plant with other sun lovers, like sages, asters, and black-eyed Susans.

POPULAR VARIETIES

P. barbatus is a loose and open variety with long, thin leaves and stems that grow 24 to 36 inches high. It blooms early to late summer. Flower color depends on cultivar.

P. b. 'Elfin Pink' has bright coral pink flowers with 1-foot stalks.

P. b. 'Prairie Dusk' has deep purple flowers on 2-foot spikes.

P. b. 'Prairie Fire' has scarlet flowers on 30-inch spikes.

P. b. 'Praecox Nanus Rondo Mix' has red, pink, and white flowers on 20-inch spikes.

P. campanulatus 'Garnet' has vibrant cherry red flowers on 24-inch spikes that bloom in May and June.

P. cobea, prairie penstemon or prairie foxglove, is native and has very large tubular

Photo 12.124 (far left)
Rock rose, *Pavonia lasiopetala*, and Brazilian rock rose, *P. Hastata*

Photo 12.125
Beardtongue, *Penstemon campanulatus 'Garnet'*

Photo 12.126
Prairie foxglove, *Penstemon cobea*

Photo 12.127
Brazos penstemon,
Penstemon tenuis

flowers. It blooms in meadows after the blue-bonnets are gone and makes a nice alternative to foxglove, which does not handle Texas heat and soil well. It blooms at the end of April through the beginning of May with flowers that are typically white with light pink or lavender throats. It is short lived, so let it go to seed to get replacements for future years' blooms.

P. digitalis, wild foxglove, is native to the Midwest. It is more tolerant of wet soils and grows 30 to 36 inches tall. It blooms in late spring and early summer with long sprays of white or light pink flowers.

P. d. 'Husker Red' has bronzy red foliage and white or light pink flowers.

P. tenuis, brazos or Gulf Coast penstemon, which is native to coastal marshes, has small lavender pink flowers in April through June on thin, 18- to 24-inch stalks. It grows best with some afternoon shade or light shade throughout the day and does best in well-drained soils, but reportedly does well in moister soils. It is short lived but reseeds easily, yet not aggressively. Remove any seedlings you do not want.

P. x 'Sour Grapes' has vivid, purple flowers on 18-inch stalks. It blooms early to late summer.

Perovskia atriplicifolia

Russian Sage

- ◆ **Zones:** 4–10
- ◆ **Light:** full sun to light shade
- ◆ **Soil:** well-drained, moist
- ◆ **Size:** tall
- ◆ **Color:** blue
- ◆ **Season:** early summer to fall

Not a true sage, Russian sage has airy gray-blue-green foliage on long stems that grow 3 to 4 feet tall. Like sages, the foliage is fragrant when bruised. In May, it comes into bloom with tiny silvery blue flowers on the ends of the 4- to 6-inch stalks. The delicate leaves and flowers have a smoky quality. Once established it is very heat and drought tolerant but will tolerate heavier moisture. Plant it with sages, *'Herbestonne'* rudbeckias, and summer phlox.

POPULAR VARIETY

'Little Spire' is a dwarf variety growing only 20 to 24 inches high.

Phlomis russeliana

Jerusalem Sage

- ◆ **Zones:** 5–10
- ◆ **Light:** full sun to light shade
- ◆ **Soil:** well-drained, dry
- ◆ **Size:** medium to tall
- ◆ **Color:** yellow
- ◆ **Season:** late spring to early summer

Jerusalem sage is not sage but is closely related. Growing in clumps of large, fuzzy gray leaves

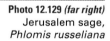

Photo 12.128 *(right)*
Russian sage,
Perovskia atriplicifolia

Photo 12.129 *(far right)*
Jerusalem sage,
Phlomis russeliana

up to 8 inches long, the foliage is fragrant and resembles large lamb's ear. In May and June, it sends up flower stalks 3 to 4 feet tall with clumps of yellow, tubular flowers clustered together and whorled around the stems. It is very heat and drought tolerant once established and can be used to cover dry slopes.

Phlox species

Phlox

Phlox is a group of popular, old-fashioned perennials that has been cultivated in gardens for generations. They have clusters of bright flowers that bloom heavily. Depending on the variety, they can be tall or short, and they can bloom in springtime or summer.

Phlox divaricata

Louisiana Phlox

◆ **Zones:** 5–9

◆ **Light:** partial shade to shade

◆ **Soil:** moist

◆ **Size:** low

◆ **Color:** blue, lavender

◆ **Season:** midspring

Louisiana phlox is a low-growing, rambling perennial native to the piney woods of East Texas. Small, thin, semievergreen leaves grow to 12 inches high and wide. In late March and April, it comes into bloom with fragrant blue or lavender star-shaped flowers. Since it grows in the East Texas woodlands, it prefers shady conditions in rich, acidic, moist soils. Plant in front of azaleas and camellias, and take care not to let it dry out in summer. In western parts of the state, it may not grow well.

Photo 12.131
Summer phlox,
Phlox paniculata

Phlox paniculata

Summer Phlox

◆ **Zones:** 4–9

◆ **Light:** sun to light shade

◆ **Soil:** well-drained

◆ **Size:** tall

◆ **Color:** white, pink, red, violet, purple

◆ **Season:** midsummer to early fall

Photo 12.132
Summer phlox, *Phlox paniculata 'Texas Pink'*

Summer phlox is an old-fashioned durable and showy favorite that begins blooming at the end of June and continues into September. Grandmothers have planted it for generations. The stems grow straight up, with long, pointed perpendicular leaves. In June, it begins to bloom with large clusters of flowers in white, lavender, pinks, and combinations of these. Trim off faded flowers to keep the plant in bloom through summer. Summer phlox suffers from powdery mildew and fungus, so keep the soil moist and the foliage dry. In Texas, where soils are heavy, plant varieties that are naturally mildew resistant, like *'Texas Pink.'* It grows 36 to 48 inches high, so plant it at the back of the border with other tall summer bloomers, like

Photo 12.130 *(far left)*
Louisiana phlox,
Phlox divaricata

'Herbestonne' rudbeckia, butterfly bush, and indigo spires sage.

POPULAR VARIETIES

'Amethyst' has lavender purple flowers.

'Bright Eyes' has light pink flowers with dark pink eyes.

'David' has clean, white flowers and is the "2003 Perennial of the Year."

'Franz Schubert' has lavender flowers.

'John Fanickk' has light pink flowers with rose eyes.

'Mt. Fuji' has white flowers.

'Orange Perfection' has orange flowers.

'Purple' has lavender pink flowers.

'Starfire' has scarlet red flowers.

'Texas Pink' has hot pink flowers and is very mildew resistant. This is probably the best one for Texas gardens.

Photo 12.133
Prairie phlox, *Phlox pilosa*

Phlox pilosa
Prairie Phlox

◆ **Zones:** 5–9

◆ **Light:** sun to partial shade

◆ **Soil:** well-drained

◆ **Size:** low

◆ **Color:** blue, lavender, pink

◆ **Season:** mid- to late spring

Photo 12.134 *(far right)*
Creeping phlox,
Phlox subulata

Prairie phlox is a Texas native that grows in grasslands and woodlands with a loose, open habit that spills naturally over rocks and paths. The look is quite similar to that of Louisiana phlox, but the leaves are a little bigger, and it grows 12 to 18 inches high and wide. In April

and May, it comes into bloom with very fragrant flowers. In the wild, prairie phlox goes dormant in summer and fall but may last a bit longer in a garden with consistent moisture. Do not forget where you planted it when digging around in the garden.

Phlox subulata
Creeping Phlox

◆ **Zones:** 5–9

◆ **Light:** sun to light shade

◆ **Soil:** well-drained

◆ **Size:** low

◆ **Color:** white, pink, lavender, blue

◆ **Season:** early to midspring

Creeping phlox is one of the first flowers to bloom in spring along with the daffodils and crocus. Its prickly, needlelike foliage grows in low, evergreen mats, growing 3 to 6 inches high and 12 to 24 inches wide, forming a nice ground cover on the front of the border, and spilling over paths and rocks. Starting in March, it blooms and completely covers the foliage with fragrant flowers. It works well with bulbs like daffodils that shoot up through it and candytuft that intermingles with it.

POPULAR VARIETIES

'Alba' has white flowers.

'Emerald Blue' has bright blue flowers with softer green foliage.

'Pink Thrift' has bright pink flowers.

'Pinwheel' has white and pink striped petals.

'Red Wings' has magenta flowers.

Physostegia virginiana

Fall Obedient Plant, False Dragonhead

◆ **Zones:** 5–9

◆ **Light:** sun to light shade

◆ **Soil:** well-drained, moist

◆ **Size:** medium

◆ **Color:** lavender, white

◆ **Season:** late summer to fall

Obedient plant, a native that grows naturally in rich, moist soils, has erect, thick stems with large glossy leaves. Named obedient plant because its stems hold the shape that they are twisted, it grows 36 to 48 inches high. In August, it comes into bloom with pink or lavender tubular flowers that resemble snapdragons on tall spikes. Plant it in the middle to the back of the border. The flowers are popular with butterflies and insects.

POPULAR VARIETIES

'Summer Snow' has white flowers and grows 24 to 30 inches high.

'Vivid' has bright pink flowers.

'Miss Manners' has white flowers and grows to only 18 to 24 inches high.

P. angustifolia, spring obedient plant, looks similar with lighter pink flowers and blooms in April and May. It does not appear to be as aggressive.

Platycodon gradiflorus

Balloon Flower

◆ **Zones:** 4–9

◆ **Light:** sun to partial shade

◆ **Soil:** well-drained

◆ **Size:** low

◆ **Color:** blue, white, pink

◆ **Season:** early summer to fall

Balloon flower is a summer blooming beauty that is slow to emerge in spring. It will quickly grow 12 to 18 inches high and begins to bloom in early June. The leaves are glossy green and oval on thin stems. The flowers start as large, balloon-shaped buds that open to large, 2-inch, star-shaped flowers. The usual flower color is a bright medium blue, although certain varieties are available in whites and pinks.

Plant balloon flower at the front of the border where you want a clear, clean blue. It looks great with yellows like coreopsis and daylily, whites like ox-eye daisy, and pinks like dianthus and phlox.

POPULAR VARIETIES

'Komachi' has bright blue flowers and grows 18 inches high and wide.

'Rosea' has pink flowers and grows 18 to 24 inches high.

Photo 12.135 *(far left)*
Fall obedient plant,
Physostegia virginiana

Photo 12.136
Balloon flower, *Platycodon gradiflorus* 'Komachi'

'Sentimental Blue' has deep blue flowers and grows only 8 to 12 inches high and wide.

P. g. mariesii has blue-violet flowers on compact stems that grow 24 inches high and wide.

Polianthes tuberorsa

Mexican Tuberose

- ◆ **Zones:** 8–10
- ◆ **Light:** sun to light shade
- ◆ **Soil:** well-drained
- ◆ **Size:** medium
- ◆ **Color:** white
- ◆ **Season:** midsummer

Tuberose is a warm-weather plant with grassy foliage. In midsummer, it sends tall flower spikes from bulbs with sweetly fragrant, white tubular flowers up to 36 inches high. After 3 or 4 months of warm weather, it will bloom. In colder regions, dig it up in winter after the leaves have died down and store it indoors in a cool, dry location. Another option would be to plant it in pots that are moved indoors for protection.

OTHER Ps

Mexican oregano, *Poliomintha longiflora,* a substitute in cooking for oregano, is a semi-woody, native, subshrub with thin, narrow leaves that are very fragrant when bruised. It grows 24 to 36 inches high and wide on woody stems, with an open habit. In June and July, 1-inch-long, lavender pink flowers bloom and continue into fall. Popular with bees and hummingbirds, it should be sheared back periodically to promote

blooming and to keep it shapely. Prune it heavily as you would any perennial in early spring to make it produce heavy growth and flowers. If it gets too much shade, the form becomes very loose, and it does not bloom as heavily.

Plant Mexican oregano in the middle to the back of the border. It is drought tolerant once established and should be used in Central and West Texas where it is hot and dry. It is hardy to zone 7.

R

Ratibida columnifera

Mexican Hat

- ◆ **Zones:** 3–10
- ◆ **Light:** full sun to light shade
- ◆ **Soil:** well-drained, dry
- ◆ **Size:** medium to tall
- ◆ **Color:** yellow, orange, red
- ◆ **Season:** late spring to midsummer

Mexican hat is a native with light, ferny foliage that grows upright 24 to 36 inches high. Deciduous in most zones, it may remain somewhat evergreen in warmer climates. It begins to bloom at the end of April and continues heavily until July. If dead flowers are removed, it will re-bloom sporadically until fall. The flowers are 3-inch daisies on long, thin stems with a brown conelike center and droopy petals. The effect of the two looks like a small sombrero. Typically, the petals are maroon or red with orange to yellow ends, but colors range in shades of oranges, yellows, reds, and browns.

Mexican hat is drought tolerant once established but will repeat bloom better with additional water in the hottest parts of summer. Plant it in the middle of the sunny border with rudbeckias, coreopsis, and gaillardia. It works very well in native, Xeriscape, and meadow gardens.

Rivina humilis

Pigeonberry

- ◆ **Zones:** 7–10
- ◆ **Light:** light shade to shade
- ◆ **Soil:** well-drained, moist
- ◆ **Size:** low
- ◆ **Color:** pink, white
- ◆ **Season:** late spring to fall

Pigeonberry is a native ground-cover-type plant with small leaves and a sprawling habit. Starting in April and May, it blooms with small spikes of light pink or white flowers, followed quickly by bright red berries, which are well liked by birds. Plant pigeonberry in a border of native-type plants along the front or under larger shrubs and trees. Provide moisture in the hotter, drier parts of the summer to keep it in bloom. It will die to the ground where temperatures get below freezing but will stay evergreen in southern Texas.

Rosemarinus officinalis

Rosemary

- ◆ **Zones:** 8–10
- ◆ **Light:** full sun
- ◆ **Soil:** well-drained, dry

- ◆ **Size:** low to medium
- ◆ **Color:** light blue
- ◆ **Season:** winter to early spring

Rosemary is an evergreen culinary herb grown for its cooking value and has become popular as a ground cover and ornament in the garden. Thin, needlelike, green foliage grows from erect stems and forms a large bush 3 to 4 feet high and wide. The foliage is full of oils that are extremely fragrant, especially when touched or bruised. In winter and early spring, it blooms with tiny light blue flowers. In the warmest parts of the state, it blooms all winter.

Plant rosemary in full sun with excellent drainage because wet soils will kill it. Drought tolerant, it makes a great ground cover but can suffer from freeze damage in northern parts of the state that experience sudden cold snaps. Plant it in the middle of the border or herb garden as an evergreen backdrop and winter accent. However, don't plant it too far from the walk because you will want to brush up against it or have it easy for cutting.

Photo 12.139 *(far left)*
Pigeonberry, *Rivina humilis*

POPULAR VARIETIES

'Hill's Hardy' has upright foliage 3 feet high and wide with lavender blue flowers.

'Huntington Carpet' is a low-growing, spreading form that grows 12 to 24 inches high and up to 8 feet wide.

'Prostratus,' a low-growing ground cover type that grows 12 to 18 inches high and 4 to 8 feet wide, is great for spilling over walls and planters. It may not be as cold hardy as the parent.

'Tuscan Blue' has upright stems 6 feet high and 2 to 4 feet wide and forms a nice hedge.

Photo 12.140
Rosemary,
Rosemarinus officinalis

Rudbeckia species

Rudbeckia, Black-Eyed Susan

Rudbeckia is a group of tough, easy to grow perennials. Most have bright yellow to orange daisies that bloom in summer and fall. Fairly drought tolerant and attractive to butterflies and insects, every Texas perennial garden should contain at least one.

Rudbeckia fulgida 'Goldstrum'

Black-Eyed Susan

- ◆ **Zones:** 3–9
- ◆ **Light:** full sun to light shade
- ◆ **Soil:** well-drained
- ◆ **Size:** medium
- ◆ **Color:** yellow
- ◆ **Season:** midsummer to fall

Easily one of the best perennials for Texas, black-eyed Susan is native in prairies throughout the state. Usually sold as *R. fulgida 'Goldstrum,'* which is an improved strain of the parent species, it has dark green, fuzzy leaves and grows in clumps up to 24 to 30 inches high and half as wide. It dies down in late fall but forms a low evergreen rosette. Starting in July, large 3-inch golden yellow daisies with dark brown or black conelike centers appear. Remove dead flowers so it will continue to bloom into fall. Leave the final flowers of fall to provide interesting winter texture and color in the yard and seeds for the birds.

Black-eyed Susan is drought tolerant once established but does well with added moisture in summer if the soils don't stay soggy. Wet soil is about its only downfall. Plant it in the middle of the border with asters, purple coneflowers, daylilies, and grasses. Attractive to butterflies and other insects, black-eyed Susan was the "1999 Perennial of the Year."

Rudbeckia hirta

Gloriosa Daisy, Rudbeckia, Yellow Coneflower

- ◆ **Zones:** 5–9
- ◆ **Light:** full sun to light shade
- ◆ **Soil:** well-drained, dry
- ◆ **Size:** medium
- ◆ **Color:** yellow, orange, red, maroon
- ◆ **Season:** midsummer to fall

The gloriosa daisy is a short-lived perennial or biennial with thick, fuzzy green stems and fuzzy dark green leaves. The clumps grow 24 to 30 inches high and wide. Starting in June, it comes into bloom with large, 5 to 7-inch daisies mostly with golden yellow daisies, but some in shades of red, orange, maroon, and brown, all with dark brown or black, thistly centers. Some varieties even have double flower heads. Gloriosa is drought tolerant but must be kept moist during the summer heat. However, if you want it to survive winter, make sure the drainage is good. Remove the faded flowers to promote continual blooming. Butterflies and other insects are wild about it. You may want to plant it as an annual because it blooms heavily.

POPULAR VARIETIES

'Becky' has large, gold, black, and bronze daisies.

'Indian Summer' has bright golden yellow flowers with black centers.

'Irish Eyes' has golden petals with green centers.

'Marmalade' and *'Goldilocks'* have bright yellow flowers and are lower growing.

'Pinwheel' has mahogany and gold flowers.

Rudbeckia maxima (R. gigantea)

Giant Rudbeckia, Giant Coneflower

- ◆ **Zones:** 4–9
- ◆ **Light:** full sun to light shade
- ◆ **Soil:** well-drained
- ◆ **Size:** tall
- ◆ **Color:** yellow
- ◆ **Season:** late spring to midsummer

Giant coneflower is a larger version of the black-eyed Susan with clumps of large, waxy, blue-green leaves that grow to 3 feet high and wide. In May and June, it sends up flower stems 5 to 6 feet high. The flowers are large, 5-inch yellow daisies. The petals droop downward, and the brown center cone sticks up 2 inches high. Keep the dead flowers removed to promote blooming.

Giant coneflower is drought tolerant once established, but it does well with added moisture in summer. Plant it in the back of the border with butterfly bush, hibiscus, indigo spires sage, and grasses. It attracts butterflies and other insects.

Rudbeckia nitida 'Herbestonne'

Herbestonne coneflower

- ◆ **Zones:** 4–9
- ◆ **Light:** full sun to partial shade
- ◆ **Soil:** well-drained

- ◆ **Size:** tall
- ◆ **Color:** yellow
- ◆ **Season:** midsummer to fall

Herbestonne coneflower grows from clumps, 3 feet high and wide, with large, deeply lobed, light green leaves. In mid-July and August, it sends up long, slender flower stalks that reach 5 to 6 feet high, holding large 4-inch canary yellow daises with bright green centers. The effect is very elegant, even though the size of the flowers is so large.

Herbestonne rudbeckia can take full sun, but a little afternoon shade may be preferable. Too much shade, though, will cause it to flop over. It is probably not as drought tolerant as the others and needs extra moisture in summer. Plant it in the back of the border with butterfly bush, hibiscus, indigo spires sage, azure sage, roses, and grasses. It attracts butterflies and other insects.

Photo 12.143 *(far left)*
Giant rudbeckia,
Rudbeckia maxima

Photo 12.144
Herbestonne coneflower,
Rudbeckia nitida
'Herbestonne'

Photo 12.145
Herbestonne coneflower
detail, *Rudbeckia nitida*
'Herbestonne'

Rudbeckia x 'Toto'
Dwarf Gloriosa Daisy

- ◆ **Zones:** 5–9
- ◆ **Light:** full sun to light shade
- ◆ **Soil:** well-drained, dry
- ◆ **Size:** low
- ◆ **Color:** yellow
- ◆ **Season:** midsummer to fall

Dwarf gloriosa daisy is similar to black-eyed Susan and gloriosa daisy but is smaller. It grows 8 to 10 inches high and wide and has small 2- to 3-inch golden yellow daisies that begin blooming in July and August and continue into fall. Plant it in the front of the border with dwarf ruellia and pincushion flowers. Care for it as you would the other rudbeckias.

Photo 12.146
Mexican petunia,
Ruellia brittoniana

Ruellia brittoniana
Ruellia, Mexican Petunia

- ◆ **Zones:** 7–10
- ◆ **Light:** full sun to shade
- ◆ **Soil:** well-drained, dry
- ◆ **Size:** medium
- ◆ **Color:** purple, blue, pink, white
- ◆ **Season:** midsummer to fall

Photo 12.147 *(far right)*
Dwarf Mexican petunia,
Ruellia brittoniana
'Katy's Dwarf'

Ruellia is an easy-care perennial that has naturalized in Texas. It has long, thin, pointed leaves on bushy plants that grow 24 to 36 inches high and wide. In July and August, it blooms with 1- to 2-inch bell-shaped flowers that resemble small petunias. The parent is lavender purple, but it ranges in shades of blue, lavender, purple, white, and pink, depending on variety. After blooming until the first frost of fall, it dies completely to the ground and doesn't return until late in the spring. It pops up easily from seed, so leave the seedlings where you like them and pull up the others.

Ruellia will grow in shade but may not bloom as well. Cut the foliage back after the first blooming push to keep the plant full and bushy. Plant it in the middle of the border where you want soft, pastel colors. Plant it with autumn sage, purple coneflower, and black-eyed Susan.

'Bonita' is a dwarf variety with pink flowers.
'Chi-Chi' has bright pink and blue flowers.
'Katy' is a dwarf variety that grows only 10 to 12 inches high and wide in shades of whites, pinks, and purples.

Russelia equisetiformis
Firecracker Plant

- ◆ **Zones:** 9–10
- ◆ **Light:** full sun to light shade
- ◆ **Soil:** well-drained, dry
- ◆ **Size:** low to medium
- ◆ **Color:** coral red
- ◆ **Season:** midspring to summer

Firecracker plant is a tender perennial that grows into a low, shrubby plant with trailing

stems that mound and flow like a fountain. The stems are bright green and nearly leafless. In midsummer, it comes into bloom with a profusion of clusters of bright, coral red, tubular flowers that look like little firecrackers. The plant mounds 4 feet high and 6 feet wide. It grows particularly well in planters and along walls where it can spill over the edges. Frost sensitive, it should be grown as an annual or in planters that can be moved indoors in northern parts of the state.

S

Salvia species
Sages, Salvias

Salvias and sages are one of the largest and most useful families of perennials for Texas gardens. Because many are native to the Southwest, salvias are suited for the summer heat, dryness, and poor alkaline soils. However, not all sages prefer full blazing sun. Lyre leaf sage and purple leaf sage, for example, prefer shady environments. Also, not all sages need dry soil. Bog sage prefers moist soils.

Flower colors range from blues and purples to reds, pinks, and oranges. The red and blue tubular flowers are magnets for insects and most hummingbirds. Sages are also important for

their fragrance, especially when touched or brushed. The common garden sage serves, of course, as an herb for cooking, as well as a nice evergreen foliage plant.

Salvia 'Indigo Spires'
Indigo Spires Salvia

- ◆ **Zones:** 8–10
- ◆ **Light:** full sun to partial shade
- ◆ **Soil:** well-drained
- ◆ **Size:** tall
- ◆ **Color:** blue
- ◆ **Season:** midsummer to fall

Indigo spires salvia is a tall, summer-flowering perennial that blooms from the end of June through October. Spikes of dark indigo blue flowers top the medium-sized dark green leaves. Small and tubular shaped, the individual flowers are popular with hummingbirds and insects. The plant grows 3 to 4 feet tall and almost as wide. It should be pruned to keep it neat, compact, and from getting leggy and flopping over. A tender perennial that should to be kept dry in winter, it likes regular moisture in summer when it is growing.

Salvia azurea var, grandiflora
Azure Sage, Pitcher Sage, Meadow Sage

- ◆ **Zones:** 6–10
- ◆ **Light:** full sun to partial shade
- ◆ **Soil:** well-drained, dry
- ◆ **Size:** tall
- ◆ **Color:** light blue
- ◆ **Season:** midsummer to fall

Photo 12.148 *(far left)*
Firecracker plant,
Russelia equisetiformis

Photo 12.150
Indigo spires sage,
Salvia 'Indigo Spires'

Photo 12.149 *(far left)*
Salvias bloom in the heat
of summer

becoming leggy and floppy. Otherwise, stake it once the flowers begin.

Azure sage is tolerant of soil types and is very drought resistant. A native to Texas and easy to grow, it emerges slowly, so be careful when you're digging around in spring and summer. Plant azure sage in the back of the border with other tall fall bloomers such as the bright yellow Herbestonne rudbeckia, goldenrods, and butterfly bush.

Salvia bicolor

Bicolor Sage, Cocoa Sapphire Salvia

- ◆ **Zones:** 8–10
- ◆ **Light:** full sun to partial shade
- ◆ **Soil:** well-drained
- ◆ **Size:** low
- ◆ **Color:** blue flowers, purple foliage
- ◆ **Season:** early summer to fall

Azure sage is a tall, late-summer flowering perennial that blooms from August through October. The foliage is light green with small leaves and a very airy texture. At the end of summer, spikes of pure azure blue flowers bloom and continue until the first frost. Small and tubular shaped, the individual flowers are popular with hummingbirds and insects. The plant grows 2 to 3 feet tall and almost as wide. Shearing in early summer will prevent it from

Bicolor sage is a low, mounding, bushy sage that grows only 12 to 14 inches high and wide. It has chocolaty bronze to purple foliage with cobalt blue flower spikes that bloom from May to October. Tough, compact, and finely textured, its only problem seems to be that it is not as hardy as most sages. Anywhere north of zone 8, it should be planted as a summer annual. Plant it in the front of the border with other sunny favorites.

Salvia chamaedryoides

Gray Shrub Sage

- ◆ **Zones:** 7–10
- ◆ **Light:** full sun to partial shade
- ◆ **Soil:** well-drained, dry
- ◆ **Size:** medium
- ◆ **Color:** blue
- ◆ **Season:** midsummer to fall

Gray shrub sage is a low-growing, bushy, evergreen salvia that has small, silvery-gray leaves and resembles germander. It grows to 2 feet high and wide, spreading by underground roots. It blooms heavily with true blue, tubular flowers in early summer, then sporadically throughout summer, and heavily again in fall. Spilling over rocks, walls, and sidewalks, it is drought tolerant once established but fairly tender. It does not survive winter in cold temperatures and wet soils.

Salvia coccinea

Scarlet Sage

- ◆ **Zones:** 8–10
- ◆ **Light:** full sun to partial shade
- ◆ **Soil:** well-drained
- ◆ **Size:** medium
- ◆ **Color:** red, pink
- ◆ **Season:** midsummer to fall

Scarlet sage is a medium tall, tender perennial that reseeds easily. The flower spikes have large, red tubular flowers that bloom in summer and are popular with hummingbirds and butterflies. The plant grows to 15 to 18 inches high by 18 inches wide. Regular shearing keeps it neat and blooming. It is drought tolerant but appreciates

ample water in the heat of summer. North of zone 8, it should be treated as an annual.

POPULAR VARIETIES

'Lady in Red' has large scarlet red flowers.

'Coral Nymph' has coral pink flowers and looks good in more pastel plantings.

'Forest Fire' is very showy and vibrant with dark red flowers and highlights of scarlet pink.

Photo 12.155
Gray shrub sage,
Salvia chamaedryoides

Photo 12.154 *(far left)*
Scarlet sage, *Salvia coccinea*

Photo 12.156 *(left)*
Scarlet sage, *Salvia coccinea*
'Coral Nymph'

Photo 12.157
Mealy cup sage, *Salvia farinacea 'Victoria Blue'*

Salvia greggii

Autumn Sage, Cherry Sage

◆ **Zones:** 7–10

◆ **Light:** full sun to partial shade

◆ **Soil:** well-drained

◆ **Size:** medium to tall

◆ **Color:** pink, red, white, violet, purple

◆ **Season:** late spring to fall

Autumn sage is one of the best performing, most consistent perennials for the Texas landscape. Despite what its name implies, autumn sage begins blooming in April and May and continues blooming consistently until October and the first frost. After that, it retains a shrubby shape with small semievergreen leaves. In average and mild winters it makes a nice evergreen bush. The flowers, whose colors vary, are tubular on short spikes that rise above the plant. They are a favorite draw for insects and hummingbirds. When crushed, the leaves give off the typical sage aroma.

Salvia farinacea

Mealy Cup Sage

Photo 12.158 *(far right)*
Red autumn sage, *Salvia greggii*

◆ **Zones:** 8–10

◆ **Light:** full sun to partial shade

◆ **Soil:** well-drained, dry

◆ **Size:** medium

◆ **Color:** blue, purple

◆ **Season:** early-summer to fall

This medium tall easy-growing perennial has spikes of China blue flowers. It grows well here in summer, but requires plenty of moisture. In winter, however, it needs a very well-drained location so it can stay dry. Mealy cup sage begins blooming in April and May and continues until the first freeze in fall. Plant it with other summer-blooming perennials that complement its clear blue color.

Mealy cup sage grows 18 inches high and 18 inches wide. *'Victoria Blue'* is a popular cultivar that displays fuller, more compact blue flowers than does the original. It is native to Texas and drought tolerant once established. It is used often as an annual.

This salvia grows with less than full sun but does not bloom as heavily and becomes more leggy and sparse. Keep the plant sheared to avoid it getting leggy and to keep it flowering more

Photo 12.159 *(far right)*
White autumn sage detail, *Salvia greggii 'Alba'*

heavily. However, prune the plant only in summer while it is growing and after a blooming spurt. Autumn sage can be killed if you attempt to prune it back too much in winter. Left unpruned, the plant grows to 30 to 36 inches high and wide. Water well and fertilize during the growing season.

No sunny Texas garden should be without an autumn sage. About the only thing it doesn't like is heavy shade or soggy soils. Pick yours according to the flower color.

POPULAR VARIETIES

'Alba' has white flowers.

'Compact Orange' has orange flowers and is more compact.

'Dark Dancer' and *'Maroon'* have burgundy flowers.

'Diana' has violet flowers bordering on purple and is not as vigorous as the other varieties.

'Moonglow' has creamy white flowers.

'Pink' has magenta flowers.

'Pink Preference' has bright pink flowers.

'Raspberry' has hot, pinkish purple flowers.

'Red' has red flowers.

'Sierra San Antonio' has orange and yellow flowers.

S. g. x lycioides 'Wild Grape' is a smaller, lacier plant with draping flowers that bloom royal purple flowers from spring to fall.

S. g. l. 'Nuevo Leon' has blue-violet flowers.

Salvia officinalis
Garden Sage

◆ **Zones:** 5–10

◆ **Light:** full sun to partial shade

◆ **Soil:** well-drained, dry

◆ **Size:** medium

◆ **Color:** lavender

◆ **Season:** midsummer for flowers, year-round for foliage

Garden sage is known mostly as a cooking herb. The grayish green leaves have a rough texture and are evergreen. The scent of the crushed leaves is fragrant. The flowers bloom in late spring and early summer and are typically lavender in color but may be pink, blue, or white. If you are not growing the plant for cooking, leave

Photo 12.160
Purple garden sage, *Salvia officinalis 'Purpurascens'*

the flowers for their ornamental value. The soils must be well-drained; otherwise, it develops crown rot and will die. The parent is hardy to 0 degrees, but the cultivars are less so. The plants are short lived, but even if they die out, they reseed easily and come up freely. The leaf color varies from cultivar to cultivar in the ranges of yellows, creams, greens, and purples.

POPULAR VARIETIES

'Purpurascens' is the most common cultivar. It has purplish leaves and makes a nice contrast with other gray-toned plants.

'Begotten' has large, rounded, gray leaves.

'Citrine' has gold to limey yellow leaves.

'Compacta' is a more restrained dwarf form.

Salvia engelmannii
Engelmann's Sage

◆ **Zones:** 7–10

◆ **Light:** full sun to light shade

◆ **Soil:** well-drained, dry

◆ **Size:** low

◆ **Color:** blue

◆ **Season:** late spring to early summer

Photo 12.161
Engelmann's sage, *Salvia engelmannii*

Engelmann's sage is low growing with finely textured leaves and has a sprawling form that reaches only 12 inches tall. The evergreen leaves are small, narrow, long, and gray-green. The flowers bloom in late April and May and are small sky blue tubular bells. Engelmann's sage does well in the front of the border, spilling out over hot paving stones or rocks with the thyme or sun drops.

Salvia guarantica
Anise Scented Sage

- ◆ **Zones:** 7–10
- ◆ **Light:** full sun to partial shade
- ◆ **Soil:** well-drained
- ◆ **Size:** tall
- ◆ **Color:** blue, purple
- ◆ **Season:** midsummer to fall

Photo 12.162
Anise scented sage,
Salvia guarantica

Anise scented sage is a tall, back-of-the-border plant that sports deep cobalt to violet blue tubular flowers from midsummer through fall. It blooms best during the heat of summer. During the hottest weeks, regular water is necessary, especially while the plants are young. The deep blue flowers grow on loose spikes on top of dark green, leggy foliage. If it grows in too much shade, it will become leggy and flop over. It requires well-drained soil with ample humus.

Photo 12.163 *(far right)*
Mexican bush sage,
Salvia leucantha

Hardy to 10 degrees, it doesn't always winter reliably. Good drainage and good mulch in winter seem to be the key, whereas frequent watering in the heat of summer helps to keep it blooming.

The back of the border is its best position because anis scented sage can grow to 4 to 5 feet tall and 2 to 3 feet wide. In ideal conditions, the spreading roots can multiply quickly. Complementary late-summer and fall plants make good companions. With the deep blue flowers, plants that have a bright canary yellow (like rudbeckia and coreopsis) and vivid pinks (like roses and asters) work well.

POPULAR VARIETIES

'Black and Blue' has striking cobalt blue to black flowers.

'Limelight' has bright, golden green foliage, and the stems are chartreuse and catch the light. They complement the bright blue flowers.

Salvia leucantha
Mexican Bush Sage

- ◆ **Zones:** 8–10
- ◆ **Light:** full sun to partial shade
- ◆ **Soil:** well-drained, dry
- ◆ **Size:** tall
- ◆ **Color:** lavender, purple
- ◆ **Season:** late summer to fall

Mexican bush sage is one of the most popular sages in Texas. Once established, it is very drought and heat resistant. A perennial that dies to the ground each year, it returns as a bushy plant growing to 3 to 4 feet tall with light gray-green, fuzzy leaves. Its flowers bloom heavily from the end of summer through fall

and are a favorite of butterflies and bumble-bees. The white flowers, set in a larger lavender subpetal, arise on stalks with many flowers blooming at the same time. Both flower and subpetal are fuzzy, giving the plant a rather soft, lavender pastel look.

Mexican bush sage prefers full sun. It will continue to bloom with some shade, but it will become leggy and flop over. Remove the spent flowers to prolong the heavy blooming. It is hardy only to 25 degrees and does not always winter dependably in North Texas. Good drainage in winter seems to be a key. Loose mulch for protection helps as long as it does not retain too much moisture. However, regular water in summer is helpful, especially with young plants. Mexican sage is one of the best for a pastel border in late summer and autumn, mixing well with the light blues of caryopteris, the soft pinks of Nearly Wild rose, and the whites and lavenders of some asters. It also looks good with other gray-green, full sun plants, like lavender and rosemary.

Salvia lyrata
Lyre Leaf Sage

- ◆ **Zones:** 7–10
- ◆ **Light:** shade to partial shade
- ◆ **Soil:** well-drained, dry
- ◆ **Size:** low
- ◆ **Color:** blue
- ◆ **Season:** late spring

Unlike most salvia, lyre leaf sage prefers at least partial shade, performing best with morning sun and afternoon shade or with light, all-day shade. It tolerates full sun and heavier shade but, like most sages, prefers dry and well-drained soils, unlike most shade lovers. The hairy, lyre-shaped leaves stay close to the ground in rosettes developing purplish splotches, which seem to fade in full sun. In late spring and early summer, the plant sends up flower stalks of small, light blue tubular flowers 18 to 24 inches high. The rest of the year, the whorls of evergreen foliage remain only about 6 inches tall.

Native to Texas, lyre leaf sage handles the alkaline soils well. It works as a front-of-the-border plant and mixes well with other late-spring and early summer plants. It goes well with the soft yellows of the Texas Gold columbine,

Photo 12.164
Lyre leaf sage, *Salvia lyrata*

which blooms about the same time and has the same moisture and shade requirements.

POPULAR VARIETY

'Purple Knockout' and *'Purple Volcano'* have purple- and bronze-colored leaves.

Salvia nemerosa 'Plumosa'
Plumosa Meadow Sage

- ◆ **Zones:** 5–10
- ◆ **Light:** full sun to partial shade
- ◆ **Soil:** well-drained
- ◆ **Size:** medium
- ◆ **Color:** dusky purple
- ◆ **Season:** midsummer to fall

Plumosa meadow sage has dusky purple flowers that form plumes, like cockscomb or astilbe. It begins blooming in May and continues through-

Photo 12.165
Plumosa meadow sage, *Salvia nemerosa 'Plumosa'*

out the summer. The plumes reach up to 36 inches in height and are best suited for the middle of the border. Like meadow sage, plant it in full sun to keep from getting leggy and flopping over. Good drainage is also necessary. *Salvia nemerosa* is a meadow sage, which may be the parent plant of *'May Night.'* The leaves are similar to those of *Salvia x superba*.

Salvia penstemonoides

Penstemon Sage, Big Red Sage

- ◆ **Zones:** 7–10
- ◆ **Light:** full sun to partial shade
- ◆ **Soil:** well-drained, dry
- ◆ **Size:** medium to tall
- ◆ **Color:** red
- ◆ **Season:** midsummer to fall

Photo 12.166
Penstemon sage,
Salvia penstemonoides

This Texas native hails from the Hill Country and grows among limestone rocks. In ideal conditions, the plant is said to grow to nearly 5 feet tall, but in most garden situations, it grows to only 24 to 30 inches tall. The plant has glossy, rich dark green leaves that stay in fairly evergreen whorls throughout most of the year. In mid- to late summer, it sends up flower stalks with deep wine red tubular flowers until early autumn. The flowers resemble penstemon when in bloom.

Photo 12.167 *(far right)*
May night meadow sage,
Salvia x superba 'May Night'

Penstemon sage prefers afternoon shade and morning to midday sun. It likes well-drained, even, gravelly soil, with deep watering in summer time. Grow it in the middle to the back of the border with other late-summer plants that complement its rich dark colors. More difficult to find in nurseries, it is well worth the try.

Salvia x superba

Meadow Sage

- ◆ **Zones:** 4–9
- ◆ **Light:** full sun to partial shade
- ◆ **Soil:** well-drained
- ◆ **Size:** low
- ◆ **Color:** blue, purple, pink, white
- ◆ **Season:** early summer to fall

Meadow sage grows easily and tolerates cold temperatures and seaside conditions. Generally a low-growing plant with medium graying green leaves, it sends up multiple low flower spikes in early summer. The low plants spread profusely in ideal circumstances. In Texas' heavier soils, it does not grow so rampantly. In fact, amending the soil to keep it well-drained is necessary.

Plant meadow sage in the front of a sunny border as it grows only to about 12 to 18 inches tall. Removing spent flowers will keep it blooming through most of summer and on into fall. Flower colors vary depending on the many cultivar types and work well with similarly colored plants, like yarrow, and with the whites, like ox-eye daisy. High humidity and poor drainage are the biggest deterrents to its performance.

POPULAR VARIETIES

'Blue Hill' has taller, 18-inch stems and light blue flowers that bloom heavily.

Photo 12.168 (far left)
Purple meadow sage,
Salvia 'East Friesland'

Photo 12.169 (left)
Bog sage, *Salvia uliginosa*

'Blue Queen' is small and compact with blue-violet flowers.

'East Friesland' has violet-blue flowers and blooms heavily on 18-inch stems.

'Lubeca' is tall and early flowering with deep violet flowers.

'May Night' is low growing with dark violet-blue flowers. It was the "1997 Perennial Plant of the Year."

'Rose Queen' is small and compact, with gray leaves and pink flowers.

Salvia uliginosa
Bog Sage

- ◆ **Zones:** 7–10
- ◆ **Light:** full sun to partial shade
- ◆ **Soil:** wet, moist, well-drained
- ◆ **Size:** tall
- ◆ **Color:** light blue
- ◆ **Season:** midsummer to fall

Bog sage grows easily with little care, producing clear, light azure blue flowers all summer long. It spreads rapidly in ideal conditions and grows quickly to 3 to 6 feet tall. In fact, when the weather is warm and wet, you may find that you need to pull the plants out because they multiply so fast by underground roots. The tubular, blue flowers bloom from early summer through early fall. The foliage, medium green with thin lance-olet leaves, is very fragrant when bruised or crushed. It will grow in almost any well-drained to moist soil but could become a nuisance if planted along a pond or creek area.

Bog sage is definitely a back-of-the-border plant. Keep it in check by planting it in dry locations or areas with barriers. It combines well with Louisiana and yellow flag iris.

Salvia verticillata 'Purple Rain'
Purple Rain Salvia

- ◆ **Zones:** 4–10
- ◆ **Light:** full sun to partial shade
- ◆ **Soil:** well-drained
- ◆ **Size:** medium
- ◆ **Color:** purple
- ◆ **Season:** late spring to fall

Photo 12.170
Purple rain salvia, *Salvia verticillata 'Purple Rain'*

Purple rain sage has vibrant grape purple flowers that appear in clumps whorled around long spikes. The flowers bloom in late spring and continue through early fall. The leaves are rosettes of velvety green that send up spikes in late spring. Plant size is 24 inches tall by about 18 inches wide. It is one of the hardier sages and can take temperatures down to 0 degrees. Although not the showiest, nor the most fragrant sage, it does nicely in the middle to back of the border, especially in a bed where dusky colors, like grays and roses, work well.

OTHER SAGES

Salvia buchananii, Buchanan's sage, grows 12 to 24 inches high with dark, glossy leaves and 2-inch magenta tubular flowers from midsummer until fall. Its size and upright habit make it ideal for midborder. It is hardy to zone 8.

Salvia blepharophylla, purple leaf sage, blooms salmon red from late spring through autumn. It grows 24 to 30 inches high and wide. The leaves are glossy green, with the undersides exhibiting a deep purple color. It is also hardy to zone 8.

Salvia texana, Texas sage, is an upright perennial salvia that produces lavender blue flowers on 24-inch-high stalks from March to May. Plant it in full sun and well-drained soils. It is also hardy to zone 8.

Santolina incana

Lavender Cotton, Gray Santolina

Santolina virens

Green Lavender Cotton, Green Santolina

- ◆ **Zones:** 7–10
- ◆ **Light:** full sun to light shade
- ◆ **Soil:** well-drained, dry
- ◆ **Size:** medium
- ◆ **Color:** yellow flowers, gray and green foliage
- ◆ **Season:** early to midsummer

Photo 12.171
Green santolina,
Santolina virens, in bloom

The santolina is a subshrub, low-growing, evergreen plant with fragrant, finely textured leaves that resemble junipers. The overall height of the mounding forms is 12 to 18 inches tall. In early to midsummer, small buttonlike yellow flowers cover the plant. Santolina needs full sun and will creep over walks and stones for more warmth. If the soil is not well-drained, during the heat of summer it will develop rot and die quickly. Add plenty of sand or gravel to the bed before plant-

Photo 12.172 *(far right)*
Pincushion flower, *Scabiosa caucasica* 'Pink Mist'

ing. Shear the plant after the flowers have faded to keep it from getting leggy and awkward. It does not seem to perform that reliably here because the soils are too heavy and the summers are too hot. If the conditions are right, it makes a nice evergreen front-of-the-border plant. It is better to keep it in a sunny part of the bed with other plants like lavenders and sages that don't get as much irrigation.

Scabiosa caucasica 'Butterfly Blue' and 'Pink Mist'

Pincushion Flower

- ◆ **Zones:** 4–10
- ◆ **Light:** full to light shade
- ◆ **Soil:** well-drained, dry
- ◆ **Size:** low
- ◆ **Color:** blue, pink
- ◆ **Season:** late spring to fall

This clump-forming perennial with gray green, low-mounding foliage produces a show of large 2-inch pincushion-looking flowers that bloom almost continuously except in the coldest weather. Good drainage is necessary to avoid root rot and powdery mildew. Keep the dead flowers removed for prolonged blooming.

Pincushion flower is an excellent front-of-the-border plant in a sunny location. It grows well in a container, too. Butterflies also love them. *'Butterfly Blue'* has a lavender blue color, and *'Pink Mist'* has a soft clear pink color. Plant it with other pastels in the sunny border, like *'Moonbeam'* coreopsis, meadow sage, and ox-eye daisy. *'Butterfly Blue'* was the "2000 Perennial Plant of the Year."

Scilla sibirica
Siberian Squil, Scilla

- ◆ **Zones:** 4–10
- ◆ **Light:** full to light shade
- ◆ **Soil:** well-drained, dry
- ◆ **Size:** low
- ◆ **Color:** blue, pink, white, purple
- ◆ **Season:** midspring

Scilla is a perennial that grows from small, crocus-sized bulbs. Plant it in fall when you plant daffodils and other spring bulbs. It has grassy foliage that grows in spring from clumps to 12 to 15 inches high. Spikes of small, bell-shaped flowers follow quickly in March and April. Remove the faded flowers. The foliage withers quickly, but do not remove it until it has dried completely. As summer perennials fill out, they will mask the fading foliage nicely. Feed as you would other bulbs.

RELATED SPECIES

Peruvian Scilla, *Scilla peruviana,* is grown from large 4- to 5-inch bulbs planted in fall or early spring. In March and April, it sends up long, straplike leaves that curve outward from the central clump. Large clusters of star-shaped, blue flowers that bloom in late April and May follow the leaves. The clusters reach 12 to 15 inches high and spread to 18 to 24 inches wide. Plant the bulbs 4 to 5 inches deep in soil with good drainage, in full sun to light shade. Trim off flower spikes after they are spent. The foliage dies away after it is finished blooming. Other cultivars are available with different colors of flowers. It is hardy to zone 6.

Scutellaria suffrutescens
Pink Scullcap

- ◆ **Zones:** 7–10
- ◆ **Light:** full sun to light shade
- ◆ **Soil:** well-drained, dry
- ◆ **Size:** low
- ◆ **Color:** pink
- ◆ **Season:** midspring

Scullcap is a low-growing, mounding plant that forms a ground-cover-type plant for the front of a sunny border. The evergreen to semievergreen leaves are tiny and gray-green resembling thyme. Scullcap begins to bloom in early summer and continues on and off into fall with lots of small bright pink flowers that are indeed shaped like skullcaps. It is very drought resistant once established.

Scullcap makes a nice front-of-the-border plant in a sunny garden and works well spilling over walls and rocks. The flowers attract butterflies and other insects. Plant with other sun lovers, like lamb's ear and sages. White and violet varieties are also available.

Sedum spectabile
Showy Sedum

- ◆ **Zones:** 5–10
- ◆ **Light:** full to partial shade
- ◆ **Soil:** well-drained, dry
- ◆ **Size:** low
- ◆ **Color:** pale pink
- ◆ **Season:** late summer to early fall

Sedums encompass a large group of plants that are drought tolerant and fleshy. Many make good ground covers in warm, dry climates.

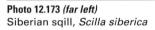

Photo 12.173 *(far left)*
Siberian sqill, *Scilla siberica*

Photo 12.174
Scullcap, *Scutellaria suffrutescens*

Good drainage is essential, and most do not do well in Texas. *Sedum spectabile* has fleshy succulent gray-green foliage that forms a thick clump 12 to 18 inches tall and wide. In late summer, it blooms with 6-inch, flat–topped, flower clumps resembling yarrow. The most common cultivar is *'Autumn Joy'* which has pale pink flowers that darken to rusty bronze with age. *'Brilliant'* has rosy red flowers that dry nicely and maintain their shape well into fall. The foliage is not evergreen and dies completely down as soon as freezing temperatures begin.

Setcreasea pallida 'Purple Heart'

Purple Heart

- ◆ **Zones:** 8–10
- ◆ **Light:** full sun to partial shade
- ◆ **Soil:** well-drained
- ◆ **Size:** low
- ◆ **Color:** lavender pink flowers, purple foliage
- ◆ **Season:** summer to fall

Purple heart is a low-growing, spilling plant that is mostly grown for colorful foliage. It sends out long runners in summer that grow 6 to 10 inches high and 24 inches wide. The leaves are pointed and slightly striped in shades of purple. Purple heart blooms with tiny almost unnoticeable lavender pink flowers on the ends of the stems. It dies down to the ground in winter, but returns every summer. Except keeping it trimmed to stay in bounds, it needs little care and looks best where it can spill over walls or planters.

Sidalcea species

Prairie Mallow

- ◆ **Zones:** 4–10
- ◆ **Light:** full sun to partial shade
- ◆ **Soil:** well-drained
- ◆ **Size:** medium to tall
- ◆ **Color:** white, pink
- ◆ **Season:** midsummer to early fall

Mallow is a group of old-fashioned plants that includes rose of sharon, hibiscus, and hollyhock. Less showy is a group called prairie mallows whose flowers are smaller, on stalks that reach 24 to 48 inches high, and bloom in summer to fall. The effect is similar to hollyhock, but it is more dependable. Because of its size and shape, prairie mallow blends well into perennial borders and works well in naturalized and meadow gardens. Plant it in the middle to back of the border.

POPULAR VARIETY

'Party Girl' has bright purplish pink flowers and grows to 24 to 36 inches tall with graceful flower spikes.

- ◆ **Color:** lavender flowers, gray foliage
- ◆ **Season:** early summer for flowers, foliage year round

Lamb's ear is a terrific, ground-hugging perennial with large, fuzzy, silvery green leaves. It is low growing and mounding to only 12 inches high. In May and June, it sends up thick, fuzzy flower stalks with tiny purple flowers. Keep the flowers trimmed after they are finished blooming. They tend to look bad quickly.

Photo 12.178 *(far left)*
Goldenrod, *Solidago sphacelata*

Solidago sphacelata
Goldenrod

- ◆ **Zones:** 4–10
- ◆ **Light:** full sun to light shade
- ◆ **Soil:** moist, well-drained
- ◆ **Size:** medium to tall
- ◆ **Color:** golden yellow
- ◆ **Season:** late summer to fall

Goldenrod is a pillar of the autumn show in Texas. It has a bad reputation, however, because it blooms when ragweed does and is mistaken as a cause of hay fever. Goldenrod has long, willowy leaves and grows 3 to 4 feet high and almost as wide. It spreads quickly by underground rhizomes and can become a nuisance if planted in moist soils. In late August, it develops sprays of golden yellow flower spikes that continue until the first frost. It can handle wet to quite dry soils.

Unless you are planting a meadow or large, naturalized beds, plant the shorter, better-behaved types.

POPULAR VARIETIES

'Gold Dwarf' and **'Golden Thumb'** grow only to 12 inches high.

'Cloth of Gold' and **'Golden Fleece'** grow 18 to 24 inches high.

Stachys lanata
Lamb's Ear

- ◆ **Zones:** 4–10
- ◆ **Light:** full sun to light shade
- ◆ **Soil:** well-drained, dry
- ◆ **Size:** low to medium

Photo 12.179
Lamb's ear, *Stachys lanata*

If kept wet, especially in high temperatures, it develops rot and dies out quickly. Do not be alarmed, however, because it reseeds easily and will pop up all over the garden. Just leave it where you like it and pull out the seedlings where you don't want them. Plant it at the front of the border with pincushion flowers, sages, lavender, and coneflowers.

Stokesia laevis
Stokes Aster

- ◆ **Zones:** 6–10
- ◆ **Light:** full sun to light shade
- ◆ **Soil:** well-drained, dry
- ◆ **Size:** low to medium
- ◆ **Color:** blue, red, pink
- ◆ **Season:** early summer to fall

Stokes aster, although not a true aster, is in the same family. It has low, gray-green foliage that is evergreen to semievergreen and grows in a clump. In early summer, it begins to flower with large 3-inch flowers that resemble an aster's. The height depends on the cultivar. The colors range from blues and purples to pinks and whites. Although drought tolerant, it

appreciates even moisture in the heat of summer. Plant it with other summer sun lovers in the front to middle of the border.

POPULAR VARIETIES

'Blue Danube' has bright blue flowers.

S x cyanea 'Purple Parasols' has purple flowers.

OTHER Ss

Strawberry geranium, *Saxifrage stolonifera,* is a member of the strawberry family. This little ground cover is more of a woodland or shade garden plant. Strawberry geranium has large 3-inch evergreen leaves that are medium dark green with silvery stripes. In April, it blooms in a mass of tiny airy white blooms that float above the foliage. The rest of the year it makes a nice edger or ground cover for the front of the border. When conditions are good, it spreads easily by runners and grows to a height of 12 inches. Slugs can be a problem for strawberry geranium. Plant it in well-drained soils in full to partial shade. Strawberry geranium is hardy to zone 6.

T

Tagetes lemmonii
Copper Canyon Daisy

◆ **Zones:** 7–10

◆ **Light:** full sun to light shade

◆ **Soil:** well-drained, dry

◆ **Size:** medium

◆ **Color:** yellow-orange

◆ **Season:** late summer to fall

Copper Canyon daisy is a tough, drought-tolerant, shrubby perennial that is related to the annual French marigold. When touched or bruised, its dark green, finely cut leaves are extremely aromatic with a fragrance of lemon and marigold. It grows into a 3-inch high and wide shrub. In most cases, it blooms in late summer and fall with small yellow-orange daisies. In mild climates, where it does not get damaged from freezing, it blooms most of the winter and into spring. Where temperatures drop below freezing, it dies to the ground and doesn't reemerge until late spring. Drought tolerant when established, it attracts butterflies and insects. It will reseed and spread quickly. Pull up the seedlings that you don't want. Plant it in the middle of the sunny border, especially in Xeriscapes and native plantings.

Tagetes lucida
Mexican Mint Marigold, Mexican Taragon

◆ **Zones:** 8–10

◆ **Light:** full sun to light shade

◆ **Soil:** well-drained, dry

◆ **Size:** medium

◆ **Color:** yellow-orange

◆ **Season:** late summer to fall

Mexican mint marigold is similar to Copper Canyon daisy, but it has darker, narrower, and less cut foliage that grows 24 to 30 inches high and wide. The foliage has the fragrance of tarragon when bruised. It comes into bloom in August with small, bright golden yellow daisies and dies to the ground in winter. Plant it as an annual in northern regions. It is very drought tolerant

the state. Plant it in the back of the sunny border or in pots that can be moved indoors in colder winter regions.

POPULAR VARIETY

T. x 'Orange Jubilee' is a hybrid that has bright orange flowers and is reported to be more cold tolerant.

Teucrium chaemedrys
Germander

- ◆ **Zones:** 5–10
- ◆ **Light:** full sun to light shade
- ◆ **Soil:** well-drained, dry
- ◆ **Size:** low
- ◆ **Color:** pink
- ◆ **Season:** early summer

Germander is a fragrant herb with fragrant evergreen foliage that is small and gray-green. It grows 12 to 18 inches high and wide and has a mounding, bushy form that spills over rocks and

when established and attractive to butterflies and insects. It will reseed and spread quickly. Plant it in the middle of the sunny border, especially with Xeriscapes and native plantings.

Tecoma stans
Yellow Bells, Esperanza

- ◆ **Zones:** 8–10
- ◆ **Light:** full sun to light shade
- ◆ **Soil:** well-drained, dry
- ◆ **Size:** large
- ◆ **Color:** yellow
- ◆ **Season:** midsummer to fall

Really more of a shrub, yellow bells is a fast-growing, heat-tolerant perennial in areas that receive frost. It has dark, compound green leaves and grows as an open bush 4 to 8 feet high, depending on the conditions. All summer and into fall, it blooms heavily with large canary yellow trumpets that are popular with hummingbirds and butterflies. It produces long pods if the faded flowers are not trimmed off. Shear back the foliage to keep it shapely. Native to South Texas, it is very heat and drought tolerant once established, but it dies to the ground with freezing temperatures in the northern parts of

paving. In May and June, it blooms with tiny pink flowers. Plant it as an evergreen edger or as part of a Mediterranean border.

It can be sheared easily and has often been used in knot gardens. Shear at least once a year to keep it from getting too woody and leggy. Heavy clay and soggy soils are its only downfalls, but it will handle consistent water if the soils drain quickly. It also works well in planters. Plant it with thyme, sages, and German bearded iris.

POPULAR VARIETIES

'Prostratum' grows only 4 to 6 inches high and up to 3 feet wide.

T. fruticans, bush germander, is an evergreen shrubby perennial that grows 3 to 4 feet high and almost as wide. It has silvery green leaves and lavender blue flowers in February to June.

Thymus vulgaris
Creeping Thyme

- ◆ **Zones:** 7–10
- ◆ **Light:** full sun to light shade
- ◆ **Soil:** well-drained, dry
- ◆ **Size:** low
- ◆ **Color:** blue, pink, lavender, white
- ◆ **Season:** early summer

Creeping thyme is a perennial herb grown mostly for use in cooking. Very low growing, it forms wiry mats that spread over rocks and paving. The overall height is 8 to 12 inches by 18 to 24 inches wide. The tiny, gray-green leaves are extremely fragrant, especially when touched or stepped on, and can be dried and used as seasoning in food. In May and June, the plant is covered with tiny flowers. The leaf color, flower color, and fragrance vary per variety.

Plant thyme at the front of the border. It is drought tolerant once established and will seek the hot areas like concrete and rocks. The soils must be well-drained, or it will rot. Add sand, gravel, and lava sand to keep the drainage good. Plant with other sun lovers, like sun drops, German bearded iris, germander, and lavender. It also works well planted between stepping-stones because it tolerates light traffic and provides fragrance as you walk through the garden. Sheer it after it blooms to keep the foliage from getting woody and sparse.

POPULAR VARIETIES

'Elfin' is a dwarf variety growing only 1 inch high. The leaves are tiny and dark green with pink flowers.

'Argenteus' has silver variegated leaves.

T. citriodorus, lemon thyme, has bright green leaves with a lemony scent and pink flowers.

T. c. 'Aurea' has golden leaves.

T. pseudolanuginosus, wooly thyme, has fuzzy gray leaves with pink flowers.

Tradescantia virginiana
Spiderwort

- ◆ **Zones:** 4–9
- ◆ **Light:** light shade to shade
- ◆ **Soil:** well-drained
- ◆ **Size:** medium
- ◆ **Color:** purple
- ◆ **Season:** late spring to early summer

Spiderwort is a Texas native that grows in clumps with leggy, arching stems and long, grasslike foliage. It grows 18 to 24 inches high and wide. In April through June, it comes into bloom with small, three-petaled purple flowers that bloom only for one day but are quickly re-

placed by others. It may self-sow and pop up in other areas. Plant spiderwort in the middle of the border with daylilies, columbine, and lyre leaf sage. Varieties that bloom in white, pink, and blue are available.

POPULAR VARIETIES

'Aurea' has chartreuse, yellow-green leaves with lavender flowers. Because of the added foliage color, this is the most interesting one.

'Zwanenburg Blue' has royal blue flowers and green leaves with purple veins.

Tulbaghia violacea

Society Garlic

- ◆ **Zones:** 7–10
- ◆ **Light:** full sun to light shade
- ◆ **Soil:** well-drained, moist
- ◆ **Size:** low
- ◆ **Color:** lavender
- ◆ **Season:** early summer to fall

Society garlic, a great plant for the sunny border, grows in clumps of thin, grassy light green foliage that resembles liriope. The foliage is extremely pungent with a strong garlic smell when bruised. It dies to the ground at the first frost. In zones 8b or warmer, it stays evergreen. In spring it shoots up forming a clump that is 12 to 18 inches high and wide. It works well with evergreen liriope and ophiopogon, blending in during the summer. Starting in May, it comes into bloom with loose lavender flower clusters above the foliage. Remove the faded blooms, and it will continue all summer and into fall.

Plant society garlic in full sun to partial shade. The soils should be deep and organic, but it will tolerate moist to dry soils. In fact, you can plant

it as a bog plant. Extra water in the hottest parts of summer will keep it in bloom. Plant it as an accent in the front and middle borders, or in mass with other evergreens. It works well planted behind dwarf daylilies, too.

POPULAR VARIETY

'Variegata' has creamy white and green striped leaves, but is not as vigorous as the parent.

Tulipa clusiana, Tulipa bakeri 'Lilac Wonder'

Species Tulip or Wild Tulip

- ◆ **Zones:** 4–8
- ◆ **Light:** full sun to light shade
- ◆ **Soil:** well-drained
- ◆ **Size:** low
- ◆ **Color:** yellow, white, pink, red, violet
- ◆ **Season:** midspring

Unlike most tulips, which require a cold period to bloom, species tulip grows well in warmer climates. Growing only to 12 inches high, it emerges in March and April and blooms with small flowers like those of regular tulips. The *T. clusiana*, the lady tulip, has fragrant, peppermint red and white striped flowers. *T. bakeri 'Lilac Wonder'* has violet pink flowers with a yellow center. Plant species tulip from bulbs in late fall and winter in deep, well-drained soils, 4 to 6 inches deep and 4 to 6 inches apart in random drifts. The narrow, pointed petals open wide in sunshine. It works best in the front of the border among creeping phlox, ophiopogon, candytuft, dwarf daffodils, and grape hyacinths.

Photo 12.187 *(far left)*
Society garlic,
Tulbaghia violacea

Photo 12.188
Lady tulip, *Tulipa clusiana*

OTHER TS

Thalictrum aquilegifolium, or ***meadow rue,*** has dainty, blue-green foliage that looks similar to columbine. It grows 2 to 3 feet wide in an open, airy form, with tiny flowers that bloom in May and June in fluffy clusters of whites, pinks, or purples. It grows naturally in woodlands and should be planted in light and dappled shade with deep, humus-rich soil. Heat tolerant once established, it works well with columbines, ferns, and lyre leaf sage in shady gardens. It is hardy to zone 4.

V

Verbena bonariensis
Upright Verbena

◆ **Zones:** 7–10

◆ **Light:** full sun to light shade

◆ **Soil:** well-drained, dry

◆ **Size:** tall

◆ **Color:** purple

◆ **Season:** early summer to fall

Photo 12.189
Upright verbena, *Verbena bonariensis*

Unlike most verbenas, which are low-growing, sprawling plants, upright verbena grows straight 36 to 48 inches high with narrow leaves. Starting at the end of May, it blooms with clusters of fluffy, purple flowers at the top of the sturdy, thick stems. The effect is very open and airy. It can be planted at the back of the border or closer to the front because it has a transparent quality. It is not long-lived but reseeds easily and may pop up in other locations. Just move these seedlings where you want them.

Photo 12.190 *(far right)*
Homestead purple verbena, *Verbena canadensis*

Verbena canadensis
Garden Verbena

◆ **Zones:** 7–10

◆ **Light:** full sun to light shade

◆ **Soil:** well-drained, dry

◆ **Size:** low

◆ **Color:** purple, white, pink, red, blue

◆ **Season:** late spring to fall

This verbena is the most familiar and is tolerant of hot, humid conditions. It has medium, finely toothed dark green leaves on stems that mound and sprawl, and it grows 12 to 15 inches high and 24 to 36 inches wide. Starting at the end of April, it comes into bloom with flower clusters that will continue throughout summer. The parent plant has rosy purple flowers, but many selections are available depending on the variety. Verbena needs good drainage, especially in winter. However, it does well with extra moisture in the hottest parts of summer. Plant it at the front of a sunny border where it can spill over rocks, walls, and walks. It is good for pots and baskets, as well.

POPULAR VARIETIES

‘Alba’ has white flowers.

V. x **‘Apple Blossom Pink’** has light pink flowers.

V. x **‘Blue Princess’** has lavender blue flowers.

V. x **‘Homestead Pink’** has bright pink flowers.

V. x **‘Homestead Purple’** has grape purple flowers and is a heavy bloomer.

V. x **‘Julian Red’** has bright red flowers.

V. x **‘Sissinghurst Pink’** has rosy pink flowers.

Verbena tenuisecta

Moss Verbena

- ◆ **Zones:** 7–10
- ◆ **Light:** full sun to light shade
- ◆ **Soil:** well-drained, dry
- ◆ **Size:** low
- ◆ **Color:** pink, purple, white
- ◆ **Season:** late spring to fall

Moss verbena has naturalized throughout much of Texas, blooming from April to November with clusters of small flowers. It is low growing, 6 to 12 inches high and twice as wide. The foliage is finely dissected and has a fernlike quality. Grow it as you would other verbenas. It is more drought tolerant than other verbenas.

Photo 12.192
Moss verbena, *Verbena tenuisecta*

summer in Texas. Too much shade will cause it to flop over. The soil should be rich with ample moisture in summer months. It goes completely dormant in winter and is a bit slow to return in spring, so be patient. *V. longifolia* tends to wilt if drainage is poor.

Veronica longifolia, Veronica spicata

Veronica, Speedwell

- ◆ **Zones:** 5–9
- ◆ **Light:** full sun to partial shade
- ◆ **Soil:** well-drained
- ◆ **Size:** medium
- ◆ **Color:** white, blue, pink
- ◆ **Season:** early summer to fall

Veronica is a great perennial for the traditional border. Both varieties have long, thin leaves that grow on upright stems in clumps 12 to 24 inches high and half as wide. *V. longifolia* has larger, crinkled leaves. In June, it comes into bloom with long, pointed spikes of tiny flowers. It continues to bloom throughout summer and on into fall, and is well liked by butterflies and bees. Remove the faded flowers to keep the plants in bloom. Plant in full sun, but some afternoon shade is preferable in the middle of

Photo 12.193
Sunny border blue veronica, *Veronica longifolia* '*Sunny Border Blue*'

POPULAR VARIETIES

V. l. 'Sunny Border Blue' has long, deep blue flower spikes and was the "1993 Perennial Plant of the Year."

V. s. 'Blue Charm' has light blue flower spikes.

V. s. 'Blue Fox' has bright blue flower spikes.

V. s. 'Goodness Grows' has blue-violet flower spikes.

V. s. 'Icicle' has clean, white flower spikes.

V. s. 'Red Fox' has rosy pink flower spikes.

Veronica peduncularis 'Georgia Blue'

Creeping Speedwell

- ◆ **Zones:** 5–9
- ◆ **Light:** full sun to partial shade
- ◆ **Soil:** well-drained
- ◆ **Size:** low
- ◆ **Color:** blue
- ◆ **Season:** late spring to early summer

Photo 12.191 *(far left)*
White Veronica, *Veronica spicata 'Icicle'*

Creeping speedwell is an extremely low-growing, sprawling plant, reaching 6 to 8 inches high and 12 to 24 inches wide. It has small leaves on thin stems and forms a low mat of foliage that is semievergreen. In April to June, it blooms with small, deep blue flowers. Shear it back after it blooms to keep the foliage neat and tidy. Plant it at the front of the border and where it can spill over rocks, walls, and planters. Good drainage is necessary to keep it from wilting.

Other Vs

Viola odorata, or wood violet (also known as sweet violet), is a low, green, lush plant with small heart-shaped leaves. It spreads underground by runners and stays very low. In February to April, it blooms with small purple flowers. Flower color depends on the variety. Closely related to viola, it has a similar flower shape that is extremely fragrant and attractive to bees and butterflies. It needs ample moisture in the hottest parts of the year and should have afternoon shade or partial shade, so it is best for the woodland or shady border. It is hardy to zone 6.

Popular Varieties

'Royal Robe' has dark purple flowers and is the most common variety sold.

'White Czar' has white flowers.

V. missouriensis, the native wood violet, is in fact native and has lavender flowers. It can be aggressive in the right conditions.

Z

Zantedeschia species

Calla Lily

◆ **Zones:** 8–10

◆ **Light:** full sun to partial shade

◆ **Soil:** well-drained, moist

◆ **Size:** medium

◆ **Color:** white, yellow, pink

◆ **Season:** early to midsummer

Calla lily is a tropical looking perennial with large, lush, arrow-shaped foliage that grows in clumps. Evergreen in southern zones, it dies down to the ground where the winters drop below freezing. In May through July, it blooms with a large bract, called a spathe, which surrounds a central spike. The standard calla has a white spathe, but it also blooms in shades of yellow, pink, and violet. Plant from bulbs 2 to 4 inches deep in soils rich in humus. It does well in boggy soils, too. It will tolerate full sun where soil moisture is consistent, but afternoon shade is necessary in drier soils. It also does well planted in pots that can be moved indoors, especially in cold climates where it is not winter-hardy.

POPULAR VARIETIES

Z. aethiopica, the common calla, has white flowers.

Z. albomaculata, the spotted calla, has large leaves with white spots. Flower color varies from white to yellow.

Z. rehamannii, the red calla, has long, lance-shaped leaves and flowers that bloom in shades of red, pink, and violet.

Zephyranthus candida
White Rain Lily

◆ **Zones:** 7–10

◆ **Light:** full sun to light shade

◆ **Soil:** well-drained, moist

◆ **Size:** low

◆ **Color:** white

◆ **Season:** midsummer to early fall

Rain lily is an easy-care plant with dark green, grassy foliage that grows in low clumps. The foliage is thick, hollow, and evergreen. It grows 6 to 8 inches high and wide, blooming in midsummer with large, white crocuslike flowers. In nature, rain lily blooms only after rain showers, but in gardens, where water is more consistent, it blooms on and off until mid-September. Plant it from small bulbs, 2 inches deep, at the front of the border. It will handle wet soils. Being evergreen, it makes a nice edger to the border and looks good planted among ophiopogon, which has similar foliage.

RELATED SPECIES

Z. sulphurea, yellow rain lily, has bright yellow flowers.

Z. robusta, pink rain lily, has bright pink flowers.

Photo 12.196
White rain lily,
Zephyranthus candida

Zexmenia hispida
Zexmenia

◆ **Zones:** 5–10

◆ **Light:** full sun to light shade

◆ **Soil:** well-drained, dry

◆ **Size:** medium

◆ **Color:** yellow

◆ **Season:** early summer to fall

Zexmenia is a durable, shrubby-type perennial native to South and West Texas. It has narrow green leaves on bushy stems that grow 24 to 30 inches high and wide. It remains evergreen or semievergreen in southern zones, but dies to the ground in Dallas and colder regions. Starting in June, it comes into bloom with small, bright yellow daisies. It is drought tolerant and long lived once established. Plant in sunny borders, especially with other natives, or in Xeriscape gardens.

Photo 12.197
Zexmenia, *Zexmenia hispida*

Chapter Thirteen
FERNS

*F*erns are ancient plants that predate
flowering plants. They are a group of
clump-forming plants that produce
fronds, which unfurl from a center point. As the
fronds develop, they produce spores, which fall
off and become new ferns. Most ferns grow in
woodlands, where conditions are shady, moist,
and full of organic matter. These are the
conditions you need or must reproduce in order
for ferns to grow and thrive. Obviously, conditions
are more ideal in the eastern and north central
parts of the state where humidity, soils, and
available shade are more prevalent.

Plant ferns in shady and semishady conditions with deep, moist soils. Provide consistent irrigation, especially in the hot summer months. Morning sun is fine for most of them, but afternoon shade is usually necessary. Fertilize them in early spring. They have few disease or insect problems and are easy to care for. They do well with spring bulbs like daffodils and summer snowflake planted among them. As the foliage from the bulbs dies, the fronds from the ferns mask it. Place them with other shade lovers like columbine, coral bells, and hostas.

Arachinoides simplicior 'Variegata'

Variegated Shield Fern

- ◆ **Zones:** 9–10
- ◆ **Light:** partial shade to shade
- ◆ **Soil:** moist
- ◆ **Size:** low
- ◆ **Foliage Color:** green and yellow
- ◆ **Season:** year-round

Variegated shield fern has dark green fronds with bright yellow stripes down the center. Evergreen to semievergreen, it is listed as hardy to

Photo 13.2 *(right)*
Southern maidenhair fern,
Adiantum capillus-veneris

Photo 13.3 *(far right)*
Japanese painted fern,
Athyrium niponicum 'Pictum'

Photo 13.4 *(right)*
Fronds of southern wood
fern, *Thelypteris kunthii*,
catch the afternoon light

Photo 13.5 *(far right)*
Variegated shield fern,
*Arachinoides simplicior
'Variegata'*

zone 9, but with some protection, it will return in zone 8 after it dies down in winter. It is low growing and reaches 12 to 18 inches high.

Adiantum capillus-veneris
Southern Maidenhair Fern

- ◆ **Zones:** 8–10
- ◆ **Light:** partial shade to shade
- ◆ **Soil:** moist
- ◆ **Size:** low
- ◆ **Foliage Color:** light green
- ◆ **Season:** summer

Photo 13.6
Southern maidenhair fern,
Adiantum capillus-veneris

Southern maidenhair fern is a low-growing, deciduous fern with light green, finely textured fronds and tiny fan-shaped leaflets. Native to eastern parts of Texas, it is tolerant of high soil pH but is intolerant of dry soils. It grows 10 to 15 inches high and wide.

Athyrium niponicum
Japanese Painted Fern

- ◆ **Zones:** 8–10
- ◆ **Light:** shade to light shade
- ◆ **Soil:** moist
- ◆ **Size:** medium
- ◆ **Foliage Color:** blue-green
- ◆ **Season:** year-round

Japanese painted fern has beautiful evergreen fronds. In spring, when new fronds unfurl, it has shades of blue, purple, and gray, turning greener in summer. It looks especially great with the purple shades of coral bells like *'Palace Purple.'* Keep it moist and protected from hot sun. It may burn a bit in winter, but the new fronds emerge

Photo 13.7 (far left)
Japanese painted fern,
Athyrium niponicum 'Pictum'

Photo 13.8 (left)
Holly fern,
Cyrtomium falcatumfgc

Photo 13.9 (far left)
Autumn fern,
Dryopteris erythrosora

Photo 13.10 (left)
Southern wood fern,
Thelypteris kunthi

wonderfully each spring. It grows 24 inches high and wide.

Cyrtomium falcatum

Holly Fern

- ◆ **Zones:** 8–10
- ◆ **Light:** shade to light shade
- ◆ **Soil:** moist, well-drained
- ◆ **Size:** low to medium
- ◆ **Foliage Color:** bright green
- ◆ **Season:** year-round

Holly fern is a sturdy, bolder-looking fern than most. It has large, evergreen fronds with thick, waxy leaflets. The spores on the underside of the leaves are very pronounced. In coastal areas it grows to 30 inches high and wide. In northern areas, it may grow to only 18 to 24 inches high and wide. The leaves may burn in winter but will be replaced in spring with the new growth. Of all the ferns, this one is probably the sturdiest and takes the most sun.

Dryopteris erythrosora

Autumn Fern

- ◆ **Zones:** 5–10
- ◆ **Light:** shade to light shade
- ◆ **Soil:** moist, well-drained
- ◆ **Size:** low to medium
- ◆ **Foliage Color:** coppery green
- ◆ **Season:** year-round

Autumn fern is another evergreen or semievergreen fern with medium green foliage. The tips are lighter and have overtones of copper and red. The glossy, new growth is especially coppery and reddish. Like other evergreen ferns, it may burn in winter, especially cold winters, but it will quickly bounce back in spring. It grows 18 to 24 inches high and wide.

Thelypteris kunthii

Southern Wood Fern

- ◆ **Zones:** 8–10
- ◆ **Light:** shade to light shade

- ◆ **Soil:** moist, well-drained
- ◆ **Size:** low to medium
- ◆ **Foliage Color:** green
- ◆ **Season:** summer

The Southern wood fern is probably the most popular fern for Southern gardens. It grows eas-ily and, along with the holly fern, is the sturdiest and most sun and soil tolerant. It has long, medium green, delicate fronds that light up when catching early morning or late-afternoon sun. The dimensions of light and shadow in a large mass of wood ferns are breathtaking. It works especially well with daffodils, which pro-vide spring color before its fronds emerge.

Photo 14.1
Maiden grass plumes,
Miscanthus species,
catch the late summer light

Chapter Fourteen
THE GRASSES

*G*rasses are perennials that make great companion plants in the border. They generally require little care, add year-round color and texture, and peak at the end of summer when the other flowers begin to wane. They dance in the breeze and catch the light of the sun as it goes low. As they wave in the hot summer wind, the rustling sounds provide a cool, soothing music. Even though most are not evergreen, they hold their form through winter and provide interest even when they are dormant. They look best planted in large drifts but also work singularly as sculptural accents. Cut them down to the base in February before the new foliage emerges in spring.

Acorus gramineus

Variegated Sweet Flag

- ◆ **Zones:** 6–10
- ◆ **Light:** partial shade to shade
- ◆ **Soil:** moist
- ◆ **Size:** low
- ◆ **Foliage Color:** creamy white
- ◆ **Texture:** fine
- ◆ **Season:** year-round

Sweet flag is a low-growing, evergreen grass with creamy white stripes. It blooms in summer, but the plumes are quite insignificant. Sweet flag grows well in moist soils, will grow in permanently wet soils and bogs, and is quite often used on the edges of lily ponds. If you plant it in full sun, plant on the edge of water. It grows only 8 to 10 inches tall in clumps. Plant sweet flag at the front of the border in large drifts.

A. calamus 'Variegatus' is another evergreen grass that grows 24 to 36 inches high with thin-bladed leaves that are ½-inch wide. Like

"Grasses dance in the breeze and are silent in the storm."

ARAB PROVERB

other acorus, it is evergreen, with creamy white stripes on top of light green. It prefers shade but will grow in sun with wet soils or on the edges of ponds.

Andropogon species

Bluestem Grasses

- ◆ **Zones:** 4–9
- ◆ **Light:** sun to light shade
- ◆ **Soil:** well-drained to dry
- ◆ **Size:** tall
- ◆ **Foliage Color:** blue-green to red and purple in fall

- ◆ **Texture:** fine to bold
- ◆ **Season:** summer to winter

Bluestem grass along with Indian grass and switchgrass makes up the majority of the grasses of the Tall Prairies, which start in Texas. Typically, bluestem is a large grass growing 4 to 6 feet high with bluish to purplish stems and green leaves that turn beautiful shades of red, purple, and cinnamon in fall and winter. Once established, it is drought tolerant and should not be irrigated on a regular basis. It is probably best used in large meadows and native plantings.

POPULAR VARIETIES

A. gerardii var. gerardii, big bluestem, grows 5 to 6 foot high and half as wide. It has blue-green foliage and forked plumes that resemble birds' feet.

A. virginicus, broomsedge bluestem, grows 3 to 5 feet tall and has green foliage in summer but turns orange-red in winter. It prefers moist to well-drained soils.

A. glomeratus, bushy bluestem, grows only about 3 feet high and has green foliage in summer that turns beautiful cinnamon in winter. It has attractive, fluffy seed heads in fall. It also prefers moist soils. Because of its size and character, this is probably the best one for the garden.

Sideoats grama is the official State Grass of Texas. It grows in low clumps that stand 18 to 24 inches high and wide. The foliage is light green and finely textured. In summer, it produces tiny seedheads that droop to the side. It will go dormant in winter and is extremely drought tolerant. This grass is best used for native-type plantings.

Schizachyrium scoparium, little bluestem, grows 3 to 6 feet high and forms tight, upright bunches. The foliage is bluish, turning cinnamon in winter. Irrigate only to get it established.

Bouteloua curtipendula var. caespitosa

Sideoats Grama

- ◆ **Zones:** 6–10
- ◆ **Light:** partial shade to shade
- ◆ **Soil:** moist
- ◆ **Size:** low
- ◆ **Foliage Color:** grayish green
- ◆ **Texture:** fine
- ◆ **Season:** year-round

Calamagrostis arundinacea 'Karl Foerster'

Karl Foerster Feather Reed Grass

- ◆ **Zones:** 5–9
- ◆ **Light:** sun to light shade
- ◆ **Soil:** well-drained to moist
- ◆ **Size:** tall
- ◆ **Foliage Color:** green with tan plumes
- ◆ **Season:** fall to spring

Feather reed grass is a cool season grass that may not handle heat, drought, and heavy soils as well as most of the others listed. It is a clumping grass with fine, dark green foliage that is very upright. Large, bronze, feathery plumes up to 6-feet tall appear in fall. The plumes grow straight up and make a wonderful accent. It also looks great planted in mass. Be sure to keep it

irrigated during the hot, dry months. It has not been planted much in Texas and is probably best for the northern and eastern zones. This feather grass was the "2001 Perennial of the Year."

Chasmanthium latifolium
Inland Sea Oats

- ◆ **Zones:** 5–10
- ◆ **Light:** partial shade to shade
- ◆ **Soil:** moist to well-drained
- ◆ **Size:** medium
- ◆ **Foliage Color:** green
- ◆ **Texture:** fine
- ◆ **Season:** summer

Inland sea oats grows naturally in East Texas in a loose, clumping form that has light green bamboolike foliage on long, delicate stems. In summer, it produces showy, drooping flowers and seed heads that resemble oats. The flowers wave in the breeze and turn golden brown before the foliage does. The effect is elegant and showy, and the plant makes a nice sound as the foliage blows in the wind. In autumn, the foliage quickly turns brown and falls down.

Inland sea oats does not seem to be particular about soil types as long as they are fairly moist. In shade, it can withstand drying soils, but it needs consistent moisture when it receives a lot of sun. The leaves are thin and do not look as healthy in full sun, either.

Elymus glaucus
Blue Wild Rye

- ◆ **Zones:** 4–8
- ◆ **Light:** light to light shade
- ◆ **Soil:** well-drained to dry

> ## BULLY ALERT
>
> Plant horsetail reed only in beds, containers, or planters where it cannot spread easily. Treat it as you would bamboo.

- ◆ **Size:** medium
- ◆ **Foliage Color:** blue
- ◆ **Texture:** fine
- ◆ **Season:** year round

Blue wild rye is a deciduous grass that multiplies by runners underground. The foliage is very blue, growing 24 inches high. Good drainage is a necessity, and blue wild rye is quite drought tolerant once established. Heavy soils will kill it.

Equisetum hyemale
Horsetail Reed

- ◆ **Zones:** 4–10
- ◆ **Light:** partial shade to shade
- ◆ **Soil:** moist to well-drained
- ◆ **Size:** medium to tall
- ◆ **Foliage Color:** green
- ◆ **Texture:** medium
- ◆ **Season:** year-round

Horsetail reed is an evergreen, moisture-loving grass that has thick, jointed reeds that grow to 36 to 48 inches high. The reeds are bright, emerald green and very exotic looking. It spreads quickly by underground runners and can be very invasive, especially in moist areas. Horsetail reed will grow in sun or shade.

RELATED VARIETY

E. scirpoides, dwarf horsetail reed, is similar but grows to only 6 to 8 inches high and is very delicate. It is not quite as invasive and is hardy to zone 5.

Photo 14.12 *(far left)*
Horsetail reed,
Equisetum hyem...

Photo 14.13 *(left)*
Weeping love grass,
Eragrostis curvula

◆ **Size:** low

◆ **Foliage Color:** silvery-blue

◆ **Texture:** fine

◆ **Season:** summer

Blue fescue is a low-growing evergreen grass that forms tight little clumps with silvery blue, finely textured foliage and grows 8 inches high and wide. Wet roots and humidity will bring about root rot, causing it to die out. Plant it where the air circulation is good. The color is outstanding and works well at the front of the border backed by other blues or bright yellows. It works well in pots and raised planters. It sends up finely textured plumes in early summer.

'Elijah Blue' variety has a more consistent blue, grows 10 to 12 inches high, and has buff-colored seed heads in spring.

Eragrostis curvula

Weeping Love Grass

◆ **Zones:** 7–10

◆ **Light:** sun to light shade.

◆ **Soil:** well-drained to dry

◆ **Size:** low to medium

◆ **Foliage Color:** green to gray-green

◆ **Texture:** fine

◆ **Season:** summer

Weeping love grass is a deciduous perennial grass that makes an excellent ground cover, especially on dry sunny slopes. It has gray-green weeping foliage that grows 24 to 36 inches high and wide and blooms in midsummer with fluffy, tan plumes. Both the plumes and foliage weep and curl under. In winter, the foliage turns a tawny buff color. Plant it as a mass at the front of the border or as an accent in full sun to light shade. It is drought and heat tolerant.

Festuca ovina glauca

Blue Fescue

◆ **Zones:** 4–10

◆ **Light:** sun to light shade

◆ **Soil:** well-drained to dry

Photo 14.14
Blue fescue,
Festuca ovina glauca

Hakonechloa macro 'Aureola'

Golden Japanese Forest Grass

◆ **Zones:** 5–9

◆ **Light:** partial shade to shade

◆ **Soil:** moist

◆ **Size:** low

Photo 14.15 *(right)*
Golden Japanese forest grass, *Hakonechloa macro 'Aureola'*

Photo 14.16 *(far right)*
Japanese blood grass, *Imperata cylindrica 'Red Baron'*

◆ **Foliage Color:** golden-yellow variegated

◆ **Texture:** fine

◆ **Season:** summer

Photo 14.17 *(far right)*
Maiden grass, *Miscanthus sinensis 'Gracillimus'*

Golden Japanese forest grass is a beautiful, low-growing deciduous grass, with finely dissected bamboolike foliage. The leaves are golden yellow with thin chartreuse stripes. The flower plumes appear in late summer. It grows 12 to 18 inches high but droops and has a flowing quality. Plant Japanese forest grass in moist, rich soils with plenty of humus. Be sure to keep it evenly moist in the heat of summer, or it will dry out. Plant it among ferns, Japanese anemones, and purple coral bells.

Photo 14.18 *(far right)*
Zebra grass, *Miscanthus sinensis 'Zebrinus'*

Imperata cylindrica 'Red Baron'

Japanese Blood Grass

◆ **Zones:** 5–9

◆ **Light:** sun to partial shade

◆ **Soil:** moist to well-drained

◆ **Size:** low

◆ **Foliage Color:** red

◆ **Texture:** fine

◆ **Season:** summer

BULLY ALERT

Japanese blood grass has become invasive in eastern parts of the United States but does not appear to be a problem in Texas.

Japanese blood grass is a striking, low-growing grass. The foliage is fine, grows 18 to 24 inches high and spreads underground. The leaves are greenish at the base and turn bright red at the tops. The color is striking and bold in summer. In Texas, afternoon shade is best to keep the foliage from scalding. It goes completely dormant in winter.

'Red Baron' variety has darker, richer red foliage.

Miscanthus sinensis

Miscanthus, Maiden Grass, Japanese Silver Grass

◆ **Zones:** 5–10

◆ **Light:** full sun to light shade

◆ **Soil:** moist, well-drained

◆ **Size:** medium to tall

◆ **Foliage Color:** varies

◆ **Texture:** fine

◆ **Season:** summer to fall

The *Miscanthus species* comprises one of the biggest and most useful groups of ornamental grasses used in the landscape industry. These grasses are tall, architectural, and easily cared for. They tolerate a variety of conditions and seem to thrive with or without regular irrigation. In fact, many native grasses will not grow with continual irrigation, but these will. They prefer acidic soils but will grow quite well where the levels are more alkaline. Many varieties have been developed within the industry, offering a variety of colors, sizes, and shapes.

Except for the dwarf varieties, plant them in the back of the border. They look marvelous in huge, sweeping drifts but work well as accents, too. The variegated cultivars look especially good as individual accents. Most of them begin blooming in midsummer, sending up feathery plumes. In late summer and fall, the plumes and the leaves catch the late afternoon sunlight and seem to glow. Although they go dormant in winter, turning shades of tan and gold, they hold their structure well through the end of February. Then, cut them off at the base, so the new year's foliage can emerge. Fertilize them in spring as the new leaves emerge.

POPULAR VARIETIES

'Adagio,' Adagio dwarf silver grass, is a dwarf miscanthus that grows only 24 inches high with silvery foliage and a mounding habit. It blooms heavily in summer with plumes up to 48 inches high. This is a good miscanthus for small gardens.

'Cabaret,' cabaret maiden grass, has showy foliage that is creamy white, green, and a little pink. The foliage is wide and grows to 6 feet high. In September, it blooms with copper-colored plumes.

'Gracillimus,' maiden grass, is the most common and well-known miscanthus. It has thin, fine green leaves with a silver vertical midrib and has extremely delicate foliage that grows 5 feet high. In September, it develops coppery plumes that catch the light in fall.

'Morning Light,' Japanese silver grass, has thin, silvery foliage and grows 4 to 5 feet high. The flower plumes are reddish bronze when they emerge in fall.

'Silberfeder,' silver feather grass, is a taller variety growing 6 to 7 feet tall. The foliage is rich green with a silver midrib. The fluffy plumes stand high above the foliage.

'Stictus,' porcupine grass, is a green grass with horizontal white stripes on the leaves. It grows only 4 to 5 feet tall and is more heat and drought tolerant.

'Variegatus,' variegated miscanthus, has creamy white bands that run vertically along the edges of the leaves. It has a bright, clean color and makes a nice accent. Growing 4 to 5 feet high, the grass develops bronze blooms that fade to creamy white in fall.

'Yaku-Jima,' dwarf miscanthus, is the smallest of the miscanthus grasses, growing only 3 to 4 feet high. It has green foliage that turns reddish in fall. The plumes are bronze in fall turning creamy white.

'Zebrinus,' zebra grass, is a larger leaf miscanthus with dark green foliage and pronounced creamy white horizontal bands. It grows to 6 feet high and has coppery pink plumes in fall. It appreciates moisture and will grow alongside ponds. However, it grows well in fairly dry sites that have some light shade.

Muhlenbergia species

Muhly Grasses

The muhly grasses, largely native to Texas, are heat and drought tolerant and can be planted in the desert with irrigation. Plant them in full sun to light shade in very well-drained soils, and they should grow and bloom with abandon. They are becoming increasingly more prevalent in Texas.

Muhlenbergia capillaris

Gulf Muhly, Hairyawn Muhly

◆ **Zones:** 7–10

◆ **Light:** full sun to light shade

◆ **Soil:** well-drained to dry

◆ **Size:** low to medium

◆ **Foliage Color:** green, red plumes in fall

◆ **Texture:** fine

◆ **Season:** summer to fall

Photo 14.22 (far right)
Bamboo muhly,
Muhlenbergia dumosa

Photo 14.21
Regal mist muhly,
Muhlenbergia capillaris
'Regal Mist'

Gulf muhly is a finely textured, clumping grass with grayish-green foliage. It is semievergreen in lower parts of the state and turns buff in winter in northern parts. The foliage grows 24 to 30 inches high and wide. The real beauty of this grass is its blooms in August and September, which are fine plumes of pinkish red, so fine that they almost resemble pink smoke. Gulf muhly is especially vibrant in the sun. *'Regal Mist'* variety has more vibrant red flowers.

Muhlenbergia dumosa

Bamboo Muhly

◆ **Zones:** 8–10

◆ **Light:** full sun to light shade

Photo 14.23 (far right)
Lindhiemers muhly,
Muhlenbergia lindhiemerii

◆ **Soil:** well-drained to dry

◆ **Size:** tall

◆ **Foliage Color:** green

◆ **Texture:** fine

◆ **Season:** summer

Bamboo muhly is a tall-growing grass with soft, billowy foliage that waves and dances in the breeze. The fine foliage resembles bamboo. The arching stems grow 3 to 6 feet tall. It goes dormant in winter and is not as hardy as the other muhlys.

Muhlenbergia lindhiemerii

Lindhiemers Muhly

◆ **Zones:** 7–10

◆ **Light:** full sun to light shade

◆ **Soil:** well-drained to dry

◆ **Size:** tall

◆ **Foliage Color:** blue-green

◆ **Texture:** fine

◆ **Season:** year-round

Lindhiemers muhly is a Texas native that grows well in many conditions. This is one of the best grasses for Texas gardens. It forms a large tuft with grayish blue-green foliage that is finely textured and arches gracefully. It stays evergreen to semievergreen in winter. In August through October, the grass sends up feathery plumes 5 to 6 feet high. The plumes are copper colored turning buff in winter and holding their form until spring. The plumes work well in dried arrangements, as well. Well-drained soils are best, but it seems to hold up in heavy clay soils. It is very drought tolerant once established, but handles a fair amount of water if the soils drain. Plant this instead of the larger, coarser pampas grass.

Muhlenbergia rigens
Deer Grass, Deer Muhly

- ◆ **Zones:** 7–10
- ◆ **Light:** full sun to light shade
- ◆ **Soil:** well-drained to dry
- ◆ **Size:** low to medium
- ◆ **Foliage Color:** green
- ◆ **Texture:** fine-medium
- ◆ **Season:** year-round

Deer grass is an evergreen grass that grows in low, mounding clumps. Extremely heat and drought tolerant, it does well in the desert, although it will also grow quite well in light shade. The foliage is medium green and coarser than the other muhlys. It has small plumes in late summer.

Nasella tenuissima
Mexican Feather Grass

- ◆ **Zones:** 7–10
- ◆ **Light:** full sun to light shade
- ◆ **Soil:** well-drained to dry
- ◆ **Size:** low to medium
- ◆ **Foliage Color:** green
- ◆ **Texture:** fine
- ◆ **Season:** winter to early summer

Photo 14.25
Mexican feather grass,
Nasella tenuissima, in winter

Mexican feather grass is a fine, delicate grass that grows in winter and early spring with bright green, hair-like foliage that is soft and wispy and blows gently in the breeze. It grows only 18 inches high and wide in a mounding, spraylike form. In spring it develops soft, feathery plumes. The grass goes dormant in summer and softens to a buff color. It is extremely heat and drought tolerant and grows well in planters and pots.

Panicum virgatum
Switch Grass

- ◆ **Zones:** 5–10
- ◆ **Light:** full sun to light shade
- ◆ **Soil:** moist to well-drained to dry
- ◆ **Size:** medium to tall
- ◆ **Foliage Color:** green, metallic blue
- ◆ **Texture:** fine
- ◆ **Season:** summer to fall

Switch grass is a tall native, perennial, bunching grass with upright, blue-green foliage that turns reddish in fall. It has delicate silvery plumes in summer, which wave in the wind. It grows naturally in moist soils but tolerates drought and heat.

Photo 14.24 *(far left)*
Deer grass,
Muhlenbergia rigens

Photo 14.26
Heavy metal switch grass,
Panicum virgatum
'Heavy Metal'

3'/4'

POPULAR VARIETIES

'Prairie Sky' grows only 3 to 4 feet high, with upright, silvery blue foliage. The inflorescences are steely blue and turn tan in fall. It tolerates areas with poor drainage.

'Heavy Metal' has striking, dark, metallic blue foliage in upright, tight clumps. The inflorescences stand high above the foliage and are metallic and shiny.

Pennisetum species
Fountain Grasses

The fountain grasses are low to medium grasses with fine texture, weeping habit, and fuzzy plumes in summer. They are tolerant of moist to dry soils and can take a fair amount of drought once established, although it is best to provide them with irrigation in the hottest months. They grow well in full sun to light shade and have few problems except with heavy, alkaline soils. In summer they do fine, but don't survive the winter well in the heavy clay. Provide rich, well-drained soils if you want them to be permanent. They are deciduous and turn golden tan in winter but hold their shape quite well. Cut down near the base in late winter before the new foliage begins to grow. Note: *Pennisetum setaceum 'Rubrum,'* or purple fountain grass, is hardy in only the southernmost regions of the state.

Pennisetum alopecuroides 'Hameln'
Dwarf Fountain Grass

◆ **Zones:** 5–9

◆ **Light:** full sun to light shade

◆ **Soil:** moist to well-drained

◆ **Size:** low to medium

◆ **Foliage Color:** light green

◆ **Texture:** fine

◆ **Season:** summer to fall

Dwarf fountain grass has a clump-forming habit with fine, light green, cascading blades. It grows only 24 to 36 inches high and wide and is covered with fluffy little buff-colored plumes in summer. This grass looks striking when planted in mass or as individual accents in a smaller garden. It is drought tolerant but needs irrigation in the heat of summer. In winter, it needs good drainage to stay dry. *'Little Bunny'* variety is similar, but grows to only 12 inches high and wide.

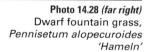

Photo 14.27 *(right)*
Fountain grasses, *Pennisetum species*, with regal mist muhly add life to the summer garden

Photo 14.28 *(far right)*
Dwarf fountain grass, *Pennisetum alopecuroides* 'Hameln'

Pennisetum alopecuroides 'Moudry'

Black Fountain Grass

- ◆ **Zones:** 5–9
- ◆ **Light:** full sun to light shade
- ◆ **Soil:** moist to well-drained
- ◆ **Size:** low to medium
- ◆ **Foliage Color:** late green with black plumes
- ◆ **Texture:** fine to medium
- ◆ **Season:** summer to fall

Black fountain grass is similar to dwarf fountain grass, except the leaves are wider and the plumes are a dark purplish black. Also, it grows only 18 to 24 inches high and wide, and it looks great in mass or as an accent in small gardens. The dark plumes look striking set off from the green foliage. This one seems to handle the heavy clay soils a little bit better than others. It is heat and drought tolerant.

Pennisetum orientale

Oriental Fountain Grass

- ◆ **Zones:** 5–9
- ◆ **Light:** full sun to light shade
- ◆ **Soil:** moist to well-drained
- ◆ **Size:** low to medium
- ◆ **Foliage Color:** late green
- ◆ **Texture:** fine
- ◆ **Season:** summer to fall

Oriental fountain grass is similar to dwarf fountain grass except it grows only 18 to 24 inches high and wide. The plumes are smaller and more delicate that those of the dwarf fountain grass. The texture is extremely fine. Being

shorter, it does not cascade as much. Care requirements are similar to the other fountain grasses.

Sorghastrum nutans

Indian Grass

- ◆ **Zones:** 4–10
- ◆ **Light:** full sun to light shade
- ◆ **Soil:** well-drained to dry
- ◆ **Size:** tall
- ◆ **Foliage Color:** varies
- ◆ **Texture:** fine to medium
- ◆ **Season:** summer to fall

Indian grass is a large, clumping grass with long, upright blue-green leaves and fine, coppery panicles, which wave in the breeze. It grows 5 to 6 feet tall and half as wide. A native prairie grass, it is well adapted to Texas soils and handles heat and drought well once established. Plant this one in natural settings and in Xeriscape gardens.

Photo 14.29 (far left)
Black fountain grass,
*Pennisetum alopecuroides
'Moudry'*

Photo 14.30 (left)
Oriental fountain grass,
Pennisetum orientale

Photo 14.31
Sioux blue Indian grass,
*Sorghastrum nutans
'Sioux Blue'*

'Sioux Blue' variety is a more refined cultivar that has striking blue-gray foliage in dense, upright clumps. It grows only 3 to 5 feet high and looks a bit more domesticated than the original. The color is beautiful when planted in mass.

Typha latifolia

Cattail Reed

- ◆ **Zones:** 4–10
- ◆ **Light:** full sun to light shade
- ◆ **Soil:** moist, well-drained
- ◆ **Size:** tall
- ◆ **Foliage Color:** green with brown plumes
- ◆ **Texture:** medium to coarse
- ◆ **Season:** summer to fall

Photo 14.32
Cattail reeds, *Typha latifolia*

Cattail is a native reed that pops up along lakes, ponds, and anywhere that it is seasonally wet. It grows 4 to 5 feet tall but will grow taller if given ample moisture. The foliage is long, green, and swordlike. In summer, it quickly develops large plumes packed with brown fuzzy seeds. This one is probably best used in native plantings where you have large bodies of water or boggy meadows. It gets quite large and can be invasive. Its smaller cousin, dwarf cattail reed, may be better.

The related *T. minima*, dwarf cattail reed, has the same look, but grows only 3 feet high and has smaller plumes. The foliage is quite thin, and the texture is very fine. Plant it in wet to well-drained soils or in bogs and water gardens. Dwarf cattail is hardy only to zone 6.

OTHER GRASSES

Carex glauca, blue sedge, is an evergreen perennial grass that forms clumps with graceful, arching foliage. The leaves are soft gray-blue and grow 10 to 12 inches high and wide. Be sure to provide even irrigation during hot, dry months. Blue sedge is said to grow better than blue fescue in Texas. It is hardy to zone 6 and grows in moist soils in shade and partial shade.

Carex marrowii 'Aureo-Variegata,' variegated Japanese sedge, is an evergreen perennial grass with creamy white and green striped foliage growing 18 to 24 inches high and wide forming a clump. It prefers moist soils and will even grow in wet, boggy areas and alongside ponds. It is hardy to zone 5.

Deschampsia caespitosa, tufted hair grass, is a native perennial with very fine, green foliage, which grows 18 to 24 inches high in clumps that curl under. The flowers are extremely fine and silvery, born on delicate stems, 24 to 30 inches above the evergreen foliage in summer. It is useful in native plantings and is hardy to zone 5. Plant tufted hair grass in moist to dry soils and sun to partial shady spots.

Photo 15.1 *(opposite page)*
Blue lacecap hydrangea,
Hydrangea macrophylla
'Bluebird'

Chapter Fifteen
Shrubs, Vines, and Roses

*S*hrubs, along with hard materials like walls, fences, paving, and edgers, provide the "bones" or structure of the garden. They give the garden distinct form as the perennials, ferns, and grasses come and go. Taller shrubs, especially evergreens, like upright hollies and Texas sages, provide backgrounds. Others, like Anthony Waterer spirea and red yucca, are lower and blend into the border while providing color for one or more seasons. Still others are very low or can be sheared low, like boxwood and dwarf yaupon holly, to provide an evergreen edge to the front of the border. Whether you have a sunny formal garden or a shady woodland, there is a shrub for every garden.

Vines, such as Confederate jasmine and Carolina Jessamine, can be trained on walls and trellises to provide a backdrop as well. Others, like clematis, are free to climb up trellises or ramble through the border.

Agave species

Agave, Century Plant

◆ **Zones:** 7–10

◆ **Light:** full sun to very light shade

◆ **Soil:** well-drained, dry

◆ **Size:** low to medium

◆ **Color:** green, blue, yellow, and variegated evergreen foliage

◆ **Season:** year-round

Agaves are clump-forming, evergreen plants with long pointed leaves. Depending on the type, they grow 15 to 48 inches high and wide. Foliage color varies. One of the most common, *Agave americana*, has large extremely sharp, pointed, blue leaves. Don't plant it next to heavily traveled sidewalks. It is extremely drought tolerant and should be planted where it always gets good drainage. Use it as an accent in a Southwestern border. It will bloom after growing 10 to 20 years. Flower stalks grow 20 feet and die after blooming. However, by that

Photo 15.2 (left)
Jackman clematis,
Clematis x 'Jackmanii'

Photo 15.3 (far left)
English rose Graham Thomas,
Rosa 'Graham Thomas'

Photo 15.4
Blooming spirea and
viburnum provide a colorful
backdrop midspring

◆ **Size:** low to medium

◆ **Color:** red foliage

◆ **Season:** summer to fall

Barberries are deciduous shrubs with small leaves and prickly thorns. Redleaf barberry has bright red foliage all summer and grows 4 to 6 feet high and wide. It can be sheared into about any shape. The color intensifies in fall before it loses its leaves.

POPULAR VARIETIES

'Crimson Pygmy' is bright red and grows only 18 to 24 inches high and wide.

'Rose Glow' has pink and white marbled leaves with. It works better with pinks and blues.

'Limemound' has bright yellow-green foliage that seems to glow.

Photo 15.5
Century plant, *Agave species*

time pups, or smaller plants, have formed at the base to replace it.

Berberis thunbergii 'Atropurpurea'
Redleaf Barberry

◆ **Zones:** 6–9

◆ **Light:** full sun to light shade

◆ **Soil:** well-drained, dry

Photo 15.6 (far right)
Redleaf barberry, *Berberis thunbergii 'Atropurpurea'*

Photo 15.7 *(far left)*
Cross vine, *Bignonia caprolata 'Tangerine'*

Photo 15.8 *(left)*
Clipped littleleaf boxwood, *Buxus sempervirens*

Bignonia caprolata (Anisostichus capreolata)

Cross Vine

- ◆ **Zones:** 6–9
- ◆ **Light:** full sun to partial shade
- ◆ **Soil:** well-drained, moist
- ◆ **Size:** tall
- ◆ **Color:** yellow, orange, red flowers
- ◆ **Season:** early spring to late summer

Cross vine is an evergreen vine that grows 20 feet high. It can be trained easily up walls and trellises. Starting at the end of February, it comes into bloom with orange-red, almost brown, tubular flowers. They bloom heavily in spring, then sporadically throughout summer. Different cultivars have different flower shades. It is good for hummingbirds. The *'Tangerine'* variety has brighter yellow-orange flowers.

Buxus microphylla

Boxwood

- ◆ **Zones:** 6–9
- ◆ **Light:** full sun to partial shade
- ◆ **Soil:** well-drained, moist
- ◆ **Size:** low to medium
- ◆ **Color:** evergreen
- ◆ **Season:** year-round

Boxwoods are tight, evergreen shrubs with glossy, tiny leaves. They can be sheared into almost any shape but work best sheared into a hedge, either as a backdrop or as a low border, only 12 to 18 inches high and wide. Left unsheared, they grow into round shrubs 4 to 5 feet high and wide. In Texas climates, regular irrigation is advised, especially in full sun.

'Wintergreen' variety has dark green leaves that are less likely to scorch in cold weather.

Callicarpa americana

American Beautyberry

- ◆ **Zones:** 4–9
- ◆ **Light:** sun to shade
- ◆ **Soil:** well-drained, moist
- ◆ **Size:** medium to tall
- ◆ **Color:** purple, white fruit
- ◆ **Season:** late summer to fall

Photo 15.9
American beautyberry, *Callicarpa americana*, in autumn

Native to East Texas, beautyberry is a large, free-form, open shrub. The spring flowers are unnoticeable, but it comes into its forte when the berries develop. They ripen in August and remain through fall into winter. The berries are bright purple, clustered in groups up and down the stems. They are especially noticeable after the leaves drop in fall. White-berried forms are available, too. The berries become food for birds and wildlife in winter. Plant beautyberry in sun or shade. It is not picky about soil types but prefers moist soils with a lot of organic matter.

Symphoricarpos orbiculatus, coralberry, is another native that looks similar. It grows only 3 to

Photo 15.10
Japanese camellia,
Camellia japonica

winter and throughout spring. They do best in shady gardens or with morning sun only. Camellias need acidic soils, so amend the bed if you are not in East Texas. Plant as you would azaleas.

POPULAR VARIETIES

Camellia japonica, Japanese camellia, has large glossy leaves and 4- to 6-inch flowers that can be single, semidouble, or fully double. Many of the varieties even have multicolored petals. It generally blooms from late winter into spring. Although it is the showiest, Japanese camellia is the more difficult to grow. It needs good soil and protection from dry summers and is hardy only to zone 8. Deep freezes below the mid-20s can damage it.

Camellia sasanqua is not as showy because it has smaller leaves and flowers. However, it is less picky about the soils and is hardy to zone 7. It ranges in size from low and sprawling to tall and upright. You may consider the new hybrids that are even less picky about soils and can tolerate more sun and heat. They tend to be more cold hardy as well.

4 feet high and has white, pink, or purple berries in winter.

Camellia species
Camellia

- ◆ **Zones:** 7–10
- ◆ **Light:** partial shade to shade
- ◆ **Soil:** moist, acidic
- ◆ **Size:** medium to tall
- ◆ **Color:** white, pink, red
- ◆ **Season:** late fall to mid-spring

Camellias are generally large, upright shrubs with glossy, dark, evergreen leaves. Depending on the variety, they bloom from November into

Campsis radicans
Trumpet Vine

- ◆ **Zones:** 5–10
- ◆ **Light:** full sun to light shade
- ◆ **Soil:** well-drained
- ◆ **Size:** tall

- ◆ **Color:** red, orange, yellow
- ◆ **Season:** all summer

Trumpet vine is a fast growing, deciduous vine that grows 20 to 30 feet high. It blooms heavily all summer with large tubular blossoms. The standard variety is orange-red and very attractive to hummingbirds. Grow it up trellises and over walls. It may even adhere to wood fences with its tendrils.

POPULAR VARIETIES

'Flava' has yellow flowers and is not very aggressive.

'Michigan Red' has darker, red flowers.

'Madame Galen' has larger, showier orange flowers but is less aggressive.

Clematis Species

Clematis

- ◆ **Zones:** 4–8
- ◆ **Light:** partial shade
- ◆ **Soil:** well-drained, moist
- ◆ **Size:** medium to tall
- ◆ **Color:** white, pink, lavender, burgundy, blue
- ◆ **Season:** spring to fall (depending on variety)

Clematis is a delicate, rambling vine with large, showy flowers in ranges of white, pink, red, and purple, and most varieties are deciduous. It should be planted in locations where the roots will be in shade. Morning sun with afternoon shade is best in hot climates. Plant clematis in deep, rich soils with lots of organic matter. It can be grown on trellises or allowed to ramble through shrubs and large perennials. It does not overtake supporters. Keep it evenly moist, especially in summer, and trim back after the blooming period.

POPULAR VARIETIES

C. armandii, evergreen clematis, is the one evergreen vine with large glossy leaves. In midspring, it has large white flowers that are very fragrant. It is hardy to zone 7 and probably should be used more in Texas.

C. paniculata, sweet autumn clematis, is the easiest to grow and the most vigorous of the species. It has small leaves, grows in full sun to partial shade, and is hardy to zone 5. It blooms at the end of August and into September with small, white, very fragrant flowers.

Clematis hybrids, large flowering clematis, bloom in three different groups: early spring, late spring, and summer. They have the big, showy flowers. Trim spring flowers after they bloom and trim the summer flowers in early spring. They bloom in the full range of colors, and some are double flowered. *'Jackmanii'* is one of the most common and easy to grow. It produces bold, purple flowers in spring.

C. picheri, Texas clematis, and *C. texensis,* scarlet clematis, are native to East Texas. They have nodding, lantern-type flowers in purple and red respectively.

Cycas revoluta

Sago Palm

- ◆ **Zones:** 9–10
- ◆ **Light:** full sun to partial shade
- ◆ **Soil:** well-drained
- ◆ **Size:** low to medium
- ◆ **Color:** evergreen
- ◆ **Season:** year-round

Sago palm is a large leathery, clumping plant with fronds that look like a cross between ferns and palms. It is neither, actually. It can take a fair amount of moisture but is drought tolerant

Photo 15.13 *(far left)*
Violet clematis,
Clematis 'Violacea'

Photo 15.14 *(far left)*
Sweet autumn clematis,
Clematis paniculata

Photo 15.15
Sago palm, *Cycas revoluta*

as well. When young, it is about 24 to 36 inches high and wide. Eventually, it develops a trunk and will get 6 feet high. It also develops "pups" or plants that grow off to the side. Remove or transplant the pups to prevent the parent from getting too wide. Plant it as a nice evergreen accent for its texture and tropical look where temperatures are warm.

Photo 15.17 (far right)
Fig ivy, *Ficus pumila*

Dasylerion species
Desert Spoon, Sotol

- ◆ **Zones:** 8–10
- ◆ **Light:** full sun
- ◆ **Soil:** well-drained, dry
- ◆ **Size:** medium to tall
- ◆ **Color:** evergreen
- ◆ **Season:** year-round

Photo 15.16
Desert spoon,
Dasylerion wheeleri

Native to the Desert Southwest, desert spoons are from the family of yuccas and agaves. The desert spoon looks like a yuccas, with thinner leaves and sharp points up and down the edges. It grows in a rounded form, 3 to 4 feet high and wide. In summer, it comes into bloom with tall flower spikes of tiny creamy white flowers atop stems that reach up 6 to 10 feet

high. Plant it as an evergreen accent in the western parts of the state.

Ficus pumila
Fig Ivy

- ◆ **Zones:** 8–10
- ◆ **Light:** partial shade
- ◆ **Soil:** well-drained
- ◆ **Size:** medium to tall
- ◆ **Color:** evergreen
- ◆ **Season:** year-round

Fig ivy is a nice evergreen backdrop vine that climbs up walls and fences easily. It has tiny, dark green leaves that lie close to the surface it is covering. It also works well in topiary forms. Plant in almost any soil, but keep it moist in the heat of summer. It can be planted in zone 8 in sheltered areas.

Gelsemium sempervirens
Carolina Jessamine

- ◆ **Zones:** 7–10
- ◆ **Light:** full sun to partial shade
- ◆ **Soil:** well-drained
- ◆ **Size:** medium to tall
- ◆ **Color:** yellow
- ◆ **Season:** early spring

Carolina Jessamine is a vine native to East Texas. It has small, pointed, glossy evergreen leaves. At the end of February and on through March, it is covered with small, tubular, bright yellow flowers which are fragrant and popular with insects. The vines twine around wires and supports, and then spill over fences and walls. It

It rots when it sits in wet soils. Keep the faded flower stalks trimmed to promote blooming. It is extremely heat and drought tolerant.

POPULAR VARIETIES

'*Yellow*' has yellow flowers but may not be as vigorous.

H. funifera, giant hesperaloe, has larger, stiffer foliage and flower spikes that shoot up 6 to 10 feet with creamy white flowers. It is not as readily available, but it is extremely hardy.

grows 10 to 15 feet high, and it is not picky about soil types, but does best if the soil is not too alkaline.

Hesperaloe parviflora
Red Yucca

- ◆ **Zones:** 6–10
- ◆ **Light:** full sun to partial shade
- ◆ **Soil:** well-drained, dry
- ◆ **Size:** medium
- ◆ **Color:** red, yellow
- ◆ **Season:** late spring to fall

Native to the Desert Southwest including Texas, red yucca looks like a yucca but with thinner leaves that are not as spiny. The evergreen leaves are gray-green and spring from a center clump and arch out. The clump is 18 to 24 inches high and wide. Starting in April, it begins to shoot out flower spikes 4 to 5 feet high. It has tubular, coral red flowers that stay in bloom from April until October and are popular with insects and hummingbirds. Red yucca will handle a fair amount of shade but will not bloom as much.

Hydrangea macrophylla
Big Leaf Hydrangea

- ◆ **Zones:** 7–9
- ◆ **Light:** light shade to shade
- ◆ **Soil:** moist, acidic
- ◆ **Size:** low to tall
- ◆ **Color:** white, pink, purple, blue, lavender
- ◆ **Season:** midsummer

Hydrangea is a deciduous shrub with very large, crinkly leaves. In June and July, it comes into bloom with huge clusters of flowers. Actually, bracts around the flowers are the showy parts: pink if the soil is alkaline, and blue to purple if the soil is acidic. Apply aluminum sulfate to the soil to get the flowers to be blue. Grow as you would azaleas, in moist, rich soils with lots of organic matter. Make sure to keep it well watered throughout the heat of summer. Trim and prune after the flowers fade. It grows 4 to 6 feet high and wide and lightens up the shadier parts of the garden in summer.

POPULAR VARIETIES

'Nikko Blue' has more dependable blue flowers.

'Mariesii Variegata' has creamy edges to the leaves and blue flowers. It is not as vigorous.

'Pink Elf' and **'Pia'** are dwarf varieties that grow 18 inches tall and wide. They have bright pink flowers and should be planted at the front of the border.

Hydrangea quercifolia
Oakleaf Hydrangea

- ◆ **Zones:** 7–9
- ◆ **Light:** light shade to shade
- ◆ **Soil:** moist, acidic
- ◆ **Size:** tall
- ◆ **Color:** white
- ◆ **Season:** early to midsummer

Photo 15.21
Oakleaf hydrangea,
Hydrangea quercifolia

Oak leaf hydrangea is native to East Texas and is easier to grow than big leaf hydrangea. It has large, oak-looking, deciduous leaves that have excellent fall color before they drop in October and November. In May and June, it blooms with large cone-shaped clusters of white flow-

ers that turn pinkish-bronze by the end of summer. Prune after the flowers have completely faded. Plant in the same conditions that you would the big leaf hydrangea, even though it is more tolerant of heat and soil conditions.

POPULAR VARIETIES

'Snow Queen,' an improved variety, has a more compact form and flowers more heavily.

H. arborescens, Anna Belle hydrangea, is less particular about soils but still needs rich, moist soil and morning sun with afternoon shade. It blooms midsummer with large white clusters of flowers. It grows 4 to 6 feet high and wide and is hardy to zone 5.

Hypericum species
St. John's Wort

- ◆ **Zones:** 4–9 (depending on species)
- ◆ **Light:** full sun to shade (depending on species)
- ◆ **Soil:** well-drained to moist
- ◆ **Size:** low to medium
- ◆ **Color:** yellow
- ◆ **Season:** early to midsummer

Several species of St. John's wort are available in the nursery trade, all of which have small, bright yellow, puffy flowers in summer. Most are deciduous, but a few are evergreen. *H. reptans*, or creeping St. John's wort, is an evergreen ground cover that grows well in shady gardens. However, it is too aggressive for the perennial border.

Photo 15.22 *(far right)*
St. John's wort,
Hypericum henryi

H. frondosum 'Sunburst,' sunburst St. John's wort, is a low, deciduous shrub that has a rounded form and grows 2 to 3 feet high and wide. It blooms in May and June with many small puffy yellow flowers. Plant it in full sun to light shade with good drainage. This one is very attractive for a couple of years but short-lived in most Texas soils. It is hardy to zone 4.

H. beanii (or *H. patulum henryi*), Henry's St. John's wort, is a mounding shrub with evergreen foliage and larger yellow flowers in early summer that may continue through fall. Plant it in moist to well-drained soils with full sun to partial shade.

Ilex species

Holly

◆ **Zones:** 6–10

◆ **Light:** full sun to shade

◆ **Soil:** well-drained

◆ **Size:** low to tall

◆ **Color:** evergreen; red berries

◆ **Season:** year-round

Hollies became popular in gardens thousands of years ago for being evergreen, being easily sheared into shapes, and providing beautiful red berries in winter. Depending on the species, they range from low shrubs to quite large trees. They also perform well in full sun to quite a bit of shade. The varieties used in Texas are more adaptable to alkaline soils and hotter climates. They bloom in spring with small, unnoticeable white flowers but are followed by berries that ripen at the end of fall, providing color for the garden and food for animals in winter. If the berries are important to you, take care in pruning. Berry production will be prevented if the flowers are sheared before they bloom in spring or if the fruits are sheared when they're setting in summer. Many species are either male or female plants. The berries set only on the female plants, but a few males must be planted nearby so the bees can pollinate the female plants.

Hollies are divided into two groups: low-growing shrub or hedge types and upright tree types. Both types work well as backdrop color for your border. Some of the low shrub types can be used in the middle of the border or as an edger to the beds.

Photo 15.23
Hollies, *Ilex species*, provide evergreen color, texture, and structure

SHRUB OR HEDGE HOLLIES

I. cornuta, Chinese holly, is a durable, evergreen shrub, hardy to zone 5. It typically has spiny leaves with bright red berries and grows in full sun to partial shade in just about any soil. It is usually planted as a hedge and can be sheared heavily. Many improved cultivars exist in the trade.

'Rotunda,' dwarf Chinese holly, has the same spiky characteristics as the parent but grows only 3 to 4 feet high and wide with few berries.

'Burfordii Nana,' dwarf Burford holly, is the most common holly used for hedges in Texas. It has glossy green leaves and is not as prickly. It will grow 4 to 6 feet high and wide but is easily sheared into any size.

'Berries Jubilee,' berries jubilee holly, and *'Dazzler,'* dazzler Holly, are both grown for

Photo 15.24
Upright shrub, Mary Nell holly, *Ilex x 'Mary Nell'*

Photo 15.25
Low shrub, dwarf yaupon
holly, *Ilex vomitoria 'Nana'*

their outstanding large, red berries. They have the more prickly foliage and get quite large, so keep them pruned back.

'**Carissa,**' Carissa holly, is a dwarf variety that grows only 2 to 3 feet tall and wide and needs little pruning. The leaves are pointed but not as prickly. It is a softer looking plant but does not produce berries.

'**Needlepoint,**' needlepoint holly, has longer, thin leaves. It naturally grows into a rounded form, 6 to 10 feet high and wide, but it is easily sheared into any shape. It has a softer appearance and produces berries heavily.

Ilex meserveae, the blue hollies, are primarily grown in the northern and eastern parts of the state. They are hardy to zone 4 and need afternoon shade and more acidic soils. Even moisture is a necessity as well. All have dark blue-green foliage and produce berries, provided you plant both the male and female cultivars.

'**Blue Prince**' and '**Blue Princess**' grow slowly to 6 to 8 feet tall and have dark purplish blue foliage.

'**China Boy**' and '**China Girl**' are denser and grow to 4 to 6 feet high and wide with smaller dark green leaves.

I. vomitoria 'Nana,' dwarf yaupon holly, is a cultivar from the yaupon holly, which is native to East and Central Texas. The dwarf variety grows to only 2 to 3 feet high and wide with small, soft leaves that resemble boxwood. Since it grows almost in any condition—sun or shade, dry or moist—it is the most adaptable of all the hollies. It makes a great substitute for boxwood in areas that are too dry and too alkaline because it can be sheared into almost any shape, including a low, evergreen hedge border for a formal perennial garden. The dwarf variety does not produce berries, so don't worry about overshearing.

UPRIGHT OR TREE FORM HOLLIES

I. decidua, passumhaw, is a small native tree that resembles yaupon holly. It is deciduous and

has outstanding winter color because the branches are covered in red berries. Keep it pruned back to maintain a shrub form for the perennial garden. Cultivars are available that have large berries or even yellow berries.

I. latifolia, luster leaf holly, has very large shiny green leaves that look like magnolias. It grows upright and conical to 10 to 12 feet high. It is very striking and prefers more acidic soils.

I. opaca, is a fairly large upright tree with an open habit. It is most often sold as one of its cultivars. All need fairly acidic soils and will grow in full sun to light shade.

'**Savannah**' is an upright, pyramidal tree, 8 to 12 feet tall, with rounded leaves and an open habit. The leaves look yellow if the pH is too high.

I. x attenuata 'East Palatka' and *I. x attenuata 'Foster'* are both bred from the American holly. They are narrowly upright or pyramidal trees with small dark green leaves and a lot of berries, eventually reaching 20 feet high or more. They are fairly slow growing and can be pruned back. Of the American hollies, Foster's holly is the most adaptable to alkaline soils.

I. x 'Nellie R. Steven's' is a dense, conically shaped holly that grows slowly 10 to 15 feet high. It can be sheared to keep it low and makes an excellent dense screen or green wall at the back of the border. It has bright red berries as well.

I. x 'Mary Nell' is similar to *'Nellie R. Steven's'* but has larger, looser leaves and gets a bit taller. It may not be as adaptable to alkaline soils.

Lagerstroemia indica

Dwarf and Miniature Crape Myrtle

◆ **Zones:** 7–10
◆ **Light:** full sun to light shade
◆ **Soil:** well-drained
◆ **Size:** low to tall
◆ **Color:** red, pink, purple, white
◆ **Season:** early summer to fall

Crape myrtles typically are small trees grown in the South for their outstanding summer color. They bloom from the end of May through October, and they tolerate heat and humidity quite well. In fact, in Dallas they don't really start blooming heavily until the temperatures reach about 95 degrees. For this reason, they make a nice addition to the border because they are in

full bloom when the perennials begin to fade from the heat. Plant dwarf varieties in the back of the border. They grow 4 to 6 feet high and half as wide.

For the middle of the border, plant miniature varieties. They grow to only 18 to 24 inches high and wide. Some have a weeping form and look good spilling over walls and pots. Some varieties have good fall color as well. Too many varieties exist in the nursery trade to start naming here. Choose from numerous varieties for color, height, and disease resistance.

Crape myrtles are not picky about soil types but prefer well-drained soils with lots of organic matter. They are fairly drought tolerant but stay in bloom with ample summer water and fertilizer. They get powdery mildew easily, so keep them sprayed with fungicide if the problem persists. Try to get varieties that have a lot of disease resistance. Plant them in full sun for best

flower shows. Keep the seed pods clipped as well. They bloom on new wood, so you can prune them back severely in winter. Pruning forces them to send up more shoots, which leads to more flowers. They are slow to leaf out in spring, so you may want to underplant them with an evergreen ground cover or spring bulbs.

Leucophyllum species

Texas Sage, Texas Ranger, Ceniza

- ◆ **Zones:** 6–10
- ◆ **Light:** full sun to light shade
- ◆ **Soil:** well-drained, dry
- ◆ **Size:** tall
- ◆ **Color:** lavender flowers; evergreen gray-green foliage
- ◆ **Season:** late summer to early fall

Texas sages are native, evergreen shrubs. Depending on the variety, they have gray or gray-green, fragrant foliage that blooms in July through September with lavender to pink flowers. They grow 4 to 6 feet high and wide in a loose, rounded shape. They are very drought tolerant. Their loose, open form does not work with shearing, so selectively prune them by removing random branches in spring or fall after they have bloomed. Do not overwater. In the northern half of the state, they may be only semievergreen.

POPULAR VARIETIES

L. candidum 'Silver Cloud,' silver cloud sage, is a compact shrub, growing 4 feet high and wide with silvery foliage and purple flowers. It is hardy to zone 6.

L. c. 'Thundercloud,' thundercloud sage, is similar to silver cloud, but grows to only 3 feet high and wide.

Photo 15.26 *(far left)*
Dwarf crape myrtle,
Lagerstroemia indica 'Purple'

Photo 15.27 *(far left)*
Miniature crape myrtle,
Lagerstroemia indica 'Baton Rouge'

Photo 15.28 *(left)*
Texas sage,
Leucophyllum laevigatum

L. frutescens 'Compacta,' compact Texas sage, has a compact form and grows 5 feet tall and wide. It has gray foliage and orchid pink flowers. *L. frutescens* is hardy to zone 8.

L. f. 'Green Cloud,' green cloud sage, has brighter green foliage and dark pink flowers. It grows up to 6 to 8 feet tall and wide.

L. laevigatum, Chihuahuan sage, has tiny green foliage and lavender flowers. It grows 4 feet tall and wide.

L. x 'Rain Cloud,' rain cloud sage, has a vertical form and grows 6 feet high and 3 to 4 feet wide. It has silvery foliage and lavender blue flowers.

L. x 'Silverado,' silverado sage, is a new introduction with gray-green foliage and lavender flowers. It grows 4 feet high and wide.

Photo 15.29
Coral honeysuckle,
Lonicera sempervirens

Photo 15.30 *(far right)*
Fringe flower, *Loropetalum chinensis rubrum*

Lonicera sempervirens
Coral Honeysuckle

- ◆ **Zones:** 4–10
- ◆ **Light:** full sun to light shade
- ◆ **Soil:** well-drained
- ◆ **Size:** tall
- ◆ **Color:** coral red flowers
- ◆ **Season:** late spring to late summer

Coral honeysuckle is a vine native to Texas. Unlike Japanese honeysuckle, this one is not invasive and grows 12 to 15 feet tall on trellises. It has rounded, evergreen, blue-green foliage. Starting in April, it comes into bloom with tubular, coral red flowers that are popular with hummingbirds. It will bloom on and off until the end of summer. Unfortunately, the flowers are not as fragrant as most honeysuckles. It is drought tolerant, but prefers extra moisture in the heat of summer.

Loropetalum chinensis rubrum
Loropetalum, Fringe Flower

- ◆ **Zones:** 7–9
- ◆ **Light:** full sun to shade
- ◆ **Soil:** well-drained, acidic
- ◆ **Size:** tall
- ◆ **Color:** pink
- ◆ **Season:** autumn to winter

Loropetalum is a large shrub with arching branches and pink fringelike flowers up and down its stems in December through March. The foliage is burgundy red and evergreen to semievergreen in northern parts of the state. It grows best in rich, acidic soil with consistent moisture and partial shade. Loropetalum does well in the same locations as azaleas but seems to handle the sun and alkaline soils better. The flowers will be knocked out by sudden cold snaps.

'Burgundy' and *'Ruby'* varieties have consistent purple-red foliage color and are a bit more compact.

Magnolia grandiflora 'Little Gem'
Little Gem Magnolia

- ◆ **Zones:** 7–10
- ◆ **Light:** full sun
- ◆ **Soil:** well-drained
- ◆ **Size:** tall
- ◆ **Color:** white
- ◆ **Season:** early to late summer

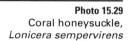

Little gem magnolia is a cultivar of the native, grand Southern magnolia. Like the parent, it has large, rounded, glossy, evergreen leaves, but it grows only 10 to 15 feet high and wide. The form is more shrubby and compact. It is slow growing and can easily be trained against a fence or wall. In May, it blooms with large 10-inch white flowers that continue to bloom periodically all summer. The flowers are luscious and sweetly fragrant with a lemony scent. It prefers moist, acidic soil but is quite tolerant of alkaline soils. Plant it at the back of the border for an evergreen backdrop and stunning flowers. There are several deciduous magnolias that are more cold hardy and bloom in early spring.

RELATED SPECIES

M. stellata, star magnolia, grows 10 feet high and half as wide. It has star-shaped white flowers in February and March. It is hardy to zone 6.

M. lilliflora, lily magnolia, is hardy to zone 5 and grows 6 to 10 feet high and half as wide. Depending on the cultivar, it has large pink to purple flowers in early spring that repeat occasionally throughout summer. Plant it in good soil with some afternoon shade.

Mahonia bealei

Leatherleaf Mahonia

- ◆ **Zones:** 6–10
- ◆ **Light:** partial to full shade
- ◆ **Soil:** well-drained, dry
- ◆ **Size:** medium to tall
- ◆ **Color:** yellow
- ◆ **Season:** late spring

Leatherleaf mahonia is a large shrub with thick, glossy leaves that resemble holly. It is a shrub with twiggy, upright stems that grow 5 to 6 feet high and eventually as wide. In April and May, it blooms with clusters of yellow flowers followed by blue berries in late summer and fall. After a few years, it gets leggy and rangy looking, so cut the longest stems back to let it fill out and get bushy. *M. aquifolia,* Oregon grape holly, has finer foliage but prefers acidic soils and cooler weather.

Myrica pusilla

Dwarf Wax Myrtle

- ◆ **Zones:** 7–10
- ◆ **Light:** full sun to light shade
- ◆ **Soil:** well-drained, dry
- ◆ **Size:** medium to tall
- ◆ **Color:** evergreen
- ◆ **Season:** year-round

Native to the Southeast, wax myrtle is an evergreen shrub with fine, aromatic foliage. The dwarf variety grows 36 to 48 inches high and wide. It has unnoticeable yellow flowers in spring and small, blue-gray berries in fall. It is planted mostly as a hedge or backdrop plant. It

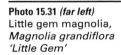

Photo 15.31 (far left)
Little gem magnolia,
Magnolia grandiflora
'Little Gem'

Photo 15. 32
Leatherleaf mahonia,
Mahonia bealei

Photo 15.33
Dwarf wax myrtle,
Myrica pusilla

followed in fall by bright orange-red berries. It gets very leggy so cut the longest branches down to the ground in early spring. However, if you cut away the branches that produce flowers, you will not get the berries, which are quite attractive and provide food for wildlife. Many improved cultivars are available that have better color and form but do not usually bloom or fruit.

can be pruned selectively and severely, but shearing does not work well with its loose, open habit. Cut back stems that get leggy and brittle. It will grow in almost any soil in sun to shade. It is even drought tolerant once established. *M. cerifera,* Southern wax myrtle, is similar and grows into a small tree.

POPULAR VARIETIES

'Gulf Stream' is very low growing reaching 12 to 18 inches high with reddish winter foliage.

'Harbor Dwarf' is a low, round form that reaches 3 to 4 feet tall with reddish winter foliage.

'Moonbay' has bluish green foliage in summer and turns purple in winter, growing 24 to 30 inches high and wide.

'San Gabriel' has very fine foliage that turns red. It is not nearly as dependable.

Nandina domestica
Nandina, Heavenly Bamboo

◆ **Zones:** 6–10

◆ **Light:** full sun to light shade

◆ **Soil:** well-drained

◆ **Size:** low to medium (depending on variety)

◆ **Color:** red to purple to green evergreen foliage

◆ **Season:** year-round

Opuntia Species
Prickly Pear

◆ **Zones:** 7–10

◆ **Light:** full sun to light shade

◆ **Soil:** well-drained, dry

◆ **Size:** medium to tall

◆ **Color:** evergreen foliage; yellow and red flowers

◆ **Season:** year-round

Prickly pear is an evergreen cactus with large, rounded flat pads and many thorns. Native to Texas, it blooms in late spring with yellow to red flowers and develops red to purple edible fruit in fall. It grows 4 to 6 feet high and eventually spreads as wide. This plant works well in gar-

Photo 15.34
Dwarf nandina, *Nandina domestica 'Gulf Stream'*

Photo 15.35 *(far right)*
Purple prickly pear, *Opuntia violacea* var. *macrocentra*

Nandina is a shrub common to Texas because it grows in almost any condition: sun to shade, moist to dry. The parent plant has evergreen, lacy foliage on long thin stems that grow 6 to 8 feet high. It is a clumping plant and will keep getting wider if you let it. In winter, the foliage normally turns red or purple. In late spring, it blooms with plain creamy-white flower clusters

dens that have a Southwest look. Spineless varieties are available. **O. violacea** has purplish colored pads.

Raphiolepis indica
Indian Hawthorn

- ◆ **Zones:** 8–10
- ◆ **Light:** full sun to light shade
- ◆ **Soil:** well-drained
- ◆ **Size:** medium to tall
- ◆ **Color:** evergreen foliage; white and pink flowers
- ◆ **Season:** late spring

Indian hawthorn is a great shrub that provides an evergreen backdrop and spring flowers in full sun where azaleas will not work. It has thick, leathery, round leaves and grows 24 to 48 inches high and wide, depending on variety. In April and May, it blooms with clusters of white or pink flowers. It needs very good drainage and can tolerate some shade but will not bloom as well. It can be sheared into a hedge, but looks much better selectively pruned to keep its loose, open habit. It gets freeze damage in the cold temperatures. Even if the foliage is not affected, the flower buds may be damaged so they won't bloom in spring. Plant it in protected areas in the northern parts of zone 8 and 7. It can develop fungal and fireblight problems, especially if the soil is poorly drained.

POPULAR VARIETIES

'Pinkie' and *'Ballerina'* are dwarfs with pink flowers and grow 24 to 30 inches high and wide.

'Clara' and *'Snow'* grow 30 to 36 inches high and wide with white flowers.

'Spring Rapture' has dark pink flowers and grows to 36 to 48 inches high and wide.

Rhododendron species
Azalea

- ◆ **Zones:** 7–10
- ◆ **Light:** partial to full shade
- ◆ **Soil:** moist, acidic, well-drained
- ◆ **Size:** medium to tall
- ◆ **Color:** evergreen foliage; white, red, pink, violet flowers
- ◆ **Season:** midspring

No plant or flower is as stunning as the azalea when it is in bloom for 2 or 3 weeks in spring. Azaleas provide an attractive dark evergreen hedge or backdrop to summer perennials. However, they need acidic, well-drained soils, even moisture, and partial shade. East Texas' acidic, sandy soils, naturally wooded sites, and heavy annual rainfall lend themselves to growing azaleas and related plants like gardenias and camellias. Because the rest of Texas has alkaline, heavy clay soils, and hotter weather, good conditions for these plants must be recreated. Therefore, do not plant azaleas unless you are a dedicated gardener who will maintain them properly.

There are a few things you need to know and do if you want to plant azaleas. Azaleas prefer shady or semishady conditions protected from hot, drying winds. Some varieties will tolerate sun if they get regular irrigation and have good soil. They need deep, rich acidic soils with regular irrigation but hate wet feet. Therefore, build up your beds to 18 inches above the soil level. Remove existing soil if you need to, but be sure the water can still drain out of the bottom. Then back fill with 50 percent peat and 50 percent commercial azalea mix. Azaleas have shallow root systems, so the roots will remain mostly in the top 18 inches of the bed, which allows extra moisture to drain away at the bottom. Mulch

Photo 15.36 *(far left)*
Indian hawthorn,
Raphiolepis indica

Photo 15.37
Azaleas in bloom,
Rhododendron species

the bed with 2 inches of shredded pine bark or pine straw to retain moisture.

You must continually care for your azaleas once they are planted. Feed with azalea/camellia food after blooming in spring, once in July and once in early September. Replace soil and mulch as needed. It will quickly decompose in hot summers, washing out with irrigation. Prune the plants back after blooming in springtime. Add acidifiers to the soil as directed on the labels. Once they are established, water deeply and allow to dry out on top between watering. Sudden cold snaps in winter will damage the flower buds if not protected. Many of the evergreen varieties will turn red or purple in winter. There are literally thousands of varieties. The following is a list of some the best types of azaleas to grow in Texas.

POPULAR HYBRIDS AND VARIETIES

Kurume hybrids have tiny, dark green leaves and grow 36 to 48 inches high and wide in a mounding form. They are hardy to zone 6. They are covered with tiny, brightly colored flowers in April. *'Coral Bells'* variety has salmon pink flowers, *'Hinodegiri'* has vibrant hot red-pink, *'Hino-crimson'* has bright red, *'Sherwood Red'* has orange-red, and *'Snow'* has white.

Satsuki hybrids are low-growing dwarfs that have small leaves and grow 24 to 30 inches high and wide. They are hardy to zone 7. They include *'Gumpo,'* which has white, pink, or red flowers.

Southern indica hybrids are larger varieties bred for sun tolerance. They have large leaves and bold blossoms that often have a different colored throat. Hardy to zone 6, they grow 6 to 8 feet high and wide. They include *'Formosa'* with lavender flowers, *'George Tabor'* with light pink flowers, *'Judge Solomon'* with watermelon pink flowers, and *'Pride of Mobile'* with bright pink flowers.

Encore azaleas are new varieties that are dark green and grow to only 4 or 5 feet high and wide. They are supposed to be more tolerant of Texas soils. They bloom in shades of pink, violet, and red and will repeat bloom in fall.

Photo 15.38 (far right)
Antique and landscape roses provide structure and summer color in the garden

RELATED SPECIES

Gardenias, *Gardenia jasminoides,* are old-fashioned, Southern favorites that grow in the eastern parts of the state where the soil is acidic and moist. An evergreen shrub with large, glossy green leaves, it comes into bloom in late spring and early summer with large, white, extremely fragrant flowers. It has some of the sweetest smelling flowers of any plant, and the fragrance will fill your whole garden, especially at night. Plant and feed as you would azaleas in acidic, moist soils. It grows 4 to 6 feet wide in the shady border. Actually, morning sun with afternoon shade is best. Drought, freezing temperatures, and nematodes can kill it. Trim off any freeze damage after winter, and shape after blooming in summer. It is hardy to zone 8.

'August Beauty' grows 4 to 6 feet tall and blooms from April until fall.

'Mystery' grows 6 feet tall, blooms in late spring, and may repeat bloom in fall.

'Radicans,' dwarf gardenia, has small leaves and flowers and grows 12 to 18 inches high and spreads out to 2 to 3 feet wide. It makes a nice front-of-the-border plant in shady gardens. This one is easier to grow and is less picky about soil pH and sun.

Rosa species

Rose

◆ **Zones:** 4–9 (depending on variety)

◆ **Light:** full sun to light shade

◆ **Soil:** well-drained, rich

◆ **Size:** medium to tall

◆ **Color:** every color

◆ **Season:** late spring to fall

Roses are probably the most beloved of the flowers. Unfortunately, they can be some of the trickiest to grow, especially the modern hybrids, which have large, breathtaking blooms but are prone to disease. Roses need to be planted in good sun, with protection from hot, drying winds, and in well-drained soil that is deep and rich with organic matter. They need good air circulation to keep from developing

fungus in humid climates, so avoid planting anything close to them to mask the ugly, thorny canes. This approach does not work in a typical perennial bed.

Many roses come under the category of landscape roses, which are grown mainly to be small to large shrubs. As a rule, they are more disease resistant, tolerate a broader range of conditions, and are much more fragrant. The flowers them-

selves probably won't be as big, but they tend to be covered with hundreds of blooms. Many are old-fashioned favorites and antiques that have survived generations. These are the types you should plant in the perennial garden, because they perform well without a lot of maintenance, and they look good mixed with other plants.

Plant your roses from bare root or by container in deep soil, rich with organic matter. For best results, plant in a raised bed, 12 to 18 inches above the existing ground level. Mix in large amounts of organic matter, washed or lava sand, well-balanced fertilizer, and commercial-grade

cornmeal to help prevent fungus. Many companies make a rose blend soil with these ingredients in it. Plant them so the crown of the roots sits right above the soil line. Cover with a 2-inch layer of mulch but don't bury the crown. Fertilize several times per growing season.

For repeat blooming varieties, cut faded flowers off to encourage more blooms. For those that don't rebloom, or for the rebloomers at the end of fall, leave flowers to develop seedpods called "hips." Generally, the hips turn bright red in fall and winter and become food for wildlife. In February or March, before the leaves emerge, prune the stems back to 12 to 18 inches above the ground. Do not prune the climbing roses back. Anytime you see leaves with blackspot or the stems are turning black, remove the stem below the infected area and dispose of it. To control fungus, spray regularly if you need to. An organic preventative spray of baking soda and water will prevent disease without using chemicals.

Literally thousands of varieties exist in the trade. Look for those high in disease resistance and easy care.

POPULAR VARIETIES

Antiques roses are a traditional, extremely durable variety.

Bourbon roses are an antique variety that have been grown in Europe for hundreds of years. They tend be heavy bloomers that are rich in fragrance.

Polyantha roses bloom continuously in large clusters. They predate the hybrid teas and grandifloras.

Musk roses were bred in England in the early twentieth century. They are vigorous and fragrant, and they bloom heavily with many small flowers.

Photo 15.39 (far left)
Nearly wild, *Rosa 'Nearly Wild,'* a popular landscape rose blooms nearly all year

Photo 15.40 (far left)
Antique rose, ballerina, *Rosa 'Ballerina,'* can be trained as a climber on fences and wall

Photo 15.41
David Austin English roses are fragrant and bloom in many colors

English roses, developed in England by famed rose breeder David Austin, are upright growing shrubs. They have very fragrant, large, cabbage-type blooms, are quite easy to grow, and repeat bloom in summer and fall.

Climbing roses do not actually climb like a vine does. Instead, they develop long canes that can be trained on trellises and arbors.

Modern shrub and **ground cover types** encompass a large group of roses grown mostly for hedges or ground covers. They tend to be very hardy and low maintenance. Choose varieties that are repeat bloomers.

Hybrid tea and **grandiflora roses** have been bred for superior flower color and size, but the actual plants tend not to look very attractive. Look for varieties that are disease resistant and fragrant.

perennial border, and it can be cut down to the ground in winter. Golden leaved varieties are available as well.

Spiraea species

Spirea

◆ **Zones:** 5–10

◆ **Light:** full sun to light shade

◆ **Soil:** well-drained

◆ **Size:** medium to tall

◆ **Color:** white, pink

◆ **Season:** midspring to midsummer

Spirea is a group of bushy shrubs that are easy to grow. They perform in any soil that has good drainage and sun. The leaves are deciduous, and many have good fall color. Cut back the stems severely after blooming when they get too large or leggy. Flower color and size depend on variety.

Trachelospermum jasminoides

Confederate Jasmine, Star Jasmine

◆ **Zones:** 8–10

◆ **Light:** full sun to light shade

◆ **Soil:** well-drained, moist

◆ **Size:** tall

◆ **Color:** white

◆ **Season:** late spring to early summer

POPULAR VARIETIES

S. japonica 'Little Princess' grows 3 to 4 feet high and wide with small pink flowers in midspring.

S. nipponica 'Snowmound' has arching blue-green foliage and grows 4 to 5 feet high and wide. It blooms with tiny white flowers in early spring. It usually has bright yellow and orange fall color.

S. prunifolia, bridal wreath spirea, has a form similar to snowmound. The flowers are double and bunched in tiny clusters.

S. x bumalda 'Anthony Waterer' grows only 18 to 24 inches high and wide. It blooms in May and June with red to light pink flowers in flat-topped clusters similar to that of yarrow. This is the most useable spirea in a

Photo 15.42 *(far right)*
Snowmound spirea, *Spiraea nipponica 'Snowmound'*

Photo 15.43 *(far right)*
Anthony Waterer spirea, *Spiraea x bumalda 'Anthony Waterer'*

Photo 15.44 *(far right)*
Star Jasmine, *Trachelospermum jasminoides*

Star Jasmine is a popular evergreen vine that grows 15 to 20 feet high. It has glossy green leaves and grows by twining around structures, so a trellis or wires are necessary. In May and June, it blooms with extremely fragrant white flowers and often blooms sporadically throughout the rest of summer. It gets freeze damage in the northern parts of the state. 'Madison' seems to be more cold tolerant and durable.

Viburnum species

Viburnum

- ◆ **Zones:** 3–8 (depending on variety)
- ◆ **Light:** full sun to shade (depending on variety)
- ◆ **Soil:** well-drained, moist
- ◆ **Size:** tall
- ◆ **Color:** white
- ◆ **Season:** early to midspring

Viburnum is a group of large shrubs that have mostly evergreen or semi-evergreen leaves and fragrant white flowers in March and April. They are tolerant of different soil types but may not all handle the heat and humidity of Texas. Selectively prune after flowering in spring.

POPULAR VARIETIES

***Viburnum x burkwoodii,* Burkwood viburnum,** is an upright shrub that grows 6 to 10 feet tall. It has evergreen or semievergreen, dark green foliage and fragrant pinkish white flowers in early March. Plant it in well-drained soil with partial shade or morning sun only. It is hardy to zone 4.

***Viburnum opulus,* snowball bush viburnum,** is a deciduous shrub that grows 6 to 8 feet tall and wide. It blooms in March with large, round clusters of white flowers before the leaves emerge in spring. The leaves are quite large and have good fall color. Plant it in full sun to partial shade in well-drained soils. Dwarf forms are available. It is hardy to zone 3.

***Viburnum tinus* 'Spring Bouquet,' spring bouquet viburnum,** is suited best for Texas gardens. It has leathery green leaves and grows 4 to 6 feet high and wide. In March to April, it blooms with clusters of small pinkish white flowers. Plant it in shade to partial shade in well-drained soil with lots of organic matter. Provide even moisture in the heat of summer. It is hardy to zone 7.

Photo 15.45
Snowball bush viburnum, *Viburnum opulus*

Photo 15.46
Spring bouquet viburnum, *Viburnum tinus*

Yucca species

Yucca

- ◆ **Zones:** 4–10
- ◆ **Light:** full sun to light shade
- ◆ **Soil:** well-drained, dry
- ◆ **Size:** medium to tall
- ◆ **Color:** white flowers; evergreen foliage
- ◆ **Season:** early to late summer

Yuccas are clumping, evergreen, shrubby plants with green or gray-green spiky foliage and large stalks of white flowers in summer that are popular with insects. Prune the stalks away after they have flowered. Depending on the variety, some slowly develop trunks and can get quite tall. They are all heat and drought tolerant. They make good accents, especially in the Southwestern garden, and they work well in planters and pots. Choose one with an appropriate scale for your garden.

Y. filamentosa, Adam's needle, is the best of the group. It has thin pointed leaves that are not

Photo 15.47
Soft leaf yucca,
Yucca recurvifolia

eventually develops a trunk. This one is native to East Texas and is quite tolerant of shade and moister soils.

Y. rupicola, twisted yucca, is native to Central Texas and grows 24 to 30 inches high and wide with thin, twisted leaves. This one is not readily available in the nursery trade, but it should be. It maintains a low profile without a trunk. The flower spikes get quite tall and can reach 8 feet high but are more delicate than the others.

A related species, **Norlina species,** bear grass, has similar foliage but is softer and grassy looking. It grows in large clumps, 3 to 4 feet high and wide, and eventually develops a trunk. In summer, it sends up large plumes of creamy yellow flowers. It is extremely heat and drought tolerant.

OTHER SHRUBS AND VINES OF NOTE

Abelia grandiflora, **glossy abelia,** is a large evergreen shrub that booms in mid- to late summer with white and pink flowers. It takes full sun to partial shade and is hardy to zone 6.

Acer palmatum, **Japanese maple,** is a small deciduous tree that has varieties that are shrub size, growing only 4 to 5 feet high and half as wide. *'Cascade'* and *'Crimson Queen'* have finely dissected foliage and a mounding, weeping habit. Foliage colors range from green to red to purple in summer, and yellow, orange, and red in fall. Plant them in very good, deep, rich soil and in partial to full shade.

Acuba japonica 'Variegata,' **acuba,** is a tropical looking evergreen plant with large pointed leaves that are speckled with golden spots. It grows 5 to 8 feet tall and half as wide. It provides color in very dark parts of the garden and is hardy to zone 7.

Caesalpinia species, **desert bird of paradise** (also known as Mexican poinciana), are tropical looking large shrubs with lacy foliage and delicate, brightly colored flowers in yellows, oranges, and reds all summer. They grow 6 to 10 feet high and half as wide. They need good sun, good drainage, and protection from freezing temperatures. Depending on the variety, they are hardy to zone 8 and die to the ground when the temperature hits 32 degrees but quickly recover in spring. In South Texas, they may be evergreen.

Cotinus coggygria, **smoke tree,** has large leaves and tiny, billowy flowers in June and July that are so delicate they look like smoke. It can be pruned back heavily to keep it as a

overly sharp. It does not produce a large trunk and stays 3 to 4 feet high and wide. In early to midsummer, it blooms with white flower stalks 5 to 6 feet high. Variegated varieties are readily available; one example is *'Golden Sword,'* which has golden yellow stripes on its leaves.

Y. gloriosa, Spanish dagger, has very stiff leaves, which can be quite dangerous. Plant it away from walkways. It also develops a trunk and reaches 10 feet high. Use this only if you have a lot of room and want a Southwestern look.

Y. recurvifolia (Y. pendula), soft leaf yucca, has large, blue-green leaves that are softer and droop over. Like the others, it sends up flower stalks with white flowers, which bloom off and on all summer. It grows 4 feet wide and high and

Photo 15.48
Variegated yucca, *Yucca filamentosa 'Golden Sword'*

large shrub. It needs full to partial sun and is hardy to zone 5. *'Royal Purple'* has very purple leaves and flowers.

Fatsia japonica, **Japanese fatsia,** is a tropical looking shrub with large, deeply lobed evergreen leaves. It grows 5 to 8 feet tall and half as wide, and it should be planted in shady gardens in deep soil, rich with organic matter. It is hardy to zone 8 but needs protection from hard freezes.

Forsythia species, **forsythia,** is a large, mounding shrub with arching branches and bright yellow flowers that bloom in March. It grows 5 to 6 feet high and wide and is best suited for northern parts of the state. It is hardy to zone 5.

Hibiscus syriacus, **rose of Sharon** (also known as althea), is an old-fashioned upright deciduous shrub that grows 8 to 12 feet high and half as wide. It blooms nearly all summer with 4-inch hibiscus-type flowers in a range of colors. Hardy to zone 6, plant it in full sun and well-drained soils.

Juniperus species, **juniper,** is a large group of evergreen plants with small prickly needles. Thousands of types are available, which range from low ground covers to tall trees. Most need well-drained soils to perform and are drought tolerant. They grow in full sun but will tolerate some light shade, and they are extremely cold hardy.

Nerium oleander, **dwarf oleander,** is a large shrubs growing 8 to 12 feet high and wide. It has long, thin leaves on thick green stems. In early to midsummer, it blooms in vibrant shades of red, white, pink, and salmon with large clusters of flowers at the end of the stems. The leaves are evergreen where it does not freeze too severely. Hardy to zone 8, it should be planted in a protected site on the south side of the house. Plant a dwarf variety that grows to only 24 to 36 inches high and wide so you don't have to keep it trimmed. Be careful with oleander because all parts of the plant are very poisonous.

Pittosporum tobira, **mock orange** (also known as pittosporum), is an evergreen shrub with thick, glossy, round leaves. The parent grows 6 feet high and wide, but more compact cultivars are available that grow to only 3 to 4 feet high and wide. They bloom in midspring with small, fragrant, creamy white flowers. However, they are usually planted for the evergreen foliage. In the northern parts of zone 8, they get freeze damage and need to be protected.

Sophora secundiflora, **Texas mountain laurel,** is a native, evergreen shrub or small tree. It has glossy, lacy foliage and grows 10 to 15 feet high and wide. However, it grows very slowly and can be trimmed into a more manageable size. In March, it blooms with purple wisterialike flowers that are extremely fragrant. Hardy to zone 7, plant it in full sun to light shade and in very well-drained soils. It is quite drought tolerant once established. Plant it in protected areas in the northern parts of the state to avoid freeze damage.

Vitex agnus-castus, **vitex** (also known as chaste tree), a large shrub, often shaped into a small tree, is an old-fashioned favorite often seen growing in older neighborhoods and farmsteads. It is a vigorous grower that reaches 15 to 20 feet high and nearly as wide. The foliage is gray-green, finely textured, and very fragrant. In June, it blooms with spikes of light blue or lavender flowers that are very popular with insects. It is hardy to zone 7.

Weigela florida, **weigela,** is an old-fashioned shrub that grows 5 to 6 feet high and wide. The foliage is deciduous and for the most part not exciting, but it blooms in March to April with showy tubular flowers in whites, reds, or pinks. Plant in full sun, but partial shade will do in Texas. Several varieties are available with different flower colors and sizes, including those that have reddish or purplish foliage and dark pink flowers. It is hardy to zone 5.

Wisteria sinensis, **wisteria,** is an extremely fast-growing vine, reaching up to 20 to 30 feet high. It climbs by twining around supports, and it can be trained on a trellis or against a wall or fence. Plant it in full sun in well-drained soils. It is hardy to zone 5.

I have chosen my top ten favorite perennials for my own garden. They are the plants I could not do without in my garden because they are always beautiful, attract butterflies, and need little attention. I have also chosen my favorite companion plants. It was difficult to limit my list to only ten. Once you begin, you will develop your own preferences for color, size, texture, and durability, and top ten plus 3.

1. **Purple cone flower,** *Echinacea purpurea,* is bold, simple, bright, and in bloom all summer. It is both simple enough to be suited for the meadow and elegant enough for any bouquet.

2. **Daffodils,** *Narcissus species,* are about the first flowers to bloom and announce spring, which is my favorite season. The standard color is sunny yellow, but many varieties exist with ranges from white and pink to red and orange. I plant a range of colors and types to lengthen their blooming period from late February to early May.

3. **Autumn sage,** *Salvia greggii,* blooms from April to frost in a range of colors. I love its fragrance and its popularity with insects and hummingbirds. I prefer the hot pinks and violets.

4. **Daylily** 'Happy Returns,' *Hemerocallis 'Happy Returns,'* has a low, neat compact form with canary yellow flowers. It adds happiness to your border all summer. No Texas garden is complete without at least one daylily.

5. **Butterfly bush,** *Buddleia x davidii,* is a large, old-fashioned, back-of-the-boarder plant that blooms with abandon all summer with loose, open sprays. It sways in the breeze and butterflies love it, of course.

6. **Liatris,** *Liatris spicata,* is a native prairie plant that grew wild in our pasture in Kansas when I was growing up. Insects love it, and its lavender spikes add a striking texture to the garden and bouquet.

7. **Lamb's ear,** *Stachys lanata,* is evergreen and highly tolerant of heat and dry conditions. I love the fuzzy texture and the small purple flower spikes in early summer.

8. **Texas Gold columbine,** *Aquilegia chrysantha 'Hinckleyana,'* is a native that grows easily. The bright yellow flowers bloom late spring and bring color to the shady garden.

9. **Siberian iris,** *Iris sibirica,* is not the toughest iris, but it is the most elegant. The leaves and flowers are more delicate than the German bearded or Louisiana varieties. I prefer the dark jeweled purples like 'Caesar's Brother.'

10. **Herbestonne rudbeckia,** *Rudbeckia nitida 'Herbestonne,'* blooms midsummer when the others are pooping out. Happy, bright yellow daisies with green eyes give life to the back of your border.

PLUS 3

Best Grass: Lindhiemers muhly, *Muhlenbergia lindhiemerii,* is an easy growing native with blue-green foliage and fanciful plumes in autumn. It grows just about anywhere and looks great year-round.

Best Fern: Southern wood fern, *Thelypteris kunthii,* is the easiest fern to grow. Although it dies back in winter, it quickly bounces back in spring. I like the way the light patterns play with fronds during afternoons.

Best Shrubs, Vines, and Roses: David Austin's English roses, *Rosa species,* grow quite well and bloom profusely in late spring and again in autumn despite the "English" in the name. The large, cabbage-shaped blooms are richly fragrant. My favorites are 'Gertrude Jeckyll,' with medium pink flowers, and 'Graham Thomas,' with bright yellow blooms. Plant them close enough to the walk so they will lean over to let you breath in the perfume.

Appendix B
WHERE TO SEE YOUR FAVORITES

Because Texas is a big state with many different regions, many public gardens can be found across the state where perennials are in bloom almost any time of year. Below is a list divided into two categories: public botanical gardens and arboretums, and private nurseries that feature large display gardens. Check local listings for telephone numbers. Many of the gardens have detailed websites as well. So next time you are out seeing Texas, drop in on one of these beautiful gardens for a little inspiration.

PUBLIC GARDENS AND ARBORETUMS

Amarillo Garden Center
1400 Streit Drive
Amarillo, TX 79106

Bayou Bend Collection and Gardens
1 Westcott Street
Houston, TX 77007

Chihuahuan Desert Research Institute
P.O. Box 905
Fort Davis, TX 79734

Corpus Christi Botanical Gardens
8545 South Staples Street
Corpus Christi, TX 78413

Dallas Arboretum and Botanical Society
8617 Garland Road
Dallas, TX 75218

East Texas Arboretum and Botanical Society
P.O. Box 2231
Athens, TX 75751

Ft. Worth Botanic Garden
3220 Botanic Garden Boulevard
Fort Worth, TX 76107

Heard Natural Science Museum and Wildlife Sanctuary
One Nature Place
McKinney, TX 75069 (near Dallas)

Houston Arboretum and Nature Center
4501 Woodway Drive
Houston, TX 77024

Lady Bird Johnson Wildflower Center
4801 Lacross Avenue
Austin, TX 78739

Lubbock Memorial Arboretum
4111 University Avenue
Lubbock, TX 79413

Mercer Arboretum and Botanic Gardens
22306 Aldine Westfield Road
Humble, TX 77338 (near Houston)

Mast Arboretum
Stephen F. Austin University
Wilson Drive
P.O. Box 13000
Nacagdoches, TX 75962

Moody Gardens
One Hope Boulevard
Galveston, TX 77554

San Antonio Botanical Garden
555 Funston Place
San Antonio, TX 78209

Texas Botanical Garden Society
P.O. Box 5642
Austin, TX 78763

Texas Discovery Gardens
3601 Martin Luther King Boulevard
Dallas, TX 75210

Tyler Rose Gardens
420 South Rose Parkway
Tyler, Texas 75701

PRIVATE NURSERIES WITH DISPLAY GARDENS

The Antique Rose Emporium
10,000 Highway 50
Brenham, TX 77833

Weston Gardens in Bloom
8101 Anglin Drive
Ft. Worth, TX 76140

Appendix C
ADDITIONAL RELIABLE SOURCES

The American Horticulural Society: A–Z Encyclopedia of Garden Plants
DK Publishing, Inc.
New York, NY 10016

Sunset Western Garden Book
Sunset Publishing Corporation
Menlo Park, CA 94025

Taylor's Master Guide to Gardening
Houghton Mifflin Company
New York, NY 10003

Appendix D
GLOSSARY

acid soil: Soil with a pH lower than 7.0, usually high in iron and common in areas with heavier rainfall.

alkaline soil: Soil with a pH higher than 7.0, usually higher in salts and found in regions with low rainfall.

annual: A plant that sprouts, grows, blooms, and dies all within one growing season, or a plant grown for one growing season.

biennial: A plant that lives for two growing seasons, sprouting and growing the first season, then blooming and dying the second.

blackspot/leaf spot: Fungus that starts on the foliage, eventually spreading through the plant system; it is most common on roses.

bracts: Modified leaves that form at the base of some flowers, they are usually colorful and resemble petals.

bulb: A large, modified rootlike organ that stores food underground.

corm: Similar to a bulb, it is a short swollen underground stem that stores food.

corolla: The petals of the flower.

corymb: A flat-topped cluster of flowers.

crown rot or root rot: The crown is the part of the plant where the stems meet the roots, and crown rot is fungus that destroys these parts.

deadhead: To remove faded flowers to encourage the plant to rebloom.

deciduous: A plant that drops all of its leaves or dies back for winter.

desiccate: A problem evergreen plants have when they dry out or scald from cold winter winds.

double flower: A flower with multiple rows of petals that form a ring and usually hide the center (i.e., a cabbage rose).

evergreen: A plant that retains its foliage year-round.

herbaceous: A plant that does not develop woody stems and usually produces new shoots every year.

humus: Organic matter used to amend planting beds and derived from decomposed plant and animal matter.

hybrid: A new plant variety bred in a nursery and often a cross between two different species.

inflorescences: A cluster of flowers arranged in a particular order on a stem (i.e., umbel, spike, and panicle).

nematodes: Microscopic worms that destroy roots, injuring or killing the plant. Beneficial nematodes attack bad nematodes, fleas, and ants.

panicle: A loose, open cluster of flowers.

perennial: A plant that lives for many growing seasons and usually flowers every year.

powdery mildew: Grey or white powdery fungus that forms on leaves and flower buds, especially in humid weather, and disfigures the foliage.

rhizome: A horizontal underground stem that stores food and spreads the plant with shoots and roots.

rosette: A low, flat cluster of leaves arranged in a circle like the petals of a rose.

semidouble flower: A flower with one and a half rows of petals that surround the center.

semievergreen: A plant the retains some but not all of its leaves in winter.

shrub: A plant that lives for many growing seasons and develops woody stems.

single flower: A flower with one row of petals that ring the center (i.e., a daisy).

stolon: A stem that runs along the ground, forming roots and new plants as it spreads.

subshrub: A small shrub that dies back in winter or can be pruned severely.

tuber: A swollen underground stem that stores food from which shoots and roots emerge.

umbel: A flower cluster in which all the stalks originate from one point and fan out like an umbrella.

variegated: Foliage with spotted, striped, or edged colors other than green.

vine: A plant that grows up other plants or structures by twinning around them or clinging to them.

Xeriscape: A landscape designed to conserve water.

Purple Heart. See *Setcreasea pallida*
'Purple Heart'
Purple Leaf Sage. See *Salvia blepharo-phylla*
Purple Loosestrife. See *Lythrum salicaria* 'Mordens Pink'
Purple Rain Salvia. See *Salvia verticillata* 'Purple Rain'
Purple Shamrock. See *Oxalis triangularis*

Rain Lily. See *Zephyranthus species*
Raphiolepis indica, Indian Hawthorn, 25, 50, 52, 57, 61, 63, 66, 75, 89, 96, *217*
Ratibida columnifera, Mexican Hat, 39, 42, 66, *67*, 75, 83, 92, *160*
Red Hot Poker. See *Kniphofia uvaria*
Red Valerian. See *Centranthus ruber*
Red Yucca. See *Hesperaloe parviflora*
Rhododendron species, Azalea, 25, 39, 42, 48, 50, 52, 61, 69, 78, 89, 96, *217*
Rivina humilis, Pigeonberry, 44, 52, 56, 61, 69, 75, 85, 92, 94, *161*
Rock Rose. See *Pavonia lasiopetala*
Romantic Landscape Movement, 16
Rosa species, Rose, 25, 39, 42, 46, 48, 50, 52, 61, 78, 80, 83, 85, 91, 93, 94, 96, *204, 218, 219*, 225
Rose. See *Rosa species*
Rose Mallow. See *Hibiscus moscheutos*
Rose of Sharon. See *Hibiscus syriacus*

Rosemarinus officinalis, Rosemary, 25, 44, 46, 56, 61, 66, 75, 78, 79, 95, 96, *161*
Rosemary. See *Rosemarinus officinalis*
Rudbeckia species, Rudbeckia, Black-Eyed Susans, 42, *62*, 66, 75, 83, 85, 92, 94, *162–164*
Rudbeckia fulgida 'Goldstrum,' Black-Eyed Susan, *162*
Rudbeckia hirta, Gloriosa Daisy, Rudbeckia, Yellow Coneflower, 39, *162*
Rudbeckia maxima, Giant Rudbeckia, Giant Coneflower, 57, 60, 73, *163*
Rudbeckia nitida 'Herbestonne,' Herbe-stonne Coneflower, 57, 60, *163*, 225
Rudbeckia x 'Toto,' Dwarf Gloriosa Daisy, 164
Ruellia brittoniana, Ruellia, Mexican Petunia, 46, 48, 50, 52, 66, *67*, 69, 73, 75, 83, 84, 92, 94, *164*
Russelia equisetiformis, Firecracker Plant, 39, 56, 59, 61, 66, *67*, 84, 92, 94, 164, *165*
Russian Sage. See *Perovskia atriplicifolia*

Sage. See *Salvia species*
Sago Palm. See *Cycas revoluta*
Salvia species, Sage, 66, 75, 78, 83, *93*, *165–174*
Salvia azurea var. grandiflora, Azure Sage, Pitcher Sage, 46, 56, 58, 59, 60, 84, 92, 94, 165, *166*

Salvia bicolor, Bicolor Sage, Cocoa Sapphire Salvia, 46, 48, 56, 61, 92, 94, *166*
Salvia blepharophylla, Purple Leaf Sage, 46, 48, *174*
Salvia buchananii, Buchanan's Sage, 46, 92, *173*
Salvia chamaedryoides, Gray Shrub Sage, 46, 54, 56, 79, 96, 167
Salvia coccinea, Scarlet Sage, *38*, 39, 50, 58, 84, 92, 94, *167*
Salvia engelmanii, Engleman's Sage, 46, 56, 59, 61, *169*
Salvia farinacea, Mealy Cup Sage, 46, 52, 92, 94, *168*
Salvia greggii, Autumn Sage, Cherry Sage, 39, 42, 48, 50, 52, 56, 61, 84, 92, 94, 96, *168*, 225
Salvia guarantica, Anise Scented Sage, 46, 58, 60, 84, 92, 94, *170*
Salvia 'Indigo Spires,' Indigo Spires Sage, 46, 58, 60, 84, 92, 94, *165*
Salvia leucantha, Mexican Bush Sage, 48, 40, 54, 58, 60, *71*, 79, 84, 94, *170*
Salvia lyrata, Lyre Leaf Sage, 46, 48, 69, 84, 89, 96, *171*
Salvia nemerosa 'Plumosa,' Plumosa Meadow Sage, 48, 58, 92, *171*
Salvia officinalis, Garden Sage, 46, 48, 54, *77*, 79, 80, 96, *169*
Salvia penstemonoides, Penstemon Sage, Big Red Sage, 39, 50, 58, 84, 92, *172*
Salvia texana, Texas Sage, 92, 174
Salvia uliginosa, Bog Sage, 46, 60, 73, 92, 94, *173*
Salvia verticillata 'Purple Rain,' Purple Rain Salvia, 48, 58, 92, *173*
Salvia x superba, Meadow Sage, 46, 48, 50, 52, 58, 59, 92, 94, *172*
San Antonio Botanical Garden, 228
Sand and Gravel, 3
Santolina species, Lavender Cotton, Santonina, 56, 61, 66, 75, 78, 79, 96, *174*
Santolina incana, Lavender Cotton, Gray Santonina, *53*, 45, 174
Santolina virens, Green Lavender Cotton, Green Santolina, 44, *174*
Saucer Magnolia. See *Magnolia x soulangiana*
Savannah Holly. See *Ilex opaca* 'Savannah'
Saxifrage stolonifera, Strawberry Geranium, 52, 61, 69, 78, 96, 178
Scabiosa caucasica, Pincushion Flower, *2*, 46, 50, 63, 66, 75, 78, 83, 92, 94, *174*
Scarlet Sage. See *Salvia coccinea*
Schizachyrium scoparium, Little Bluestem, 193
Scilla peruviana, Peruvian Scilla, 46, 175
Scilla sibirica, Scilla, 46, 48, 50, 52, 78, 89, *175*

Scutellaria suffrutescens, Pink Scullcap, 50, 56, 61, 66, *74*, 75, 83, 84, 92, 94, *175*
Sedum spectabile, Showy Sedum, 39, 44, 50, 57, 61, 63, 75, 83, 85, 94, *175*
Setcreasea pallida 'Purple Heart,' Purple Heart, *47*, 48, *176*
Shasta Daisy. See *Chrysanthemum maximum*
Showy Sedum. See *Sedum spectabile*
Shrimp Plant. See *Beloperone guttata*
Siberian Iris. See *Iris sibirica*
Sidalcea species, Prairie Mallow, 39, 50, 52, 83, *176*
Sideoats Grama. See *Bouteloua curtipendula var caespitosa*
Smoke Tree. See *Cotinus coggygria*
Snowball Bush Viburnum. See *Viburnum opulus*
Society Garlic. See *Tulbaghia violacea*
Soils, 3
Solidago sphacelata, Goldenrod, 42, 58, 73, 83, *93*, 94, *177*
Sophora secundiflora, Texas Mountain Laurel, 25, 46, 48, 56, 66, 75, 78, 83, 89, 96, *223*
Sorghastrum nutans, Indian Grass, 44, 46, 60, 66, 73, 75, 79, 92, 94, *201*
Sotol. See *Dasylerion species*
Southern Maidenhair Fern. See *Adiantum capillus-veneris*
Southern Wax Myrtle. See *Myrica cerifera*
Southern Wood Fern. See *Thelypteris kunthii*
Spanish Lavender. See *Lavandula stoechas*
Speedwell. See *Veronica species*
Spider Lily. See *Hymenocallis species, Lycorus radiata*
Spiderwort. See *Tradescantia virginiana*
Spiraea species, Spirea, 25, 50, 61, 78, 83, 89, 96, *204*, 220
Spiraea japonica 'Little Princess,' Little Princess Spirea, 220
Spiraea nipponica 'Snowmound,' Snowmound Spirea, 52, *220*
Spiraea prunifolia, Bridal Wreath Spirea, 52, 220
Spiraea x bumalda 'Anthony Waterer,' Anthony Waterer Spirea, 39, 63, 91, *220*
Spirea. See *Spiraea species*
Spring Bouquet Viburnum. See *Viburnum tinus*
Spring Obedient Plant. See *Physostegia angustifolia*
St. John's Wort. See *Hypericum henryi*
Stachys species, Lamb's Ear, Betony, 79, 177
Stachys lanata, Lamb's Ear, *34*, 48, *53*, 54, 61, 66, 75, *78*, 96, *177*, 225